Ideas. Action. Impact.
Wharton School Publishing

In the face of accelerating turbulence and change, business leaders and policy makers need new ways of thinking to sustain performance and growth.

Wharton School Publishing offers a trusted source for stimulating ideas from thought leaders who provide new mental models to address changes in strategy, management, and finance. We seek out authors from diverse disciplines with a profound understanding of change and its implications. We offer books and tools that help executives respond to the challenge of change.

Every book and management tool we publish meets quality standards set by The Wharton School of the University of Pennsylvania. Each title is reviewed by the Wharton School Publishing Editorial Board before being given Wharton's seal of approval. This ensures that Wharton publications are timely, relevant, important, conceptually sound or empirically based, and implementable.

To fit our readers' learning preferences, Wharton publications are available in multiple formats, including books, audio, and electronic.

To find out more about our books and management tools, visit us at whartonsp.com and Wharton's executive education site, exceed.wharton.upenn.edu.

BUILT FOR GROWTH

Expanding Your Business
Around the Corner or Across the Globe

Arthur Rubinfeld
Collins Hemingway

Ideas. Action. Impact.
Wharton School
Publishing

Upper Saddle River, NJ • New York • San Francisco • Toronto
London • Munich • Paris • Madrid
Capetown • Sydney • Tokyo • Singapore • Mexico City

Library of Congress Publication in Data: 2004114697

Publisher: Tim Moore
Acquisitions Editor: Paula Sinnott
Editorial Assistant: Richard Winkler
Development Editor: Russ Hall
Marketing Manager: Martin Litkowski
International Marketing Manager: Tim Galligan
Cover Designer: Chuti Prasertsith
Managing Editor: Gina Kanouse
Project Editor and Copy Editor: Ginny Munroe
Indexer: Angie Bess
Interior Designer: Kim Scott
Compositor: Kim Scott
Manufacturing Buyer: Dan Uhrig
Cover Photo Artists: Nancy LeVine and Bob Woodward

Wharton School Publishing offers excellent discounts on this book when ordered in quantity for bulk purchases or special sales. For more information, please contact U.S. Corporate and Government Sales, 1-800-382-3419, corpsales@pearsontechgroup.com. For sales outside the U.S., please contact International Sales at international@pearsoned.com.

Printed in the United States of America
Fourth Printing June 2005
ISBN 0-13-146574-0

Ideas. Action. Impact.
Wharton School Publishing

Bernard Baumohl
THE SECRETS OF ECONOMIC INDICATORS
Hidden Clues to Future Economic Trends and Investment Opportunities

Sayan Chatterjee
FAILSAFE STRATEGIES
Profit and Grow from Risks That Others Avoid

Sunil Gupta, Donald R. Lehmann
MANAGING CUSTOMERS AS INVESTMENTS
The Strategic Value of Customers in the Long Run

Stuart L. Hart
CAPITALISM AT THE CROSSROADS
The Unlimited Business Opportunities in Solving the World's Most Difficult Problems

Lawrence G. Hrebiniak
MAKING STRATEGY WORK
Leading Effective Execution and Change

Robert Mittelstaedt
WILL YOUR NEXT MISTAKE BE FATAL?
Avoiding the Chain of Mistakes That Can Destroy Your Organization

Mukul Pandya, Robbie Shell, Susan Warner, Sandeep Junnarkar, Jeffrey Brown
NIGHTLY BUSINESS REPORT PRESENTS LASTING LEADERSHIP
What You Can Learn from the Top 25 Business People of Our Times

C. K. Prahalad
THE FORTUNE AT THE BOTTOM OF THE PYRAMID
Eradicating Poverty Through Profits

Scott A. Shane
FINDING FERTILE GROUND
Identifying Extraordinary Opportunities for New Ventures

Oded Shenkar
THE CHINESE CENTURY
The Rising Chinese Economy and Its Impact on the Global Economy, the Balance of Power, and Your Job

David Sirota, Louis A. Mischkind, and Michael Irwin Meltzer
THE ENTHUSIASTIC EMPLOYEE
How Companies Profit by Giving Workers What They Want

Thomas T. Stallkamp
SCORE!
A Better Way to Do Busine$$: Moving from Conflict to Collaboration

Yoram (Jerry)Wind, Colin Crook, with Robert Gunther
THE POWER OF IMPOSSIBLE THINKING
Transform the Business of Your Life and the Life of Your Business

*This book is dedicated to my parents, Max and Jeannette,
for encouraging me to "soar with my own wings."*

*And to Ellen, Benjamin, and Lauren—thank you all for
enriching my personal journey.*

Contents

Foreword xi

Introduction xv

PART 1   Make No Little Plans

Chapter 1   It's About Your Values 3

Chapter 2   Opportunities, Ideation, and Concepts 27

Chapter 3   The Importance of the First Store 49

Chapter 4   Maximizing the Retail Experience Through Design 63

Chapter 5   Seamlessly Connecting Design to Brand While
Staying on Budget 79

Chapter 6   Merchandising: Maximizing Your Profits 97

Chapter 7   Customizing Customer Service 121

PART 2   Go Long

Chapter 8   Blueprint for Execution 131

Chapter 9   Taking Your Organization Long 149

Chapter 10   Kicking the Economic Model Into Gear 169

Chapter 11   Wellsprings to Expansion 185

PART 3   Own Main & Main

Chapter 12   How to Grow Rapidly Without Stumbling 203

Chapter 13   Hot Spots, Oil Stains, and the Perfect Location 221

Chapter 14   A Walk Through the Locationing Process 247

Chapter 15   Real Estate: Who Needs Who More, When 261

PART 4   Push the Envelope

Chapter 16   Innovation as the Path to Growth 291

Chapter 17   Defining Your Mission in the New Age of Retail 313

Index 331

About the Authors

Arthur Rubinfeld, the architect behind Starbucks' expansion, helped build Starbucks into one of the world's top brands.

As executive vice president at Starbucks, Rubinfeld built a multi-faceted store development and design organization with the talent, in-house processes, and systems necessary to execute rapid expansion. Under his leadership, Starbucks grew from 100 stores to more than 3,800 stores worldwide, and it established innovative co-tenancy and co-branding concepts with companies ranging from Wells Fargo to Barnes and Noble. Starbucks' store development capabilities remain the standard by which the industry measures brand presentation, real estate site selection, store design, construction management, and asset management.

In 2002, Rubinfeld founded AIRVISION, one of the world's leading innovators in integrated brand positioning, retail design, strategy, and operations. Since its founding, the Seattle-based AIRVISION team has worked closely on the development of many of the nation's most recognized brands including Oakley, Gateway, adidas, and Washington Mutual.

Arthur can be reached at arthur@airvision.net.

Collins Hemingway is best known as the coauthor with Bill Gates on the #1 best-seller, *Business @ the Speed of Thought*, and has worked in the business and technology arena for 30 years. A Microsoft director of business development and international marketing, Hemingway was an integral part of the company that virtually defined the digital revolution. Through his firm, Escape Velocity Ventures, he lectures and writes on topics as diverse as management, aviation, medicine, technology futures, and the importance of conscience in creating profitable enterprises.

Collins can be reached at collinshemingway@hotmail.com.

Foreword

When I was starting out in the retail business a long time ago, first working for my father's clothing store and then starting a couple of retail businesses with my brother, I could have benefited from this book by Arthur Rubinfeld. *Built for Growth: Expanding Your Business Around the Corner or Across the Globe* is a valuable primer on all aspects of retail: brand, location, people, finance, property management, expansion strategy, and long-term thinking. He understands the difficulty of the small guy getting started and the big guy keeping the brand fresh. This book contains a lot of information that will not be obvious to most people. Even an experienced retailer should stop and reflect on Arthur's insights, which come from many years of experience in every aspect of the business. (Arthur and I first met in the early 1990s, when he directed Starbucks' retail expansion and I was on the Starbucks board.)

At Costco, we follow many of the precepts that Arthur describes here. We are fairly sophisticated about analyzing data versus going with our gut, but senior management is also hands on. We go out to the stores. We try to know as much about what is happening on the stores' floors as our sales associates. We are actively engaged with the people involved in evaluating and selecting our merchandise. I am personally involved in real estate and site selection, which remains one of my primary responsibilities. Of course, Costco has fewer stores than most other retail concepts, so each decision is very, very important to us. I recommend that every senior manager stay in touch with the practical day-to-day functioning of the business, especially site selection. Putting together a great team is also important, as is treating employees well. Our management team has been together since our founding more than twenty years ago, and our benefit package is designed to encourage long-term employee retention. Arthur explains the benefits of such practices to retail businesses of all sizes, particularly how investment in quality can provide a better return on investment than the usual approach of cost cutting.

Built for Growth should benefit a wide audience, especially people who are out of the retailing mold who want to start their own business. The practical advice is good, and the book provides a broad understanding of brand, an insider's perspective on retail strategy, and a professional's approach to structuring the business. *Built for Growth* is also easy to read, and Arthur's warmth and intellectual curiosity come through. I agree with him that retail is more difficult than it looks. When you're out there on your own, just getting into the business, you don't know what you don't know. Arthur fills in the blanks.

Jeff Brotman
Chairman, Costco Corporation

Acknowledgments

This book began when I met my agent, Kelli Jerome, through a mutual friend, Anne Whitney. Finding Kelli proved fortuitous. Our early conversations validated the concept of this book, and concept validation turned out to be as fundamental in developing a book as it is in developing a retail idea. Kelli assembled an outstanding team that was dedicated to the book from its birth, to the related Web site, and to the marketing and publicity efforts.

Co-author Collins Hemingway was invaluable in framing and fleshing out a topic as broad and complex as retail. He challenged me to articulate my ideas in the broadest possible ways, while still ensuring that we expressed those ideas in the most concrete and meaningful manner. Collins' business background contributed greatly to the content, and our personal rapport provided encouragement as we wrestled with numerous drafts, often late into the night.

Many other professionals deserve acknowledgement, beginning with Tim Moore, Publisher at Prentice Hall's Wharton School of Publishing. Tim initially saw the potential in our book. I also want to acknowledge Paula Sinnott, who stepped in and took the project enthusiastically under her wing. Russ Hall tirelessly read early versions of the manuscript. His perceptive feedback enabled us to develop content more fully. Insightful comments about the manuscript by William Ghormley and Stephen J. Hoch led to substantive improvements. We are grateful to the many others at Wharton School Publishing who helped produce, market, and sell the book.

CKA Creative's Dan Fraser produced the artwork in the book and Mark Anderson designed the Web site. Megan McKenzie of McKenzie Worldwide helped immeasurably with the publicity. I also appreciate the efforts of Amy Hatch in helping to keep all of us on track.

Special thanks to Jayson Tipp, Dave Barrows, Mark Austin, and Ada Braswell, my colleagues at AIRVISION; to M. Mark Albert, my partner at AV CAPITAL; and to Bill Sleeth and Shauna Stinson at Vizwerks for their important contributions and support.

Many people fostered my career. I am extremely grateful to Jeff Brotman, who has shared his wisdom and sound advice with me over the years, and to Michael Epsteen, who has generously given his time and energy to mentor me in the retail business.

As you will shortly learn, much of my business maturity developed during my tenure at the Starbucks Corporation. For my experience there, I am deeply indebted to Howard Schultz, Orin Smith, Howard Behar, and Dave Olson. It was an honor to be part of such an extraordinary, inspirational team. Also deserving of recognition are Michael Casey, Georgette Essad, Cydnie Horwat, Nancy Kent, and many other Starbucks partners.

Several people shared their insights and experiences with me or contributed to the book in other ways. Thanks to Pat Ackerman, James Allard, Joel Benoliel, Wayne Bettis, Colin Baden, Kjirsten Doole, Amy Dowless, Robert A. Fulton, the late Irving Getnick, Neil Getnick, Wendy Hemingway, John Heubusch, Mike Hislop, Mark Jaffe, Thomas S. James Jr., Tom Jednorowicz, Bryant L. Keil, Dave Lorenz, Kathleen Mazzocco, Mike McClure, David Meckler, Mike Morgan, Link Newcomb, Jeff Obtsfeld, Danny Piecora, Michael Raskin, Steve Rosen, Ellen Rubinfeld, Engle Saez, Bruce Simon, Todd Simon, Brad Shaw, Stuart Skorman, David Smith, Craig Tall, TMB members Richard Cogan and Denis Woychuk, Bob Tiscareno, Ted Waitt, and Gary Wenet.

We make a vessel from a lump of clay;
It is the empty space within the vessel that makes it useful.
We make doors and windows for a room;
It is these empty spaces that make the room livable.
Thus, while the tangible has advantages,
It is the intangible that makes it useful.

—*Lao Tzu*

Introduction: The Hardest Easy Business

Who doesn't want to run his own business? Who doesn't want to have her own store? If you're young, you think about it from time to time. If you're older, you wish you had opened that little shop before the kids came—or you plan to open it when you retire. We all want to control our destiny. We all want to express our creativity. We all want to build something that will last.

But how do you start a retail operation? That's the question I am most often asked. How do you create a going concern, one that will grow and build long-term value? That is another common query. *Built for Growth: Expanding Your Business Around the Corner or Across the Globe* answers these and related questions. The book is primarily geared at helping a retailing entrepreneur rapidly expand into a powerful market presence. The same principles that drive an entrepreneur, however, can also reinvigorate the brand for an existing retail chain and trigger new growth. These principles also help carve out a profitable, defensible niche against potential market invaders for the retailers who want to keep their business small. Small retailers must be even better than bigger competitors at understanding and applying the basic principles: As a small retailer, you don't have a portfolio of other stores to help establish your brand or to offset poor overall financial performance.

Retail is the hardest business that is easy to get into. People have an idea, borrow against their house, find a location, buy some inventory, and open their doors. They hope to be successful, expecting business to pour in. Most often, however, business doesn't pour in, it dribbles. Given the haphazard way most entrepreneurs begin, the fact that many succeed is a testament to their energy and determination. However, approximately half of all startup businesses fail, usually within a year.

The immediate cause is usually a lack of cash; however, the fundamental cause is a lack of knowledge of how to avoid pitfalls, how to think through the business and brand positioning issues, how to efficiently operate and execute the business, and how to systematically build new stores. In short, how to create, establish, and maintain a retail brand that can survive in the short term and succeed in the long term.

Things are not much easier for existing retailers. The Big Box stores and Internet vendors have knocked the bottom out of prices for an increasing number of consumer products. Very few top-of-the-line brands are dominating the concepts that have not been commoditized. "General retailers"—everybody else—are having the oxygen sucked out of them by the pressure at the top and bottom. Many well-established retail brands have faltered in the last few years, some after a century or more of existence. They have either lost the price wars or failed to keep their brands relevant to today's consumers. Two prime examples are Kmart and Sears, which after years of separate struggle decided to merge in an effort to compete with Wal-Mart. Even new retailers, who have started off well with successful stores in local markets, do not understand why their concepts stall once they enter new markets, or why the cost of new store development spirals upward while sales at new stores fail to meet expectations.

Solutions exist for all of these problems, as long as the problems are viewed in context. You the retailer need a *holistic* approach to conceiving, designing, and carrying out a retail business plan. You need to understand how to create an exciting concept and grow it to fruition in the local market. You need to understand how to rapidly expand from one market to dominate other markets at the regional, national, or even international level. You need to understand how to keep your brand fresh and relevant as it matures. *Built for Growth* covers these topics and uses examples from some of the most innovative and well-regarded retailers in the industry. The book describes a new way of thinking about retail, an approach that embodies strong personal values, creativity toward concept, an artistic approach to design, a scientific methodology in finance and market analysis, and "old-time" customer service that seeks to personalize the experience. *Built for Growth* offers a comprehensive strategy to differentiate your retail brand and a set of practical, street-wise actions to achieve success.

Delving for New Ideas

In a typical day at the office, I may propose to a CEO ways to extend his $2.5 billion retail business and brand before his current concept runs out of runway. I may advise a nationally known confectioner that he needs to expand into a seemingly different area to keep his concept relevant. I may counsel the head of a major fast-food chain on ways to redefine his value proposition to jump to the head of a crowded pack. My passion is growing retail businesses, and I work with companies to develop new retail concepts or bring new ideas to existing concepts. My expertise comes from more than 20 years of work in brand positioning and retail expansion. For 10 years, I led Starbucks Corporation's retail growth from 100 stores to more than 4,000, evolving from a unique and relatively unknown coffee vendor to one of the world's most recognized brands. Since going out on my own, I have helped many companies build or expand their retail success in a variety of enterprises ranging from outdoor gear to food service to fine women's apparel. *Built for Growth* distills what I have learned into a comprehensive view of what it takes to develop a winning retail concept. This shows you:

- How to combine core personal and company values with your business expertise to create a meaningful brand.
- How to creatively craft your on-the-street retail presence to capture the essence of your brand and develop customer loyalty.
- How to identify the best locations for your concept.
- How to build your management team, organization, and systems—whether you want to have one store or 1,000.
- How to systematically and aggressively execute your plans.
- How to successfully operate your business to keep customers coming back.
- How to innovate and renew your brand.

Other books deal with one or two of these topics, but none has taken a *holistic* approach to retail development, combining theory and practical ideas to cover the entire scope of what it takes to succeed in retail.

Building Big Principles on Simple Ideas

The book is organized into sections based on four fundamental principles. Each of the four sections covers a major aspect of retail strategy, in the order in which you will normally experience them as you grow your business. They are:

PART I, "MAKE NO LITTLE PLANS"

Have the imagination, courage, and drive to believe that you can become a nationwide brand. The most dominant retail brands in the world began as small operations run by people with no more experience than you. Some had no retail experience at all. Ray Kroc was selling milkshake machines to the McDonald brothers for their hamburger shop when he recognized that the retail operation had more potential than equipment sales. More than a quarter-century later, Howard Schultz was selling drip coffee containers to a small chain of stores called Starbucks Coffee when he had a similar epiphany. Each man ended up buying the business and ... well, you know the rest. Other people may have been as talented, but Ray Kroc and Howard Schultz had the ability to think about the potential and the energy to push the brand forward. They both showed a capacity for making big, long-term decisions. An integral part of their vision was optimism. No cynic invests in the future. Thinking big entails hope. It entails a positive vision of the world as well as big ideas on how to improve it.

Making big plans has other meanings as well. You need to think big about concept. The obvious concepts have been done. You need to reinvent concepts and categories or develop new ones. This first section describes the steps you can take to dig into your core values, to understand what you are really good at—and enjoy doing—and how to translate that knowledge into a unique, authentic working concept. Thinking big also means you need to be imaginative in design and merchandising, so that you do not repeat the look of competitors. This section describes ways to create a distinctive visual appeal that attracts customers. It also explains how to build stores with great appeal, using high-quality materials, while staying on budget.

PART II, "GO LONG"

The phrase, which originates in American football, means to throw long passes in an effort to move the ball downfield, score quickly, and demoralize the opposition. The San Diego Chargers, Oakland Raiders, and St. Louis Rams perfected the strategy in different eras. In retail business, "going long" is a strategy designed to rack up points (profits) and quickly put the game out of reach of would-be competitors. As in football, the "go long" approach is not a "Hail Mary" pass—a desperate effort to score when you're behind—but a mindset and a game plan designed to push so hard that you always keep a step ahead of competitors. Your plan, your investors, your organization, your economic model, and your expansion strategy are all of the plays that position you to "go deep." This section shows how—*because you have prepared for expansion from the very start*—you can strike quickly and grow rapidly when you
decide to expand.

PART III, "OWN MAIN & MAIN"

The "corner of Main & Main" is an expression we used at Starbucks to describe any urban street corner that offered high customer traffic counts, great visibility, and high-quality co-tenancy (quality companies located around us). By targeting the best "Main & Main" locations, we achieved not only significant sales, but also brand prominence. The brand prominence helped lift sales in future locations. Over time, the phrase "Main & Main" has taken on an expanded meaning—the best location in any trade zone, whether this is urban or suburban, on a street corner, or in a shopping center. This section describes how to aggressively seek the best markets, how to scientifically determine the best areas in those towns according to demographics, and how to identify the best sites in those areas from both a technical and "street-wise" standpoint. This section also includes detailed, real-world specifics that demonstrate the principles. By claiming "Main & Main" for yourself, you make competitors constantly play catch-up.

PART IV, "PUSH THE ENVELOPE"

The final section shows how a retailer can maintain brand leadership over time. The chapters detail the dangers of "falling into the middle" and the importance of invigorating all aspects of the concept over time—product, design, service, and quality. Pushing the envelope requires constant innovation, as the material describes. The section also describes the future of retail and the role that retail plays in the revitalization of American cities and towns.

As with any complex subject, some chapters in this book could be placed in more than one section. Depending on your interests or where you are in growing your retail business, you might want to read the chapter on leaseholds and landlords first or the chapter on the economic model. You might already have a couple of stores, so the chapter on developing a strategic plan for growth might hold the most interest. Feel free to tackle the text in whatever order is most relevant to you, but note that some chapters naturally cluster together and should be read in order. The most obvious of these are the opening chapters on developing a concept and the chapters that show the progression in finding new markets and the right locations within those markets.

In addition, different chapters reference letters of intent, lease agreements, site surveys, sample financial statements, and a variety of other forms and checklists of general interest to the retail community. Samples of these and other supporting materials can be found on www.builtforgrowth.com.

Ideating, Creating, and Executing

A framework is needed to tackle a topic as complicated as retail development. A three-step approach ensures the right combination of creativity and discipline. The holistic approach is to *ideate, create,* and *execute.* I usually express them as a unity, like this—*ideatecreateexecute*—because they relate so closely and one flows out of the other seamlessly. To *ideate* is the act of generating ideas, to imagine all the different possibilities for your business, to think about your concept in every way possible, to examine it from every angle, to challenge your assumptions and think about all the options, and to brainstorm all the possible ways you might develop the concept. You ideate when you seek to freshen or even recreate an existing concept. All the aspects of this phase must be built on your established purpose and core values.

To *create* is the next step, which is to develop a specific business solution that embodies your concept and expresses your values and brand. It's the actual "thing" you want to do, the kind of retail approach you want, and how you will proceed with it. In the creation process, you do the research, establish the financial model, and develop the strategic operating plan.

To *execute* is to carry out your plan, beginning with the design, store location, and opening of your first store and continuing through the building of your business empire. Execution includes listening to customer feedback, evaluating the success of the concept and the various products that you sell, tweaking the concept, and constantly updating your concept and brand as needed.

Ideatecreateexecute is the mechanism that drives the work to be done in each of the major parts of this book. Each problem and opportunity begins with ideation, follows with creation, and concludes with execution. For any concept to reach its maximum potential, a retailer must become skilled in carrying out all three steps within each of the four phases of developing a retail business.

My retail career began in a greeting card store, where as a teenager I learned early lessons in merchandising from Mr. Levy, the owner, and in an Italian restaurant that had a very demanding clientele, where I learned the importance of customer service. My love of building design began in upper New York State, where my parents took my brother, Josh, and me every summer to get us out of the heat of Brooklyn. Playing in and around concrete foundations for new houses in the rural area of Spring Valley, I began to wonder about space and the function of buildings, and that curiosity led me to an initial career as an architect. I later served as the project architect and construction manager for The Palace Hotel in Manhattan, under the Helmsleys, before embarking on a career in retail real estate development on the West Coast. The twists and turns of my career brought me back to brick-and-mortar retailing where I had started as a young man, but now with experience in all aspects of the business. *Built for Growth* is intended to convey my passion for this field as well as a depth of working knowledge. Nothing, I have found, has provided quite the enjoyment as helping people create and build successful, growing retail brands.

Built for Growth cannot be a cookbook for success. No one has a formula for Insta-Brand or Insta-Riches. Any such recipe must be followed by the label, "Just add talent, imagination, discipline, and hard work"—rare and magical ingredients indeed. However, *Built for Growth* provides a methodology for approaching the most vexing problems of retail, provides insights into the best ways to proceed in the most difficult passages, and provides numerous approaches to practical problems that *do work*. The book contains many practical tips and warnings about pitfalls, but the greatest value is in the principles themselves. *Built for Growth* provides a vessel into which you can pour your best ideas and out of which will come a coherent and exciting framework for growth. You will be on your way to developing the next great retail brand. And with a little bit of luck, your concept will be opening soon.

PART 1

Make No Little Plans

Make no little plans, they have no magic to stir the blood and probably themselves will not be realized.

Make big plans, aim high in hope and work, remembering that a noble, logical diagram once recorded will never die.

—Daniel Burnham

CHAPTER 1

It's About Your Values

NOT TOO LONG AGO, on a hot, summer night, I took my family to a quick-serve restaurant, a franchise known for its ice cream. The place was dirty. Service was slow. Other customers stacked up behind us. Finally, somebody took our order, and we experienced another long delay while sitting at a table that had not been recently wiped. The employees did not seem to care that we and others were waiting. We could hear them talking in back somewhere. A few other customers, frustrated with the wait, left before being served. When we finally got our treats, we ate them hastily, a nice evening gone flat. A few months later, the city tore up the street at that intersection. The construction caused temporary problems for all the surrounding businesses, but this restaurant closed permanently. The franchisee complained in the local newspaper that "the city" had put him out of business. I remember thinking that what put him out of business was having the most unappealing eatery and the worst service in town.

You see this kind of thing in retail all too often—a disconnect between the promise of the retail brand and its execution. Mediocre service and dirty tables do not make for happy customers. Sometimes the disconnects are accidental or unforeseeable. Perhaps that restaurant had people call in sick and the crew was worn out near the end of a double shift. (Couldn't they at least have given us a frazzled smile?) More often, poor results come from a superficial understanding of brand, or wishful thinking, or plain laziness. You cannot promise quality and follow through with half-hearted execution. I wonder how many times that franchise owner—the one so angry at the city—checked on his store at odd times to see what was happening. I wonder whether he ever did a reality check on his operations after his sales started to slide, which I suspect was long before the street reconstruction began.

What we saw as customers that night was a brand breakdown. Every breakdown in brand occurs because of a lack of corporate values or an insufficient effort to execute on those values. This chapter begins with a brief discussion of brand, follows by relating the brand to core values, and shows how core values are instrumental in a retailer ideating a compelling concept, developing a meaningful mission statement, and creating a compelling customer experience out of that mission.

"Brand" is a complex subject issue because for retailers the "brand" consists of both the brand image of the products being sold and the brand presentation of the store itself. For a retail concept that sells only or primarily its own brand of products—Armani clothing, Starbucks coffee, or Goodyear tires, for example—the situation is simpler, but the overall retail brand still has two elements: the quality level and packaging of what is being sold and how it is being presented and sold within the four-wall retail environment. Most brand discussions focus only on what is being sold—products—rather than the manner in which the products are offered to the public. Even here, the brand discussion often degenerates into superficial or temporary aspects of brand, such as the creativeness of the logo, the freshness of the packaging, or the jazziness of the ad campaigns. This approach trivializes the basis of a product brand and does not begin to grapple with the concept of brand as it relates to retailing.

For these reasons, it is necessary to briefly define brand as it relates to both product and retailing and to discuss the issues that affect both.

For a product and for a product company, "brand" is the product or corporate image, the positioning asserted in various marketing campaigns and supported by product quality, customer service, and overall business behavior. A retail brand builds on these same elements, benefiting from the quality and the features of the products, the packaging, and related product marketing. The retailer's overall business behavior also shapes the customer's perception about the brand. However, the retail brand is so much more than any of these individual elements. Brand is the design and presentation of your building. It is whether you can deliver the product in a timely and consistent way. It is your company policy on returns and exchanges. (This includes how easy and pleasant it is for customers to engage with store personnel to make the exchange.) It is whether your store has parking and whether, if it supports your positioning, you pay for validated parking. It is the comfort level of your store when customers shop. It is your employees and their attitudes. It is how they dress and whether they smile. It is whether they know when to assist and when to let the customer browse. It is their knowledge about your products. When customers leave the store, it is whether employees say "thank you" in a way that makes customers feel appreciated. Ultimately, a product brand comes down to the customer's belief in the quality or the value of the product. A retail brand comes down to the overall experience of the customer in the store, of which product quality or value is only one part.

For long-term success, all of the attributes of a product brand must be aligned, but a strong positive image for a product can create a "grace" period in the public's mind. Corporate image can carry a product company for a while when its products trail those of competitors, and product quality can carry the company for a while when its corporate image is less than perfect. Because the retail brand rests upon an actual, personal, encompassing experience, however, no one element can "carry" all the others. The potential buyer comes face to face with every aspect of the brand at once. Store design and appearance, product quality and presentation, and customer service will overwhelm any brand impressions the customer might have had before entering into the establishment. *For retailers, the store experience is the brand.* Because the customer is *there*, in the store, the reaction to any slippage in any brand attribute is immediate. The ice cream store failed on its appearance and service, so our confidence in the brand collapsed in a single visit, despite its fine products.

Even more than with an individual product, a brand attribute for a store is not something you can slap on, a sticker that proclaims "high quality." Whatever you assert, the customer has to merely look around to decide whether you meet your promise. Brand does mean a unique positioning—the best, the brightest, the fastest, the "something" that nobody else has. But that *something* has to come from within, not from "without." Just as a product brand cannot long retain credibility by shouting, "New and improved!" if the product is old and unchanged, neither can a retailer long survive with advertising proclaiming the latest fashion trends if the clothing line has the same styles season after season. Maybe the hard truth is that your only unique positioning is that old *Mad Magazine* maxim—"Our price, cheap"— but at least the positioning is an honest one. Whatever claim you make for your brand, it must be an intrinsic part of who you are as a product company or retailer.

To become a powerful brand, every retail concept must be based on strong, core personal values and business values. Because of the personal nature of retail and the customer's direct presence, you cannot fake who you are and what you stand for. As you look to create a new retail brand or to invigorate an existing one, you must look inside to your own ideas and standards. Make no little plans, and have no small values. The word "value," as used in branding, can mean either *principles* (of the business person or company) or *worth* (to the customer, as in the value proposition). Here, "core value" means a blend of the two because your worth to the customer must spring directly from your principles. Personal honesty and honest treatment of your customer are two sides of the same coin.

Each exciting, new concept begins with ideation—idea generation— and the first step in idea generation is to determine these core values. Without building on your own core values, it is highly unlikely that you will create a concept that differs from a dozen other similar concepts that are already out there. Basing the concept on a core value provides a fundamental and sustainable differentiation. The difference is not in a transient value, such as the flash of a particular marketing program, or even in the particular product you sell, however good it may be. It is in the way you run your business, which, in turn, determines the product you sell and also the *other* attributes of business (brand!) that you embody. Core values lead to corporate values. Corporate values lead to product and store values. Product and store values lead to store branding. Store branding leads to corporate branding. Corporate branding reinforces corporate values. All of these ideas roll one into the other to create a self-perpetuating wheel of value, action, and perception. A specific example helps illustrate how core values pertain to both product and retail branding.

The adidas sports brand takes its values from its founder, Adi Dassler, an athlete who played soccer well into his 60s and who spent his entire life creating equipment for athletes. Beginning with his first hand-made shoe in 1920, Adi personally created the category of athletic shoe. He made the first spiked track shoe; the first screw-in cleats, which helped Germany claim a World Cup victory on a muddy field; the first bobsled shoe; the first ski-jump boot; and the first ultralight sprint shoe, among many other inventions. Once, while watching the Montreal Olympics from home in Germany, he called Alberto Juantoreno and advised him to reposition his spikes to avoid drifting around the turns—a problem Adi had noticed on television—and the Cuban runner became the first person to win gold medals in both the 400-meter and 800-meter run.

Adi's passion for athletes carries through in adidas's innovation and brand positioning today. With more than 700 patents on sports equipment, adidas's focus remains on athletes and equipment that makes athletes better performers, whether this is a new design for a soccer ball or a special shoe for high jumpers. In the company's retail stores, these values are celebrated in a dual-store format. One concept is the Heritage store, the smaller of the two concepts at about 4,000 square feet. These stores feature several iconic displays, such as historical prototypes of some of Adi's shoes, to ensure that the company's legacy is communicated at the retail level. The other brand-defining concept is the large-store format, at between 12,000 to 25,000 square feet. These stores feature breadth and depth, the company's complete line of equipment and clothing in all sports, which range from track and field to soccer to golf to snow sports. In both formats, store personnel offer technical expertise to complement the company's background and to ensure a positive store experience for the customer and a position of category leadership.

SPORT HERITAGE

SPORT PERFORMANCE

SPORT STYLE

FIGURE 1-1

The heritage of Adi Dassler, who invented an athletic shoe for almost every category of competition, led to the creation of the first legitimate sports brand in the world, adidas, and to one of the most recognizable logos, the adidas trefoil (top). The solid grounding of the brand in the company's mission and corporate values has helped the company continue to innovate for more than 80 years. The company's brand strength has led to natural brand and logo extensions into high-performance gear (center) and lifestyle-fashion gear (bottom).

For the retailer especially, branding really does go back to its original sense of *imprinting*. Brand is every way you touch the customer, and *branding* is the overall personal experience your customer has with you. The slick aspects of packaging, ads, logos, store signs—all the visual, sensual stuff—summon up those experiences, but they cannot replace the experience itself. Neither can a good product make up for a poor in-store experience. If the experiences are good, the logo (as one example) becomes an icon that draws customers. If the experiences are poor, the logo deflects customers toward the competition. Retail is about the here and now, the quality of the experience *today*. The power of the retail experience is why many product brands would love to have a direct experience with the customer, rather than relying on another company to present the brand to the public. The power of the retail experience is why many product brands, from shoes to clothing to computers, open their own shops after testing their concepts within another company's retail shops to determine their differentiating factors and the "sweet spot" for both pricing and presentation. The power of retailing is why a number of companies that sell primarily through other retailers also open their own stores. In addition to emphasizing the company's history and showing customers the full range of the brand's products, for instance, the adidas's retail stores also demonstrate to other resellers of their products unique ways to merchandise them.

In contrast, the power of the retail experience is why even one poor store can be so damaging to the brand. The ice cream shop where we stopped that one summer night was just one outlet of the many 100s of good ones around the country, but the experience has remained. To this day, we generally choose another stop for our dessert. Because of my work, I may have a sharper eye than most, but my kids are the ones who made the decision not to return to this company's stores.

Clearly, the operator of this one store did not carry within himself the values that the franchise attempted to create nationally. Likewise, the operator of the store evidently made no effort to pass these values on to his shift managers or employees. Perhaps the effort was not necessary at one time. A number of years earlier, this franchise was the only ice cream shop in town, and the location was ideal. Customers flocked to it, despite the restaurant's shortcomings. Now several similar shops exist, and new roads have diminished the value of this location.

Given a choice, customers are going elsewhere. In this one spot, the retail brand failed.

When you make a mistake—poor product, poor value, poor behavior—you break a pledge to your customer, a pledge based on your marketing or on the customer's previous experiences. You are far less likely to tarnish your brand with mistakes or inconsistency if you forge your corporate behavior in the fire of your core values. At Starbucks, our determination to be the "premier purveyor of the finest coffee" led to a fanatical approach to quality in everything we did. In addition to sourcing, roasting, and serving the highest quality coffee, we targeted the best locations and used high-quality materials in everything we did—from wall graphics and flooring materials to the lighting fixtures and table designs. When faced with the usual financial constraints and tradeoffs in building each store, we needed only to reflect back on the words "premium" and "finest" to guide our decisions. Given our core values, the decisions were usually easy. Another company might have "low prices" as a core value to customers. This does not mean the retailer can ignore quality, but it means that the tradeoffs might be different. Although this book describes ways to incorporate high-quality materials into stores inexpensively, a "price" retailer still expresses quality less in terms of store ambience and more in terms of premium goods at a discounted price. Different values make for different choices.

Defining Principles Mean Defining Brand

Every successful company establishes itself in a well-defined set of ideas. For example, the following companies define their ideas as:

- 3M—To solve unsolved problems innovatively.
- Merck—To preserve and improve human life.
- Walt Disney Corporation—To make people happy.

This section examines the importance of such defining principles and how retailers can develop them. An example from both a new retailer and a well-regarded existing retailer shows how defining principles have a profound impact on the company's mission and its brand. The examples show how having well-defined principles more crisply defines the retailer's purpose—and hence, the meaning of the brand—while at the same time expanding the retailer's view of the role it can play in the world beyond making money.

Jim Collins, author of *Built to Last: Successful Habits of Visionary Companies*, worked extensively with Starbucks after we had reached a billion dollars in sales in the mid-1990s. Jim is a pretty matter-of-fact guy, but his challenge to us was substantial. "You want to be the biggest coffee roaster in the world, so what?" he said. "Anybody can do that. What's different about you?" He reiterated one of his constant themes: Over time, the most important product of a company is the company itself. Jim defines core values as the organization's "essential and enduring tenets—a small set of timeless guiding principles that require no external justification" and notes that a company "need not have customer service as a core value (Sony doesn't), or respect for the individual (Disney doesn't), or quality (Wal-Mart doesn't), or market responsiveness (HP doesn't), or teamwork (Nordstrom doesn't). ... The key is not what core values an organization has, but that it has core values." I would add that these values must emanate from within the individuals that operate the company.

Who are you, and what kind of company do you want? The answer begins with an honest and rigorous look inside yourself. Determine what is really important to you, to see what you really care about, not just in business, but in life. This self-evaluation includes a hard look at your personal strengths and weaknesses, which are the expression of your values. If you are unsure about your strengths, tell your friends and business associates that you want to start your own company. Ask them what kind of business you'd be good at and what kind of people you would need around you. You might discover that others perceive strengths you never recognized or weaknesses you might not have been aware of. Do not get discouraged if you hear something that puts you off. This feedback is just one more piece of information to consider along with everything else. I was surprised when I was once told that I needed to listen more carefully to see whether people just wanted to air their feelings or they actually wanted me to help them solve a problem. It seems that if someone mentioned a difficulty to me, I'd immediately say something like, "Okay, here's what you need to do." This feedback—yes, it was from my wife—has helped me communicate better with everyone.

To look beyond the quantitative aspects of your business, dig deep into the qualitative *human* aspects of intent, drive, and attitude. The goal is to find your core values, to determine the connection between the human being and the business—to get beyond the public presentations and the finely honed "remarks for attribution" and get to the soul of your company. Leaders get forced into managerial and organizational roles in which they feel compelled to speak and act in "reasoned tones." They get so used to answering formal (and formulaic) questions about their company that they go on autopilot. They begin to think in externalities from the perspective of "the company." Having worn the corporate mask for so long, having engaged in "corporate speak" for so long, they often forget who they really are and what they and their company really represents. They cease to tap into their original passion or stay in touch with the company's current passion. You need to see beyond this.

Ask yourself such things as:

- Where did you grow up? How many brothers and sisters do you have? Are you the oldest or youngest? How did your family dynamics shape your view of the world?
- What do you do outside of work?
- What do you view as your biggest success and feeling of accomplishment, and why? What do you view as your biggest failure, and why?
- What do you believe about contributing to your community?
- What do you believe about a commitment to excellence?
- What do you as the founder or CEO, along with your key senior team members, believe in?
- How should and can your company contribute positively to the world?
- What kind of people do you want to surround yourself with? How do you view your colleagues and would you want them with you in a foxhole?
- What is your attitude and your team's attitude toward winning? Do you want to win at all costs, or do you strive for win-win solutions?

- What are your personal core values? What are your company's core values? How are they aligned, and do you see a discontinuity between them?
- How do you impart these values to your employees? How do you impart them to your customers?
- What part of the customer's experience does your company truly value?

Consider, for instance, a kaiten sushi restaurant named Blue C Sushi. A kaiten restaurant presents sushi on plates on a conveyor belt that runs through the restaurant, continually presenting choices to customers. The guests take their choices from the conveyor belt as the plate passes by. When I first started working with James Allard and Steve Rosen, two friends since high school who are the two primary partners of Blue C Sushi, I asked what led them to this particular venture. I was not sure how their previous jobs—both worked for a young Internet company—had taken them down the path to sushi. The question led to an in-depth discussion of motivation, and soon I was listening to James speak of his admiration for Japanese culture, particularly its sense of honor, dignity, and resilience. He had been intrigued with Japan since childhood, although he did not pursue the interest until college. Rather than take his second year of French, an impulse caused him to sign up for Japanese. That experience led him later to take off from law school to do a year's immersion study in Japan. There, on a "poor student's budget," he ate regularly at an inexpensive kaiten restaurant around the corner from his apartment. When he returned to the U.S., he finished school, practiced law for three years, joined Microsoft in operations, and then became senior vice president of operations at Go2Net as it grew from less than a 100 people to 500. But even with all those "real jobs," James never forgot about those kaiten sushi houses that served healthy, inexpensive food. When he and Steve left their high-tech jobs, James thought that it was time to do something different. The more they thought of bringing Japan's healthy dietary habits—high protein, low fat—to their fellow citizens, the more they liked it. They soon "talked each other into it."

When they brought the idea to me, I gave them a homework assignment to do before they put any energy into the concept itself, into designs, into location, or into anything else. "Figure out your core values," I said. They sat down at a coffeehouse (you know the one) and went to work. Here is what they came up with:

- We bring healthy, delicious sushi to sushi novices and experts alike.
- Our sushi is only of the highest quality.
- We practice absolute integrity in everything we do.
- We offer heroic customer service (friendly service and excellent value).
- We demonstrate corporate and environmental social responsibility.

Their core values and commitment to the concept meant that we had a lot to work with.

A deep and persistent link connects the spirit of the founders and the spirit of a company. If you know the people at the top, you have a good sense of a company and how it will work through its good and bad times. If you know, for instance, that Howard Schultz, now the chairman of Starbucks, once lived in one of the poorer neighborhoods in Brooklyn, and that from the age of 12 years old and on, he did a succession of menial jobs to help out his family, you will correctly surmise that any company he runs will treat its employees with respect. And not just hallway politeness: Starbucks annually grants stock options to many of its employees, and it was the first major U.S. company to offer healthcare benefits to most of its part-time workers.

Starbucks, in fact, is a good example of how you can use core values with an established company as a way to instill fresh vigor into the organization and to help a company grow. Prior to Jim Collins working with us, our mission statement had expanded in geography, but not in significance. We wanted to be the leading purveyor of the finest coffees in the country, then the continent, then the world—bold goals, certainly. However, shouldn't our purpose in life be more than having the biggest pile of beans? On an offsite retreat with senior management, Jim split up the group of ten into two teams. I was on the team assigned to crafting a new mission statement. All five of us were asked to individually craft an updated mission statement for the company. When we came back together and read our compositions, something wonderful emerged: Four of the five of us had all included the word "spirit" in our proposed mission statements.

Spirit! This was a pivotal moment for me. Almost all of us who made up the task force had independently incorporated a higher value into our view of what the company could and should stand for. "To be the leading purveyor of the finest coffees in the world and to nurture and inspire the human spirit" was the statement we developed from that exercise. Months later, because of that exercise, the formal mission statement that is used to this day emerged: "To establish Starbucks as the premier purveyor of the finest coffee in the world while maintaining our uncompromising principles as we grow." (The phrase "to nurture the human spirit" seemed a shade grandiose for the formal mission statement, but it has appeared in many internal documents and graced the front of the 2003 annual report.) The mission expressed our relationship with the local communities in which our stores were located.

This new value statement was something that all employees could carry out in their daily interactions with customers. The statement also directly affects corporate behavior. For example, although we already strongly supported CARE, a relief organization, we expanded our involvement in local communities as noted in the following:

- Using the substantial advance from the book he was writing about his career, Howard funded the Starbucks Foundation to support local literacy programs wherever Starbucks has coffeehouses. We also formed an alliance with eight companies to provide more than 320,000 new books to children.
- We partnered with Earvin (Magic) Johnson to open coffeehouses in inner cities.
- We established a $1 million philanthropic partnership with Jumpstart, a national organization that provides tutors to needy children.
- We developed a number of programs to help improve circumstances for many small, independent coffee growers in regions that supply the coffee.

Starbucks has done much, much more that continues today in local communities worldwide. The entire company rallied around a common view of our role—a successful company has a responsibility and opportunity to use its good fortune to do something good for society.

Doing a reality check about a company's mission is a good way to find out at any point in its development whether everyone in the company is marching in step. At a recent client meeting, I asked the 18 senior people in the room to write down what they thought their company's mission was, or should be. I also asked them to finish the following sentence: "Our company provides customers…" The results produced roughly six different mission statements and six different customer statements. This is one red flag that shows the company lacks a compelling vision. The other red flag is that ten of the 18 mission statements were, in various words, "to be profitable" or "to produce profits." The customer-related questions were similarly short in reach. After the meeting, I told the company president that until everybody was singing off the same song sheet—and the song was something everybody believed in and wanted to sing—the company was not going to be as successful as it could be.

Initially, the mission statement defines your company and gives it direction. Over time, during different phases of growth, revisiting that mission enables a company to reach something bigger than the product or service it sells. As Starbucks grew, it became clear that we could leverage each step in growth to realize more ambitious manifestations of our values. These included new partnerships, new products, and corporate initiatives targeted at addressing global issues relevant to us and meaningful to our customers.

Translating Core Values into Mission into Action

Think of the mission statement as the way your company translates its core values into a call to action. Blue C Sushi's mission statement ended up being this:

> To provide our guests with the finest **value**-oriented sushi experience possible, as reflected by the **natural purity** of our sushi, the simple **elegance** of our surroundings, and the **pride** of our sushi chefs. We treat our food with **reverence** and our guests with **honor** and **dignity**.

A lot of people make the mistake of believing that the mission statement should be some kind of slogan or tagline. The opposite is true. You should try *not* to come up with a catchphrase or verbal short-hand at first. Use as many words as you need to fully flesh out everything the company is, stands for, and does. The goal is to be complete, accurate, and aspirational.

To ensure that you consider your mission in the broadest terms, you should list all the customers and other constituencies that your company touches, what benefit they get from your company (or product), and how they receive those benefits. A simple matrix will help for this step. For example, a pharmacy has patients who benefit from their medicines and from information about prescriptions and generic equivalents; doctors and health-care facilities that benefit by having a knowledgeable dispenser of medication; and insurance companies that benefit from modern bill-processing systems the pharmacy should have. Do not forget to include partners, employees, and shareholders (or investors) and how they benefit. The goal is to broaden your awareness of what you really do while also describing what you do in concrete terms. As you fill in the matrix of customers and benefits, you put together a full picture of how you actually play in the world, and you look for the larger concepts that tie all of the elements together.

With your preparation done, write up what you do *completely*. The initial mission statement for the pharmacy, for instance, might read something like this:

> The Hankins Hall Pharmacy recognizes that today's customers want more than just prescriptions. They want a healthy lifestyle and complete information about their medicine. We provide the highest-quality pharmacological services, educate our clientele, and offer additional products to enhance health and fitness. We ensure that customers understand their prescriptions and possible side-effects, and we are actively alert to conflicts between any prescriptions. We offer lower cost alternatives where possible. We treat our employees well and provide the most up-to-date training possible to ensure the highest customer satisfaction. We provide the most modern systems possible to ensure promptness in the ordering and delivery of medicines and in the billing and payment process. We strive to maximize returns for investors in keeping with good healthcare standards.

A mouthful, no question. There is also no question what this pharmacy stands for. From here, it is relatively easy to come up with a pithier mission statement or (my preference) a three-word mantra; that is, three words or short phrases that define the essence of the brand or company.

The formal mission statement might ultimately read something like this:

We provide the highest quality medicines at the lowest possible price, educate our clientele about their prescriptions and all health matters, and offer additional products and services to support healthy life choices. We provide the finest training possible for our staff and reward them fairly. We strive to achieve an equitable return in keeping with good healthcare standards.

The three-word mantra for the company might be this:

QUALITY

We offer the best medicines, personal service, and education.

VARIETY

We offer a range of health and lifestyle products and services.

ACTIVITY

We offer wellness and fitness programs to promote healthy lives.

Putting the Mantra into Action

Properly done, the mantra for a company that is primarily retail can serve as the corporate mantra as well as the design mantra for the actual stores. This is evident in the "Quality, Variety, and Activity" phrase for the pharmacy example. If the company has other major sales channels, such as wholesale or mail order, then for our purposes— developing a new retail business or energizing an existing one—the mantra should focus primarily on the retail business. All aspects of branding should be aligned with the mantra, however. A retail mantra that speaks of "quality" will lead to a certain design concept, and the packaging for mail-order products needs to convey the same sensibility. It is not sufficient to use the same corporate logo on the mail-order products if the retail presentation is high quality, but the mail-order packaging is inferior. The customer should have the same brand impression regardless of the sales vehicle.

For existing companies, it is often easy to jump quickly from the mission statement and existing values to the three-word mantra. The following examples illustrate how we *ideated* with clients to create a three-word mantra that distills the core values. The mantra can serve as a focus in the development of business strategy. Strategic planning is covered in Chapter 9, "Taking Your Organization Long," and other chapters are devoted to the many other business actions that derive from the strategy. Because so much of retailing rides on the *customer experience*, this chapter focuses on how the mantra can be translated into the physical expression of the retail idea.

Il Fornaio Café and Bakery

Il Fornaio is an established "white tablecloth" restaurant chain mainly focused on the West Coast. Seeking to extend the brand into the fast, casual dining market, Il Fornaio began work on a new café and bakery concept that would not compromise the brand's quality image in the fine-dining category. The core values were Il Fornaio's roots as an Italian bakery: an authentic Tuscan tradition that evokes simple, timeless quality, a combination of sophistication and approachability, and a desire to be the preeminent bakery café brand. These values led to the three-word mantra for design:

AUTHENTIC
The Tuscan ideals of style, simplicity, beauty, and utility.

WELCOMING
A warm, friendly, and comfortable community gathering place.

FRESH
A distinctive, high-quality product that is quickly made to order and delivered with exceptional customer service.

Omaha Steaks

Omaha Steaks has been producing and distributing a variety of premium beef, poultry, seafood, and other gourmet foods for five generations, and it now has more than 1.6 million customers, mostly through mail order. Seeking to grow its retail business, Omaha Steaks began a reevaluation in 2004 of its retail concept, its offerings, and its design. To frame our process we ideated the following three-word mantra:

PREMIUM

Omaha Steaks' quality inspires me to create great meals for my family and friends.

PANTRY

The store experience reminds me of the pantry in my home. [The store has a complete supply of related products, and I know just where to find everything.]

CONVENIENT

Shopping here makes it easier to plan my family's meal program.

For Il Fornaio, the design concept of the new café and bakery that emerged from the mantra was a "Tuscan ideal." In contrast to a highly ornate and opulent "Roman" concept, for instance, the design values of the Tuscan ideal would be a very high quality concept that is more honestly and simply expressed. For Omaha Steaks, the mantra led to a design concept that would create more reasons for consumers to use the existing product line, develop a new store environment to improve awareness of the company's complete meal offerings and the variety of its products, and make it easier for the customer to navigate the store. These values would increase the frequency of shopping and raise the level of the brand.

Both projects were unfolding as this book went to press, and we cover various aspects of the work in later chapters. In particular, the results of the design effort for Il Fornaio are covered in detail in Chapter 4, "Maximizing the Retail Experience Through Design." The mantra becomes the basis on which you can ideate, create, and execute a new store concept, as the next example involving Gateway Computers shows. Although the business outcome of Gateway's retail experience was unexpected—and to us, disappointing—the process shows how core values should drive all the thought that leads to a new retail approach.

Gateway Computers

Ted Waitt, Gateway's founder and chairman, returned to the company as CEO after a three-year absence and invited my company to help with an ambitious turnaround and reinvention of the company. Ted wanted to create a new category—an end-to-end consumer connection from the Internet to flat-screen television—and to transform Gateway from a PC maker to a "branded integrator" for all these products. He sought a company that could help consumers put together their various home systems to get more education and enjoyment from them—PCs, personal digital devices, DVD players, high-definition televisions, stereo components, games, printers, plasma screens, and whatever else comes along. The approach would create a strong alternative to Best Buy or Circuit City, with their huge, impersonal stores and the sensory overload caused by massive displays of televisions and computer monitors and aisles and aisles of other equipment.

As with other clients, we used the ideation process to come up with three key words to shape the retail experience and store design behind Ted's idea:

> **INVITING**
>
> *A welcoming, comfortable, and communal atmosphere.*
>
> **ENERGIZING**
>
> *An exciting place that makes one feel creative and productive.*
>
> **EDUCATIONAL**
>
> *A playful, interactive experience that promotes learning.*

At the center of our design concept was the area called "hearth," a central area situated at the entry that felt like a family room or den and invited customers into the store. The couches, counter stools, and cocktail table sent an overall subliminal message that this was a place to relax. One side was devoted to a floor-to-ceiling, wood-faced slab that could display various items such as a plasma screen. Merchandise was placed together the way people actually used products, so that customers could see what they needed and what was involved in putting a system together. The setting encouraged a purchase because customers could visualize the items installed in their own home, and training was part of the package. We incorporated Gateway's new logo, a variant of the computer "on" button, in various graphic displays along with several new icons unique to Gateway and subtly infused the company's old black and white cowhide pattern in the artwork.

We designed the store's physical environmental changes to be relatively inexpensive to implement so that we could move very rapidly to execute the concept's rollout to one hundred eighty stores. A modular fixture and graphics package made the design easy to retrofit into existing stores to keep upgrade costs modest. We went from ideation to complete concept design in less than ninety days, and the first store with the new design opened within five months from when we first met with Ted. *See Figure 1-2.*

FIGURE 1-2

The hearth design for Gateway retail stores felt like a family room or den and invited customers into the store. The comfortable setting encouraged individuals to visualize digital systems installed in their own home, which led to increased sales and won a design award. However, a strategic business conflict led Gateway to withdraw from the retail market shortly after the new stores opened, leaving an opening in the "high-touch" home electronics market. (Photo by John Durant. Reprinted with permission.)

In short order, remodeled stores were doing 5 percent more business than they had done previously, and some new pilot stores were doing *42 percent* more business compared to existing stores. In early 2004, however, Ted let me know that Gateway was closing its retail operation! The company had just purchased another PC maker, eMachines. The acquisition gave Gateway a strategic price advantage that greatly enhanced its chances for distribution through other retailers worldwide—but not with the substantial channel conflict created by Gateway's own retail stores. Ironically, the Gateway store redesign project won a SADI (Superior Achievement in Design and Imaging) Award the same week that the company announced the closing of the retail business unit.

Proud as we were of our work in the renewal of the retail concept, we understood the company's need to take another direction. In business, sometimes strategic conflicts can trump the role of any one sales channel, no matter how promising.

Standing for Something and Delivering

Core values for Il Fornaio, Omaha Steaks, and Gateway became both the literal and figurative cornerstones of their retail experiences. Their values led to unique store presentations, unique materials, unique layouts, and these led to unique experiences. For every company, distilling the spirit of the company's retail operations into three key words serves as a useful discipline and provides a focus for business decisions and marketing and operational activities still to be undertaken (many of which are covered later in this book). Equally important, the three-word mantra enables everyone in the company to rally around the company's mission in a way nothing else can.

Where you see a lame mission statement, you see a lame company. Every company must stand for something, and the mission statement says what that is. No matter how mundane its concept might seem, the company must stand for something special and *specific* about its offerings. A local diner might not aspire to be the next national chain, but it can aspire to be something more than a greasy spoon: "We serve the finest breakfast in town." What it stands for can translate into something bigger that resonates with customers, something with *touch*.

"As part of our breakfast," the diner mission statement might say, "we give you 15 very pleasant minutes before the start of your hectic workday." What it stands for can translate into specific systems put in place to benefit customers: "We use the latest, cutting-edge equipment and systems to guarantee the prompt delivery of hot, satisfying meals." And what it stands for can translate into specific behaviors of employees toward customers and of the company toward employees: "To ensure that you have a pleasant experience, we invest in ongoing employee training. We treat our employees well so that they treat you even better."

Your corporate values, which derive from your personal strengths and values, are the intangible but absolutely necessary qualities that ultimately affect the most important ongoing decisions and operations of your company. You have to look deep inside yourself to understand your core values and to develop your core purpose from them. After you do, you will have gone a long way toward creating an enduring brand. Core values and business or company purpose apply whether you launch a new venture or you embark on a new growth strategy for an existing venture. Core values lead to guiding principles, which determine the mission statement and ultimately every aspect of the brand. Strong core values make it unlikely that a retailer will overlook the many components that make up the retail brand and create the customer experience. Core values eventually express themselves in every detail in the implementation and operation of every store, whether the company has one store or thousands or some number in between. As adidas and Starbucks illustrate, a company grounded in strong values has a solid frame of reference from which to evaluate operational and branding decisions and a better likelihood of consistently implementing the brand values in each retail store. As the ice cream store illustrates, even a single failure to connect values to the brand position can have serious detrimental consequences. Thus quality control and consistency become major issues for every chain, and for every new retail concept that seeks to grow. The proof of the core values is the willingness of the retailer to put the considerable effort and time required to provide that quality control in every retail setting. Protecting and projecting the brand is much easier with strong core values. They are the very heart of your enterprise. If you believe, as I do, that growth is an organic and dynamic process, then core values represent the seeds of an organization. From a tiny seed—the right seed—a mighty oak will grow.

CORE VALUES CREATE CORE PURPOSE

- adidas—To be the leading sports brand in the world.
- Cargill—To improve the standard of living around the world.
- Fannie Mae—To strengthen the social fabric by continually democratizing home ownership.
- HP—To make technical contributions for the advancement and welfare of humanity.
- Lost Arrow Corporation—To be a role model for social change.
- Mary Kay—To enrich women's lives.
- McKinsey—To help leading corporations and governments be more successful.
- Sony—To experience the joy of advancing and applying technology for the benefit of the public.
- Wal-Mart—To give ordinary folk the chance to buy the same things as rich people.

CHAPTER 2

Opportunities, Ideation, and Concepts

JUST AS SOME PEOPLE KNOW from an early age that they want to be a doctor or lawyer or writer or actor, some people know they want to have their own business. Others fall into business by accident. This happened with a fellow who installed drywall in my house a few years ago. He went out on his own because he discovered he was good at installing drywall and did not like depending on others. Desire for independence propels a lot of people into business—from the handyman who opens his own hardware store to the mechanic who opens her own auto-repair business.

As with these people, your new business may stem directly from what you do today for someone else. Or, your best opportunity may lie in an area that is a small part of what you do now, but you enjoy immensely. Your opportunity may lie on the edge of your current skill set, the next logical extension of your work. A chef might think, "I should open my own restaurant." However, thinking big means thinking beyond the obvious, the automatic natural choice. Maybe you are a famously temperamental chef and do not have the people skills to successfully run a restaurant. Maybe you would enjoy the variety of a catering business versus the routine of a restaurant. Maybe you love teaching and should open a cooking school. Or, maybe your real skill is organization at large, and you should create a business that supplies fine restaurants with the latest gourmet items.

My own background—architecture, which led to construction management, which led to real estate development, which finally led to retail business development—indicates that some of the best opportunities come when several of the skills you accumulated in a variety of jobs intersect. This often occurs at the juncture of all of the most interesting or challenging things you have taken on to date. Take a close look at such areas. I have an acquaintance who worked as a marketer and customer representative for a high-tech software company. His avocation was flying airplanes. He could have had any number of jobs in the computer industry, but he realized that what he liked best was working with customers involved in manufacturing. He combined all of his interests to take a senior role in production with a startup aircraft manufacturer. He followed his bliss.

When I was growing up, it seemed important to take a specific direction. To be "successful," you were expected to choose one field and stick to it. A person who meandered through different careers was considered aimless. That view is no longer true in today's marketplace, and I am not sure that it ever should have been an expectation. A lot of entrepreneurs seem to follow a winding path. It's not that you get bored with what you have done; it's just that you are eager to learn about new things. This is why, as you consider your business, you should ask what the market really wants that nobody but you can deliver, or that you can deliver in a unique way.

Chapter 1, "It's About Your Values," describes the first step in ideation as the definition of core values. The next step in developing a concept is to ideate on the possibilities in the broadest possible way. Finding the perfect thing for you is the main reason to separate ideation from creation. You want to totally exhaust all the possible ideas for what you *might* do before you start forming a concrete notion of what you *will* do. In considering possibilities, you have to balance the real with the possible. You need an open mind, but not an empty one. If you do not know whether you want to sell flowers on the earth or repair spacesuits on the moon, you will have some difficulty in getting started. However, if you hone in on a specific idea too soon, you limit your vision. Immediately jumping on the idea you "should" do limits your possibilities.

Thus, ideation initially centers on ways to differentiate your concept from every other. Later chapters cover strategic planning and all of the elements that go into it, various legal and operational issues, the need to understand the competitive situation and locate potential markets, and so on. These and other issues are part of the due diligence needed to take a retail concept forward, but before strategic planning can proceed, the retailer has to have reasonable confidence that the concept being developed is unique, fresh, and defensible against competitors. For this reason, this chapter focuses on the ways that a retailer can create a unique concept that has the best opportunity to stand out in a crowded market. The two most important steps toward differentiation are to make your concept both *authentic* and *on trend*. Authenticity, which directly springs from core values, is necessary to ensure that the concept finds a niche. Being on trend is necessary to provide the customer base required for the concept to prosper and grow. The following sections cover these ideas in detail.

Authenticity and High Touch

As competition increases, "high touch" becomes a major way to differentiate any retail offering. As a way of contrast, let's first look at the rise of the Web, a "non-touch" environment. Web pioneers, such as Amazon.com and eBay, sell exclusively on the Web. Amazon and eBay have the powerful brand of successful retailers, but Amazon serves customers with the anonymity of a distributor and eBay functions as a middleman disguised as an invisible auctioneer. Web-only vendors are software platforms that enable commerce. They move products for others and serve as efficient distribution channels. They may be a new mechanism for supply chain management, but they are still evolving as merchants. They have not yet found a way to connect—in the pre-digital sense of the word—with their customers. They are the convenience stores on the information superhighway. Little brand loyalty exists. Price and convenience determine purchases. If a cheaper "candy bar" is being sold down the digital road, you will head over there, and probably soon.

The generic and impersonal nature of the medium drives down prices, which is good for customers, but it makes differentiation difficult for businesses. This is why many Web-only vendors, despite siphoning sales from traditional retailers, have yet to make significant profits.

For all that they live in the virtual world, I have no doubt that Amazon and eBay would love today to have a physical existence to take advantage of their palpable brand identity. However, they can't. The minute an Amazon.com store opened, the minute an eBay-owned boutique opened, their valuations would collapse. The business model for Web-only companies is just too efficient, at least in theory. Their stock valuation is based on the idea that, without brick-and-mortar expenses, their potential for profit growth is exponential. To date, however, most Web-only companies have struggled to make a profit. The most successful company, eBay, does not actually sell anything—it takes a cut from what other people sell. Established brick-and-mortar companies have moved to the Internet to complement physical stores; the "real" and "virtual" activities reinforce the brand. You would think a Web retailer could go in the opposite direction to exploit another sales channel. Nonetheless, Wall Street would interpret the opening of a physical store as a sign of weakness for a Web business. The stock of Web-only companies would collapse, and none of them so far has risked that disaster. The smart ones, however, should be looking for ways to partner with brick-and-mortar companies, as Amazon has begun to do.

The second category of Web vendors is the traditional retailer who uses the Web to supplement physical locations. This group includes catalog vendors who use the Web as an enhanced version of what they have always done. By and large, these are existing national brands. Late to the Web, most major retailers do a good job today of enhancing their brand with Web promotions and with Web stores that complement their physical stores. Websites are valuable as an outlet for overstocks and discounted wares, and an electronic "mailer" is a powerful and inexpensive promotional tool. The number of companies that are a true blend of Web and brick-and-mortar—the clever "click-and-mortar" category—is small, but increasing. Barnes & Noble is one company that makes the physical and virtual realities interchangeable. Customers can order products at a store or online, and they can return them to a physical store or to the online store. The B&N Reader's

Advantage discount card and various gift cards work at a store or on-line. Because the customer experience is integrated, the intangible Web experience and the tangible store experience reinforce a single "easy-to-shop" brand.

Web vendors provide items that are difficult to find, such as clothes in uncommon sizes or unusual designs. It is much easier to Google "sweater with reindeer," to search eBay for *Lord of the Ring* swords, or to go to a retailer's website to find a size 44 pair of slacks than it is to cruise a mall or phone different retail outlets to find a particular style, model, or size you want. This is the one value-added proposition unique to the Web.

In the real world, only three general retail positions have any future. Each one involves different degrees of customer perception and "touch"—human interaction.

EXCLUSIVE SPECIALTY RETAILER

These retailers (Cartier, Furla, Prada, Tiffany's, Williams-Sonoma, and others) offer high-end products, often hand-made, sometimes one-off, that customers cannot find elsewhere. These retailers are the leaders in fashion trends. Customer service is one on one. Prices reflect the perception—and usually the fact—of the highest quality. This category also includes fine restaurants, the "white-tablecloth" category.

THE TARGETED LIFESTYLE RETAILER

These retailers (adidas, Banana Republic, REI, Starbucks, The Body Shop, Victoria's Secret, and others) are personally relevant to the consumer in some way. They are often fun, and they reinforce the lifestyle of an individual. Service is not one on one, but the smaller stores enable the staff to engage customers personally. This category also includes ethnic dining that is not quick serve. An important point of differentiation for this category is that these retailers develop deep loyalty and strong connections with their customers through their political, social, and environmental contributions.

PRICE/VALUE RETAILERS

Big Box concepts are taking most of the remaining volume business, whether the products are underwear, stereos, or plumbing supplies. Most price/value participants are self-serve or have relatively few staff for the size of operation. They are "low touch." The price/value retailers (Wal-Mart, Target, The Home Depot, Costco, Best Buy, Circuit City, and others) use huge volumes to reduce pricing below what smaller retailers can match, as small-town merchants have learned to their dismay. Quick-serve restaurants follow the same general approach. Price/value retailers turn so much volume that they can under-price the typical hometown hardware store, grocery, or bicycle shop.

Between Web vendors cherry-picking the easiest sales, national retailers using the Web as discount outlets, and the price/value retailers dominating commodities, many traditional retailers are losing large chunks of business. Unless your concept lends itself to another Big Box approach—the number of opportunities are limited—some kind of specialty or lifestyle retailing provides the best way to create and differentiate a new brand. Neither a Web experience nor a price/value experience is "high touch." You can be in the middle—neither highest quality nor lowest price—but only if your offerings are unique. When a category collapses to a commodity, when convenience and price are the only drivers, it is time to find a niche. Specialty retailing and targeted lifestyle retailing are the only places where most retailers—small or large—can expect to play with any success. If you are in retail and you are not a Big Box category killer, you better be unique. You must find a way to touch the hearts and minds of customers. Otherwise, your business will be short lived.

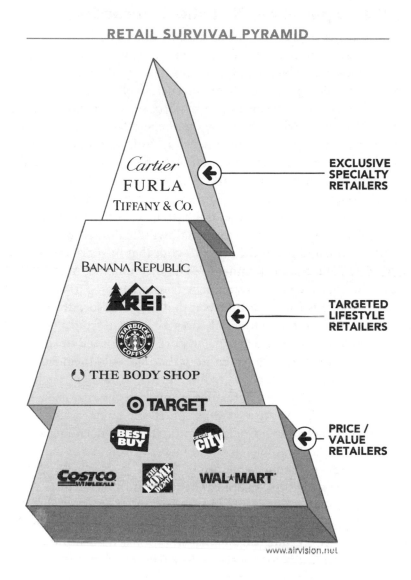

FIGURE 2-1

Only three retail positions now have economic viability: exclusive specialty retailers at the top of the price pyramid; targeted lifestyle retailers, who make a personal connection with consumers in some way; and price/value retailers, who compete on price. Representative brands are shown in each section of the retail survival pyramid. Target is one of the few companies capable of straddling the line between price/value and lifestyle, appealing to both segments.

It's the Experience, Not the Transaction

Niche categories take advantage of the consumer's desire to connect on a personal level and to be treated in a special way. The more hours a person spends in a cubicle conducting business on the phone or staring at the monitor doing work over the Internet, or the more hours a person spends wandering the aisles of a Big Box store, the more that person needs to engage with others one on one and face to face. It could be in a coffee shop, a shoe store, a bench in front of the courthouse, or in the mall. The need to "reach out and touch someone" is more than a metaphor (and more than a marketing phrase for an enterprise that never has *touched* anyone). The simple concept of "high touch" provides great power. When you found the perfect garment at a department store and the salesperson tracked down the desired color and size at another store and had it delivered to you, that memory remains with you. Chuck Williams, the founder of Williams-Sonoma, once took a bus to deliver a cake mold to a panicked customer preparing for a dinner party. A Nordstrom's legend has it that a sales associate once graciously accepted a set of automobile tires as a return from a confused but insistent old lady. The department store does not sell tires, but the associate took the tires over to the store that had sold them and saw that the customer was properly credited. Providing a high-touch experience in this way changes the retailer as much as the customer. You will enjoy knowing you are providing something unique and interesting. You will enjoy your customers as more than an unending stream of tired faces at a checkout line. You will find that you like going out of your way to make customers happy.

It's not as if a Big Box vendor cannot provide a meaningful experience too. Sam Walton was a straightforward, no-nonsense fellow, and Wal-Mart's plain retail experience reflects his personality. To this day, Wal-Mart's success is built on an efficient purchasing distribution platform. To bring a human scale to the cavernous facilities (150,000 square feet and growing larger every year), Wal-Mart has three or four employees stationed at the front to serve as greeters. Greeters, who are usually older because seniors convey trust, direct customers to the right aisles, answer questions, and assist customers however they can. However, their overriding purpose is to individually welcome customers to provide a moment of community at the start of a potentially impersonal shopping expedition. Lowe's, a warehouse-style concept, seeks personable staff who are knowledgeable about home-improvement projects. Although often swamped, they are helpful when available. In such ways, a low-touch concept can provide a high-touch moment—if not a high-touch overall experience.

The best way to deliver high touch is through authenticity. A good example comes from Potbelly Sandwich Works, a rapidly growing chain of restaurants based in Chicago. In 1996, entrepreneur Bryant Keil purchased Potbelly Sandwich Works. At that time, it was a single sandwich shop on Lincoln Avenue in Chicago. The store had been founded by a local couple as an antique shop. They began selling sandwiches to supplement sales. Eventually the food became such a success that the sandwiches developed into the main offering. On his first visit, Bryant was charmed by the store's décor and atmosphere. He was also smitten by the toasted sandwiches made on fresh rolls. Bryant sought the owners out. Once, while the owner was stoking the potbelly stove, Bryant asked him if he had ever thought of opening more stores:

"I haven't met the right person to do it with," the owner said.

"You have now," Bryant said, shaking his hand.

Eventually the owner decided he would rather not be involved in a larger operation and sold the store to Bryant for $1.7 million. "You bought a sandwich shop for *what*?" That is what all his friends asked—but I did not. Not when I saw what he had and what he wanted to do with it.

Although customers came in for the inexpensive, high-quality sandwiches, Bryant understood the need for something more, which is why the quirky atmosphere of Potbelly attracted him. He and I share a common view of the lack of character and charm of the typical quick-serve place. It seems as if all the thought put into them is to make the restaurant cheaper to build and easier to swipe clean. They reflect efficiency, yet they do not reflect anything about how they will be used: as a welcoming spot for customers. The way a typical quick-serve restaurant comes together feels contrived—from the big plastic signs and neon lights to the synthetic tables and chairs to the way the employees speak from scripts instead of thinking and acting on their own. "Anyone can sell a sandwich," Bryant says. "You need to sell an experience." I agree. Customers want to have a natural interaction, not an artificial transaction.

Bryant's goal with Potbelly is to make each store authentic—a real place where you feel you can pull up a chair by the big old stove and sit for a spell. As Bryant attracted investment capital and grew the company from one Chicago store to more than 60 in the eastern United States, he has preserved and elaborated on the atmosphere of the original site. Every Potbelly store has wood countertops rather than lamination, wood floors rather than manufactured floors, period light fixtures rather than cheap fluorescent lighting, eclectic antique furniture, and vintage signs and pictures. A few small stores lack the potbelly stove. Bryant does not duplicate the design mechanically. He chooses the layout, furnishings, and fixtures based on the unique aspects of each site. If a store is in a modern skyscraper with metalframed windows, he might use some wooden millwork to soften the look. Rather than install a wooden floor as he would in an old brownstone building, he might use a terrazzo floor. Keeping it real is the watchword. He is the high sheriff of what he calls his "hokey police" to make sure designs do not go too far. On college campuses, for instance, he shows support without going totally rah-rah. At the University of Michigan store, touches of maize and blue, the school colors, are worked naturally into the décor; the University of Maryland store has touches of Terrapin red. No two stores look the same. They are true to their neighborhoods. They are different, but comfortable. They all have a common theme and the same warm atmosphere.

The point of high touch is to make your customers feel at home. This approach means you treat them with courtesy and respect, to make them feel more like a valued friend than a commercial visitor. Once again: Create an experience rather than a transaction. A real sense of personal involvement by the retailer with the customer creates a personal connection with, and trust in, the brand. Authenticity helps achieve this goal. Because authenticity is hard to fake or copy, by definition an authentic concept gives you a very strong point of differentiation. You must always ask, "What is the distinctive and intimate experience that you can provide for your audience?"

Being On Trend

By the time you read this, more than half the population of the state of California will be of Hispanic descent. When I mentioned this demographic projection to a friend he said, "Boy, now's the time to open a restaurant specializing in local Mexican fare." "You don't know Mexican foods," I said. "You've never run a restaurant. And you don't know Latino neighborhoods. Other than that, it's a great idea."

No one should rush out to open a business strictly because of a trend. However, to avoid being swept out to sea by a contrary tide, you also should not rush out to open a business without *evaluating* trends. Significant trends in population—the growth of one group or the shift of another—can override short-term economic issues, such as interest rates or inflation rates. Such trends may cause your town to grow when others are shrinking or stagnate when others boom. Trends provide context for your business concept, a reality check for whether the concept is likely to succeed, and an insight as to how it might best succeed.

Thus, it is unlikely that genetic engineering will have much effect on the fall rollout of your jewelry line, but the location of a new R&D science center might tell you which neighborhoods could be suitable for upscale shops such as yours. The Hispanic trend in the American Southwest and other major U.S. markets might be a major boost to your concept if you have the expertise to cater to that demographic. The influx might be detrimental if you want to open a restaurant featuring heavy German fare. Or it might be neutral, depending on many other factors. The primary thing is to learn to recognize change and exploit it when possible to your advantage. If you open a clothing shop in a Hispanic area, for instance, you might offer specialty clothing that appeals to young Latinas, or you might have employees that speak Spanish. Even better, you would offer clothing proportioned for Hispanic women. If your concept does not appeal to Hispanics, it must have a *very strong appeal* to another demographic in your area.

Of all the trends, the most important one to consider is the Baby Boomer generation, the huge group born in the decade after World War II. The sheer size of this population group, coupled with a large immigrant segment of similar age, creates an economic impact four times that of any other age group. In the mid-1980s this group bought houses in huge numbers, fueling the growth of suburbs, forcing up home prices, and sending overall consumer debt to unheard of heights. In their twenties they drove the expansion of skiing, tennis, and other outdoor sports. In their thirties they caused the explosion of health clubs. In their forties and fifties, they are accelerating the growth of golf. The cumulative buying power of this group drove increased consumption and the rise of the shopping malls, the growth in eating out and the proliferation of quick-serve restaurants, and most of the other elements we associate with today's popular culture. Clever business-people pay attention to them. Joe Nevin in Aspen, Colorado, noticed that these people—some 80 percent of all snow skiers—were now avoiding the more difficult trails and back-country for fear of injury. Joe created the Bumps for Boomers program, designed to teach older bodies how to engage the whole mountain safely, including moguls and diamond-marked terrain. By opening up the rest of the slopes to this demographic, he hopes to rekindle the interest of the sizable group that fueled the ski boom of the 1970s.

Today's most important economic fact is that these same Boomers are hitting their peak in discretionary income, the result of high income and relatively low expenses as the last of their children leave home. High disposable income implies luxury items, fine shops and services, travel and leisure activities. The Boomers are also starting to move to smaller houses. They are returning to urban condos from the suburbs to re-immerse themselves in city culture, or they are settling in resort areas or non-urban villages with active lifestyles. As they age, Boomers will create new opportunities in the area of senior activities, services, and care facilities.

For a good overview of this and other megatrends I recommend Harry Dent's *The Roaring 2000s: Building the Wealth and Lifestyle You Desire in the Greatest Boom in History*. Dent provides a solid grounding in the biggest long-term cycles involving population growth and movement, technology innovation, and economic patterns world-wide. You may not agree with all his analyses or predictions, but before you get into the construction of subdivisions or shopping centers, you might want to know when the last of the Boomer kids will leave the nest (2009). Or you might want to know which areas are likely to remain boomtowns that will see an influx of prosperous young families who will still need the big homes and malls. Beyond Dent's suggestions on particular locales and investment opportunities, the greatest value of the book is the way it will prime your thinking about the kinds of new goods and services this affluent decade will require, and where the affluent areas are likely to be. After all, a boomtown requires just as many traditional retail businesses as any other town, plus many new services suitable for a dispersed economy shifting more toward telecommuting and small-town business hubs.

From the overall economic context that trends provide you still have to extract some fairly concrete ideas of how to apply them to your situation. A large in-swell of working-class immigrants might bode poorly for a chic restaurant in a particular location, but it could represent a heyday for blue-collar restaurants and shops. All customers—long-term urban dwellers, recent immigrants, and well-established suburbanites alike—are historically very loyal to businesses that do right by them. So a bank might invest in a "lower demographic" location today, catering to hard-working immigrant or inner-city families in order to reap a future return when the families get established, trade up to bigger homes and get loans for their kids' college educations. American Savings Bank in the mid-1990s had created a "doughnut" of bank branches in Los Angeles—a ring of bank branches around the city but none in the center. When the bank responded to community wishes and opened a branch in central L.A., it became the highest-producing branch from its first month, and remains that way to this day. An automobile dealer could adopt the same strategy by selling older but reliable cars in such areas knowing that over time the families will move to more expensive transport.

But if you want to appeal to the high-end Hispanic families—the second or third or fourth generation families that have done very well—you may require a different strategy. The interests and needs of this group will likely parallel those of their non-Hispanic neighbors in the upper-class suburbs rather than those of newly arrived immigrants. The trend informs your approach, but it does not define it.

Many opportunities will emerge to service the Boomers, who are the upcoming "senior generation." Right now about the most exciting "senior concept" in retail is the discount: the 10-percent markdown for seniors, the senior discount for movies, and the half-price, "early bird" dinner. Few businesses other than resorts have figured out that the new seniors-to-be—those turning 50 now—are much wealthier and much healthier than preceding generations. (This sub-group has been labeled the *Zoomers* for their active lifestyles.) Maybe you will open the first nationwide senior gym or an international senior dating service or a national chain of senior discos. Ideation on any concept should at least question how your concept might anticipate the upcoming senior boom. Merrill Garden Intrawest, which is building retirement centers in the American Northwest geared toward the well-to-do, illustrates the potential. People can move into an upscale cottage or condo at age 55 and have in place all the levels of assistance that they might need for the rest of their lives, up to and including assisted living. Personal service for all needs, whether hanging pictures or getting nursing care, is comparable in quality to a high-class hotel.

As Merrill Garden has done, you must funnel a trend down to an actionable level. Consider the current popularity of Altoids, the "curiously strong mint" that has become ubiquitous in convenience stores and supermarkets. A few years ago Altoids was a little-known item produced by a British company with a small but loyal customer base. Kraft Foods realized that the growing number of Thai and Mexican restaurants in the U.S. meant that more and more mainstream individuals were eating spicy fare, heavy on garlic and curry and cilantro. And the more coffee people drank, the more people had "coffee breath." In general, the trend did not mean a lot. To Kraft, the trend offered a specific opportunity. In a genius acquisition, Kraft acquired the granddaddy of all breath mints and made it available broadly. Altoids is now part of millions of people's daily habit. Ten years ago, offering a breath mint would insult someone. Today, Altoids has made offering a mint a social courtesy. (Kraft later sold Altoids along with its Life Savers brand to the Wm. Wrigley Jr. Co. for a substantial profit.)

Make sure you read a trend going forward, not backward. As the Boomers entered the work force, some prognosticators predicted a collapse in casual wear and a boom in traditional business attire as young employees adopted their parents' coat-and-tie business style. Instead, the Boomers brought their casual preferences with them to the office. Now, even U.S. presidents make major appearances in "casual Friday" attire so as not to appear stodgy. As the Boomer children enter society, creating a Boomer echo, they will create similar changes in culture and taste—though it remains to be seen whether the bare midriff will reach the boardroom.

Being smart about applying trends applies to niche concepts as well as niche products. Say you are an expert bicycle mechanic thinking of opening your own store. You have read that Boomers are shifting from running to bicycling to reduce stress on their aging joints. Maybe you uncover a statistic that biking is growing by 15 percent annually in your state. If you live in Aspen, not only are Boomer statistics relevant, but local demographics reinforce them. Your clientele will be industry and movie tycoons who want only the best. Your business could be selling hand-built mountain bikes for $5,000 each. On the other hand, the Boomer trend may be irrelevant for a bike store in a blue-collar neighborhood in Oakland. The primary clientele here would be children and young adults. The right business model is probably high-volume, low-cost street bikes. The questions would be whether the particular area will support this business, and whether that business interests you. Figuring out your specific niche from the broad trend is where—with bicycles particularly—the rubber meets the road.

Successfully Riding Trends

None of the previous examples are new concepts. They are extensions of existing concepts to take advantage of trends. McDonald's did not invent the hamburger joint, but McDonald's was the first quick-serve restaurant to perfect the science of affordable, consistent meals nationwide. Howard Johnson did not invent the motel, but Howard Johnson was the first motel to put together a chain of decent lodgings and restaurants along America's newly completed interstate highways. Starbucks did not invent the coffee house, but Starbucks was the first company to provide high-quality coffee in a high-quality setting worldwide. All three companies repositioned an old commodity or concept. The first two took advantage of the rapidly increasing mobility of the American populace. The latter took advantage of the urban worker's desire for a minute's pampering during a hectic day. Baby Boomers were part of the core audience for all three.

You could say that these companies expanded on an existing concept to create a trend, then rode the wave they created. Other successful concepts are likely to follow the same formula: expansions or variations on existing concepts, or the merger of two existing, related concepts. These success stories provide an important insight to a new retailer: Do not come up with a concept that tries to change consumer behavior but rather one that builds on existing behavior in some way. Elephant Pharmacy in Berkeley, California, for example, represents a cross between the depth and selection of a Walgreens Drugs and the high-touch human atmosphere that Whole Foods Market, the Austin, Texas, chain, has brought to supermarkets. As the name implies, Elephant Pharmacy is big: 12,000 square feet incorporating eleven different departments, from fresh flowers to organic toothpaste and natural cosmetics. The pharmacy quickly differentiates the customer experience. Instead of standing behind an imposing counter, the pharmacists come out to talk with customers. The pharmacy is complemented by a huge assortment of alternative health, beauty, and lifestyle products, including a full-service herbal pharmacy. About the only non-organic business is DVD rentals, and that product ties the store to the neighborhood.

In many ways, Elephant is a convenience store for healthy and educated people, but its primary mission is to educate customers about all their choices in health and beauty. Elephant has a bookstore with 3,000 titles on health-related topics. Every shelf display includes background information about the product for the customer to review. The section on Vitamin C has scientific data that shows that massive amounts of Vitamin C will not necessarily help to prevent a common cold. This information may not sell more Vitamin C, but it builds trust with the consumer, which will lead to greater sales in other areas over time. Every day customers can speak for free with a rotating staff of experts that includes registered nurse practitioners, dieticians, naturopathic doctors, and homeopaths. A classroom on site offers up to six free classes every day. My favorite is the infant massage class. Who wouldn't want to come back to a store where mothers and babies are smiling?

Elephant Pharmacy, so named in order to bring to mind an animal that is large, intelligent and gentle, is a perfect example of innovative retailing hitting an "on trend" niche: well-educated consumers who are willing to pay for the personal attention and care they can receive from a superior pharmacy. The goal of every company is to find such opportunities in an area of retail that's become static, to find a way to break out of a mold. Sometimes the solution is as simple as improving the design or aesthetics of a store or modifying the brand's position to raise the level of customer service. Sometimes the solution is to improve the location of stores. Other times it is to totally reposition the brand. Hip young women buying Burberry clothing or Coach purses would be surprised to learn that these were "old lady" brands a few years ago. Other times, you try even more radical approaches. Recently, a financial institution came to us for advice. They did not come to us and say they wanted to do something "on trend." They did not ask us what the Next Big Thing was. They asked, "How can we logically expand our business? What hasn't been done before in our category? How can we continue to innovate in our retail category and build customer loyalty?"

We proposed that they redefine themselves from being a "financial center" to being a "community center." We suggested that they provide areas for the following: tax preparation, copying and shipping, Internet access, eBay services (including packing and shipping products), and coffee and beverage service. In effect, we proposed a "category killer," a concept that rolls up all related concepts into a new, bigger one. (Think Wal-Mart and shopping or The Home Depot and hardware.) Such new services might sound radical for a bank, but shortly after our proposal we learned that ING Direct, an East Coast bank, had opened three "bank cafés" featuring cappuccinos, Internet connections, and the occasional mortgage loan. New services from banks not only meet additional consumer needs but also put a personal touch back into a business that has too often become sterile. Redefining the concept is also good business. You can open 1,000 bank branches to increase your overall revenues, but federal lending rates will still dictate your profit level. Non-financial services create new revenue sources that have much higher margins.

We are not the only ones to think of combining or expanding concepts, of course. Different fast-food companies are placing their taco, chicken, and burger brands physically together in order to sweep up customers regardless of the type of cuisine they want. One small restaurant has an American burger concept at lunch, run by the husband, and a Thai concept at dinner, run by the wife. Staples, the office supply company, now offers shipping and delivery service via in-house UPS Stores. Seeing a similar synergy between copying and delivery, FedEx bought Kinko's. (We had proposed to our financial institution that it buy Kinko's, only to read in the newspapers a week later that

FedEx had beat us to the punch!) UPS bought Mailboxes Etc. and is rebranding most of the MBE stores to UPS Stores, bridging the gap between service behind the scenes (delivery and inventory management) and service behind the counter (retailing).

Such combined operations raise tough questions about brand. Should each concept remain separately branded? Should one brand disappear to the betterment of the other? Should a new brand be created to encompass the new entity? There is no pat answer. UPS and FedEx bring a distinguished brand quality that Joe's Delivery would not, but Staples and Kinko's are well respected too. The decision rests on the strategic direction of all the parties involved. For example, if Kinko's is simply a way to supplement FedEx's delivery business, then Kinko's should remain a separate brand. If FedEx wants to expand its consumer concept from delivery to a number of new services with delivery as a component, then FedEx should swallow Kinko's and the Kinko's brand should go away. FedEx's advertising of the "FedEx-Kinko's" service shows the difficulty of combining brands or changing over from one positioning to another. Combining the names implied that FedEx would eventually phase out Kinko's. The problem is, the primary personal interaction with the general consumer (as opposed to the corporate shipper) was with Kinko's rather than with FedEx. Further, FedEx's service was part of Kinko's overall offering, making FedEx (psychologically) the subsidiary brand. The combined name did not exactly roll trippingly off the tongue. Was the new branding an example of a non-retailer, FedEx, missing the key consumer touch points? Or was this awkward positioning part of a necessary transition? Ultimately, FedEx must have hoped that its own brand name was powerful enough to overcome short-term consumer confusion.

To extend its services quickly and credibly, a bank might partner with Starbucks for coffee and FedEx-Kinko's for copying and shipping. But, over time, a multi-brand approach might help the brand partners more than you. If a huge Safeway market has a small Starbucks counter in front, nobody is confused about which brand experience predominates and which supplements. But if three equal brands have roughly the same share of a location, the bank may not get "credit" for the new services. Customers might perceive the experience as a trip to a mini-mall when you want them to think, "Wow, look what my bank is doing for me now!"

Changing the experience means changing the brand, and you can extend the brand only as far as the customer will let you. Safeway can logically extend its proposition of selling consumables to include the idea of selling gasoline. The two are a similar experience, and it is convenient for a customer to stop only once for related errands (getting groceries, getting gas). Service stations have long since flipped the idea by selling a variety of quick-food items along with gasoline. A financial services firm can extend itself into a host of business-related services, but lending money *to buy* a car would not relate to pumping gas *into* a car. The two experiences do not compute. Brand *extension* needs to be just that, a process of accretion. Think of it as extending the brand into the welcoming arms of your customer. It is what your customer would want you to do, if only you put yourself in the customer's place. A giant leap into unrelated areas will diminish rather than strengthen the brand. Consumers will not know what you stand for if your brand pillars are too far apart. Extending branded bank services to include coffee and other beverages is probably at the edge of customer acceptance. A bank could partner with Starbucks to test the concept and determine whether, at some point, it is "safe" to bring the service in-house. A final possibility is to sub-brand the entire multi-service concept to keep the primary brand intact and superior. Such decisions often require considerable consumer research as well as a gut feel.

Blue C Sushi: Pulling the Ideas Together to Validate the Concept

After you have developed the concept and know the trend on which it rides, you need to do some initial research to validate the concept. For example, Steve and James of Blue C Sushi took a hard look at the market before proceeding. Three kaiten houses operated in the American Northwest for comparison (James ate at the local one regularly), and of course James had his memories of kaiten restaurants in Japan. The two men got comments, descriptions, impressions, and photographs of kaiten houses from James's friends still living in Japan, and from other friends who traveled to Japan during this time. This up-to-date research enabled them to proceed with a reflection of a "modern Japan" aesthetic. James and Steve also had the opportunity to fly to London to evaluate the two major kaiten chains there. One had three restaurants that were more exclusive and expensive than Blue C Sushi envisioned. The other had fifteen restaurants that were of lower quality (but slightly higher prices) than Blue C Sushi was considering. Both of the concepts were succeeding. Finally, the would-be restaurateurs went to the Internet to examine the many comments and reviews about existing kaiten restaurants to determine how to improve upon the existing offerings worldwide.

When Steve and James first broached the concept to me, I was dubious. "What's another sushi house?" I thought. "What would be different?" But they took me to the local kaiten house one evening. It was in an out-of-the-way spot. The restaurant was a cluttered eatery with light pink Formica countertops and matching floor tiles. The interior was poorly lit. It did not smell particularly fresh. Despite these shortcomings, the place was packed with customers, who were from a variety of economic and ethnic backgrounds. I had never seen a conveyor-style sushi house before, and the flexibility and informality of the operation created an atmosphere that encouraged talk and laughter.

You can tell a lot from the daily operations of similar concepts. (No matter what your idea is, someone has done something similar enough to compare.) Careful observation at the ideation stage provides a good seat-of-the-pants analysis of the market. You can get a good feel as to whether the economics work, whether "the juice is worth the squeeze." Scrutinizing the traffic over several days, we could calculate that the kaiten restaurant was easily doing a million dollars a year in sales! This and the other factors were enough to convince me of the appeal of the concept, not just in Seattle or on the West Coast but throughout the United States. Japan's population of 130 million supported 5,000 kaiten sushi houses, or one restaurant for every 26,000 people. The much larger U.S. population could theoretically support 10,000-plus such restaurants.

Our observation provided the last way to parse a market, which entails looking for what is *not* there. The goal is to find the Achilles" heel of the current leader and determine how you can position your concept to exploit that weakness. As you may have figured out, the weakness of local competitors in kaiten sushi was a lack of quality. Nor was there any aggressive marketing. Of the three kaiten restaurants in the Pacific

Northwest, none was poised for ownership of the category. The owners had done nothing in terms of location, service, branding, or expansion to claim the dominant position. An opportunity beckoned for a new entry.

Blue C Sushi's opportunity presents a textbook example of process for ideating any retail concept. The concept sprang from within them, from their interests and values. Authenticity came from James's background. The trend came from a rising Asian-American population on the West Coast and from a general American desire to eat healthier foods and a willingness to try new cuisines. Taking as ancient a concept as probably exists, the restaurant, they created a variation—and established a niche. They did not plan another generic seafood restaurant or even a generic sushi restaurant but a particular kind of sushi restaurant, the kaiten. They established a point of differentiation, quality. They did enough financial research to establish the concept's economic feasibility. With all this deliberation they were able to both define and validate the concept: a kaiten sushi house that has high quality to win against competitors and low prices to bring in the general public. Validating the concept is the last step in ideation. After that, you begin the process of creation, of developing the concept in specific form. Steve and James had a real opportunity to elevate the concept. "Do it right," I told them, "and you will blow the others away." The same applies to any retailer who finds a new concept or a new variation on an old concept, who identifies the trends that will support the concept, and who focuses on creating a high-touch, authentic experience.

CHAPTER 3

The Importance of the First Store

EVERY ONCE IN A WHILE I meet someone who tells me that he is a real estate developer. "Really?" I ask, "Who are you with?" Usually the person says that he is with Trammell Crow, Opus, or another large development firm. I ask, "Have you ever put up your own personal money for a real estate project? Have you ever had to 'go hard' on a deposit for land and write a nonrefundable check with your own funds?" Almost always the answer is no. I tell them, "If you haven't, you are not a real estate developer—you *work* for a real estate developer." I see something similar with businesspeople in corporations. They say they have a great retail idea and want to go out on their own, but they are making boatloads of money, they have a corporate expense account, and they have the security of running a $50 million corporate operation. They talk about opening their own business, but because "Dad" will not be paying anymore, they become scared. Now it is *my* credit, *my* lease payment, *my* monthly expenses, checks from *my* own account. This fear, which keeps a lot of people tied to corporate apron strings, creates an efficient self-selection process for entrepreneurs. Lee Trevino, who hustled a living from golf before making it on the professional tour, says he never felt pressure in million-dollar tournaments. Pressure, he said, is a five-dollar bet when you have only two dollars in your pocket. Everything changes when it is your money. Until you have had those sleepless nights worrying about the next rent payment or the next payroll, you are not really in business. Your real business education does not begin until you pay the bills out of your own pocket.

Writing that first check begins after you have validated your concept and you move to the actual design and development of your first store. Design of the store also takes you from the stage of ideation (idea generation) to the creation of a physical embodiment of the concept. The implications and consequences of store number one are huge. The first store introduces your brand to the world, and you get only one chance to make a first impression. The store establishes the level of quality and customer service that customers will come to expect. It establishes the points of differentiation between you and competitors. It functions as a laboratory, a living experiment to work out the kinks in operations and merchandising. It presents your store's unique point of view on the respective retail category and demonstrates to employees the kind of person you will be to work for. Not least, the first store establishes to potential investors that you have a practical and potentially profitable business model. Just as your first child is more than a child, but the means by which you establish the basis of your future family life, the first store is the platform for the future of your company. Even if this is the only store you envision ever operating, the guidelines for creating it are the same. Because this is now your check being cashed, you should develop the first store with the same special care you took before you purchased your first new car with your own money!

Done properly, the first store has another role—one of history and perspective. From time to time, Howard Schultz visits Starbucks' first store in Pike Place Market in Seattle, Washington. The Market, a rambling collection of buildings that overlook Elliott Bay, is the cornerstone of Seattle, a "must see" place whenever you are in town. The Pike Place Market board does not allow for modernization of designs. As a result, the original Starbucks store has had only minor interior changes since 1976. The design controls have enabled the Market as well as the individual stores to maintain their original charm. The "soul" of Starbucks is evident in this small building, which is rapidly becoming a historical place. Howard can "return home" whenever he feels the need to connect to the soul of the brand. The first store should always be able to ground you in the values that first established your concept and your brand.

Locationing: Selecting the Perfect Real Estate to Present Your Brand

The two most critical elements in creation of the first store are location and the presentation of store design. Because location is so important to the first store, this chapter concentrates entirely on this topic. Store design and related issues follow in the next two chapters. Too many people treat their first store almost as an orphan, thinking that a "good enough" site is in fact good enough to get started. You should be disciplined in your search for the best location to open your first store. I have met many entrepreneurs who say that they specifically selected an "off-target" location because they wanted to be able to perfect the concept quietly before presenting it to the market. Nonsense! In these cases, the rent is lower, but so what? You still must pay your employees and your operating costs, as well as the rent, lower or not. The only thing you are likely to "perfect" in a sub-par location is bankruptcy. Rule Number One is: Always open your first store in the best location. Rule Number Two is: See Rule Number One. You should be disciplined in your search for the "best" location. Your objective is to find a Grade A site in a Grade A trade area that generates the right kind of traffic, offers great visibility, and has good aesthetics.

Later chapters go into great detail about methodologies to develop the criteria to obtain "A" properties. The point to make now is that there is more to a good site than just a property's X and Y coordinates on a map. Too often in retail real estate, people think in a literal, two-dimensional way. They speak of "the site at the corner of so-and-so." You would think they were targeting a cruise missile. To separate myself from the two-dimensionalists who speak of *siting*, I speak of *locationing*, which defines real estate in terms of branding.

Locationing

lo·ca·tion·ing [lōkáysh'n ing] *n*. The combination of physical and aesthetic attributes of a specific piece of real estate that shapes the consumer's reaction, establishes the retailer's brand positioning, and strongly indicates the potential for sales.

Locationing is the combination of the location of the site itself and its physical layout and characteristics—the specific feel of the surrounding area, the physical presentation of the building to the street, and the way the building and the site will present your business to the customer. Locationing encompasses all the components that enable you to create something physically unique and special for your concept. The examples that follow in this chapter about locationing show the many opportunities to find good properties to establish great brand positioning or to modify properties to improve the brand positioning of the site—that is, to create a brand-building location of an otherwise unremarkable site.

When it comes to locationing, people tend to stumble. Having ideated their concept, they rush to complete the first step toward opening a store, that of securing a location. Staying *disciplined* is the key to doing this step right. When searching for your first location, establish your site criteria and do not waiver from meeting them. Because by definition your first store must be a flagship store—a store that establishes your brand—it is imperative that you put your money into a location that creates a marketing buzz in the community. If you have a new on-trend concept, your flagship store or the initial group of stores needs to be located in the market's core business district (if it caters to business), or in an area that has "influentials," such as individuals with high per capita income, professors in a college town, or trend-setting young singles.

Sometimes landlords, recognizing the benefit of having an intriguing new concept in their building (or just wanting to lease the space), will make a persuasive offer. To lure you into the space, landlords might offer such terms as a large tenant cash allowance to pay for the store build-out or a lease with overly generous and lenient terms. No buyer would knowingly order the wrong product when buying merchandise for a store because the payment schedule was more favorable than the product needed. Neither should a retailer settle for a less than ideal store location because of a "good" lease offer.

People also trip up because they do not think they can afford to pay the higher rents for the better locations. In actuality, you cannot afford *not* to pay the higher rent to get the best location. Securing a great store location is always difficult. In a good economy, finding the perfect available location is a daunting and arduous task. A growing economy creates a landlord-driven leasing market, just as it drives a seller's market in residential real estate. Do not let this difficulty deter you. Saving 30 percent on rent is meaningless if poor storefront visibility and low pedestrian traffic limits the concept's potential sales over a ten-year lease. Short-term thinking on the cost of rent leads to long-term disaster on store revenue. Being even a few doors away from the perfect store location may have serious consequences. One final strategic reason exists to grab the preferred location. By leaving the best place open, you run the risk that a competitor might take it one day and out-position you, like a military force securing the high ground for strategic purposes.

Locationing: Conventional Versus Timeless

Assume that you are considering two locations for your first store. The two are identical in terms of demographics with equal traffic during different day-parts, and so on—both have the usual attributes of a good potential site (without considering the previous attributes of locationing). One site is in a strip mall set back from the street with all the cookie-cutter aspects of typical strip building design: metal doors, anodized aluminum window frames, stucco exterior material with a four-foot high fascia for signs. (The fascia is the location on a building's storefront elevation where a tenant's sign is mounted. The façade is the front or main face of a building.) The other location is a former bank building. Built in 1940, the classic building has a unique architecture and high-quality detailing. The interior has vaulted ceilings and plaster walls. Assuming it fits with your concept, good taste says you would choose the bank. Good business would confirm that decision, even if it costs more money to convert the bank building to suit your new concept's presentation than it would to convert the strip-mall site. The consideration is how the dull conventionality of the strip mall will be perceived from the outside versus the timeless grace of classic unique architecture. The retailer must ask, "How will the customer first react upon viewing and approaching the store by car or foot?"

Properly executed, a strip-mall storefront can adequately present the brand, but it is not usually the best choice of locationing to distinguish your brand and establish your unique presence. In Woodinville, Washington, for instance, a small restaurant known as Italianissimo developed a loyal local dinner clientele, but because of its location in the corner of a strip mall, the establishment never became *the* place to eat. Eventually, the restaurant moved about half a mile away into a new, elegant little center in which it was the primary or anchor tenant. Now, the restaurant is jammed on weekends. It is a place where people want to come. (The owner was clever enough to keep the old location as a bistro for light fare.) You need to ensure that your first store is in a location that presents your brand to the customer in a way that differentiates your business and its offerings. The first store location is as much about exterior aesthetics as it is about being on a great intersection and having great co-tenants.

Banking on Classic Designs

I confess that I am partial to good architecture and stylistic classic buildings with clerestory glass storefronts and humanly scaled detailing. Starbucks was growing at a time when regional banks were consolidating. As a consequence, many banks closed branches all across the country. We converted more former bank spaces into coffeehouse/general retail use than any other company in the world. If we had shipped all the vault doors back to Seattle, we could have opened a museum. (I wanted to preserve the vault doors in some way, and we talked about converting them into tables to use in the coffeehouses; however, bank vault doors made of lead and steel were not designed to be moved easily. It would have cost at least $5,000 to remove and reset each one! So we typically sealed them open and designed the former vault spaces to be used for storage or, in a few cases, for secluded seating areas.) Many banks had been remodeled and updated in the 1950s in ways that covered up the original quality detailing and design of the buildings. It was always an adventure to peel off the existing layers to rediscover the underlying architecture. It is amazing to see what you can find beneath surfaces in older buildings that have been "modernized" over the years—too often in inexpensive or tacky trendy ways. At one early Starbucks store in New York, we stripped away several layers of dropped ceilings and a number of interior wall layers to expose the original brick walls. We used this unique character and refinished the wood floors to create a warm, comfortable, open sitting area on the second floor. We added an eclectic collection of tables, chairs, and couches from garage sales in New Jersey. The total cost of the furnishings was $1,200, keeping the price of authenticity within reason. Part of proper locationing is choosing a building so that, on opening day, your concept looks and feels to the customer as though it has been there for years.

As important as it is to respect the architecture of the building, it is equally important in urban locations to respect the neighborhood that surrounds the store. The store will be more successful if it is an integral and intimate part of its locale. Its "look" should be seamlessly woven into the fabric of the street. With the right real estate, the retailer should strive to present the brand in a way that promotes the business and seamlessly connects to the character of the street. At Oak and Rush in downtown Chicago, we relocated from nearby to take advantage of the opportunity to design a new two-story building on a vacant lot. For our design direction, we picked up the physical proportions of the two-story buildings on the block. The main influence was the window pattern and general curb appeal of the Barneys store opposite us. The result was a flagship store presentation for Starbucks in the major market of Chicago, helping to position us as the leader in the coffee category.

In Vancouver, B.C., we redesigned a former restaurant; among other changes, we reused operable overhead garage doors that roll open, enabling customers to look out on a lake in an indoor/outdoor design and directly connect to sidewalk activity. This is another example of the use of unique physical design elements to build brand awareness. The distinctive storefront gives the customer something to talk about and relate to, supporting the brand's position in the community's eyes. Across from the ABC television headquarters in the upper west side neighborhood of New York, we painted a mural of a theater audience on a wall looking toward the customers inside the Starbucks store as a thematic connection to the Lincoln Center and the ABC neighborhood. The mural not only connected our store and brand to the work of most of our customers there, but it also served as a backdrop for the television interviews that are held in the store on a regular basis. On Chestnut Street, a favorite neighborhood strolling street in San Francisco, we were the first to install operable, sliding-glass storefront windows to bring the street into the store and allow our customers to connect to the activity on the sidewalk. At a location in Seattle, we transformed a rundown hamburger outlet by peeling away the walls and ceiling layers to reveal the building's structural beams and columns. The store design fit in well with the Northwest architectural style. Like many others, that Starbucks store has a fireplace. I have seen parents in there dressing their kids for weekend snow skiing outings, people assembling to meet their carpool there, and lots and lots of meetings taking place. I knew that we were succeeding with our designs when customers were so comfortable in the store that they relaxed as they would in their own living rooms.

Making the Most of Physical Presence

Even if you do not have a landmark location, you can still demonstrate vision in the way you use the physical presence of the site to best present your brand. Rather than accept an existing building design formerly leased by a fast-food chain in Vancouver, Washington, we added a two-story tower element to display the Starbucks sign for the 60,000 vehicles passing daily. Here is the idea again of the "brand beacon," of using your real estate to build brand awareness. We used architectural tower elements elsewhere when they effectively served to highlight the brand. In a shopping center near the University of Washington in Seattle, we were offered a great corner location in an older shopping center that was undergoing renovation. We created a new two-story façade with a steel and glass awning that wrapped around the entire storefront. The design was so exciting that other retail shops around the store picked up the motif. In Sacramento, California, we added on an outdoor pergola to an existing nondescript building that not only served as a brand beacon but also served to create and enclose an inviting shaded outdoor sitting area. In Santa Barbara, a city well known for its agreeable year-round climate, we wanted to offer outdoor sidewalk seating to our patrons. The store is located in a typical neighborhood shopping center. The sidewalk was too narrow to allow us to set out tables and chairs, so we pulled back the actual storefront to create an outdoor space for five or six tables. This amenity for customers immediately differentiated our location from that of our competitors.

One of the biggest challenges for restaurants is that many city building codes discourage outdoor café seating areas. San Francisco is a city where you might expect a lively café life, but for a while San Francisco had such restrictive codes that it was almost impossible to open a new restaurant. What had happened is that in the 1980s, the original Gianini Bank building, now known as the Bank of America building, was vacated and ultimately leased to a Carl's Jr. hamburger franchise. The citizenry, who pride themselves on the town's culture and architecture, went berserk at the sight of one of the oldest and most important buildings in the city becoming a fast-food restaurant. To avert the spread of other fast-feeders, the planning commission adopted a rule to prevent the conversion of any existing retail uses to restaurant sit-down service. To open a restaurant in the City of San Francisco, you effectively had to buy an existing one, and for a chain that would have been economically unfeasible.

At that time, I was a principal in the real estate brokerage representing Starbucks in Northern California. In 1991, I identified three great available locations in the city that had been formerly occupied by general retail users. Because each of them had an existing built-up window display platform from the previous use, they could be used as benches for perhaps a dozen Starbucks customers. Because the beverage line would efficiently serve the majority of customers, I knew Starbucks would be successful in these units despite the lack of other seats. Yet I could not believe the city would continue to forbid restaurant development. I had lived in San Francisco for a number of years. It is a beautiful city, a lovely place to walk, one of the most livable cities in America in its atmosphere and outlook on life. Yet it had little night life and lacked the most visible feature of Mediterranean towns: outdoor cafés. When I joined Starbucks as senior vice president that year,

I offered up my idea for the company to be the catalyst to convince the city of San Francisco to modify the planning code to allow more sit-down uses. Starbucks agreed to support the effort. We found a land-use attorney and a public relations expert who understood how to move changes through the political process. Our proposal would enable a general retail space to be converted to allow sit-down food consumption if the dedicated seating area in the new store was limited; the final proposal specified that such areas would be no greater than 400 square feet with no more than 15 seats. The "beverage house" code, as it became known, quickly developed support and appeared to be heading for passage.

Then, four days before the code's proposed adoption, one of our supporters had a "slight" change of mind and wanted to exclude from the new rule the North Beach neighborhood, which had a number of Italian restaurants and coffeehouses that served primarily cappuccino drinks. The North Beach neighborhood also had plenty of restaurants, and its sidewalks were the most vibrant in the entire city. Our supporter, who had decided to run for mayor, could not be seen allowing Starbucks to "threaten" the restaurants in North Beach, her political base. We did not argue, as long as the rule applied to the rest of the city. To this day, Starbucks still has no stores in the core of the North Beach commercial district.

Obviously, Starbucks benefited from the addition of the new code. We also opened the door to many other coffee and dessert shops, juice shops, bagel shops, pizza shops, and innumerable small cafés. As more restaurants came into being, more of them also began to use outdoor seating, which was reasonably easy to obtain under the rules. It took several years for the change to take hold, but by 1996 the city's street life had become visibly richer. ... And that is how a coffee purveyor from Seattle helped improve the street ambience of San Francisco.

Two lessons emerge from this story. The first lesson is that if government regulations prohibit the development of reasonable retail activity—activity that improves the quality of life for local residents—then you can work within the system to create change. It will take time, energy, and money, but if you create a proposal that takes into account the genuine concerns of the government and the populace, you usually will be successful. The second lesson is not to be deterred by obstacles. Starbucks refused to accept the status quo. We persevered in taking the steps necessary to create brand-building locations for this market.

To show how the wheel keeps turning, San Francisco recently enacted another ordinance that requires any "formula retailers" with a dozen or more stores—in other words, any retail chain—to notify residents of any plans to locate a store in their neighborhoods. The goal is to give residents a chance to comment on new retail stores, but the reality is that the law will stop retailers from coming in. The ordinance also banned chains entirely from one business district. At the minimum, the ordinance will increase costs for retailers and delay openings, and opposition by even a small number of determined activists could prevent any "outsiders" from opening. The law also could have the perverse effect of slowing down the growth of any rapidly expanding local businesses, such as Andronico's, a Bay Area supermarket with 11 stores. Though it is understandable that citizens do not want their streets and neighborhoods to be homogenized by cheap, generic store designs, the ordinance as written is too severe. A better approach would be to limit each chain to one store per neighborhood, with the definition of neighborhood left to the planning department, and to insist on better designs.

San Francisco's reaction is a long-term warning to all retailers of the need for interesting, fresh, varied, quality store presentations. A "one design fits all" mentality no longer suffices. A major national chain store in Seattle's Capitol Hill neighborhood is a textbook case of visual insensitivity. The standard materials used in the building conflict with the materials of the neighborhood. The sign is the biggest sign for four blocks. The parking lot is in front, breaking the plane of the pedestrian sidewalk. A slightly different choice of materials would have blended in the building with others nearby. A scaled-down sign would still have provided great visibility without overwhelming the area. The parking lot could have been put in back, keeping the street and entrance pedestrian-friendly. Three changes, only one of which would have cost more, and the positive impact would have been enormous. In most cases, neighborhood-friendly designs make the initial cost for chains a little higher. However, the increased acceptance by the community and the loyalty that such sensitivity shows drives higher revenues. Only the law of bad design says a chain store has to look like a chain store.

Discovering the Sense of Place

When we first talked about Blue C Sushi, James Allard and Steve Rosen told me that they expected their first store to be open in four to six months. Doing it right, I told them, would take at least three times as long. They laughed at me ("guffawed" is James's recollection). Their restaurant opened 18 months later.

Much of that time was spent in finding the right location. They looked at more than 50 places in the Seattle area. They would bring me in whenever they identified an interesting potential site for the first store, and I would match it up to our site criteria and shoot it down. They particularly wanted one site in the heart of downtown Seattle. To the inexperienced eye, the site was great. It was on the same block as a three-story Niketown flagship store and an Old Navy clothing store. But the other smaller co-tenants on the block would not drive enough midday traffic to Blue C Sushi during the week, and the building façade had no "pop" to it, no visual draw. If it were located mid-block with a non-descript storefront, Blue C Sushi would not be able to distinguish itself. They would be just another retailer located on just another downtown street. The lesson here is to strive to occupy a storefront that serves as a marketing beacon for your brand. In building Starbucks' brand we took highly visible corners to shout the name out to pedestrians. We always looked for "the corner of Main & Main," as we called such spots. Because of locationing, you could not miss learning the brand. If James and Steve could have secured space on the other side of the street I would have approved it. The reason is that the western side of the street featured more opportunities for storefront design on a human scale, more retail shops in total, and more varied retailers whose appealing window merchandising resulted in *30 percent more* pedestrian traffic on that side.

They also looked in Bellevue, which is an affluent community 20 minutes east of Seattle across Lake Washington. In the last 15 years, the eastside, high-tech boom has turned Bellevue's sleepy downtown into a steel-and-glass high-rise core. Its major shopping intersection is anchored by Bellevue Square Mall, a huge, constantly expanding complex. Several sites in this area offered good traffic flow and visibility, but every potential location was situated in buildings set back on the site; large parking lots separated the storefronts from the street. The sites looked too similar to the existing downscale kaiten sushi competitor already operating in town. A stylish concept will never lift up a poor real estate location, but a poor real estate location will always bring down a stylish concept. In addition, none of the shopping districts in Bellevue offered a neighborhood location that would be busy seven days a week and in which the concept could take root and build a loyal local following. In other words, we were looking for a location that was neighborhood-oriented and also could draw customers from out of the area.

Eventually Steve and James identified a terrific location in the Fremont area, otherwise known as the Greenwich Village of Seattle. Recognized for its eclectic retailers, creative architecture, and the public art displays on its streets, Fremont is a well defined and growing neighborhood much desired by singles and couples. It is considered a hip area to office. There is a high daytime population of businesspeople working in newly constructed office buildings during the weekdays and plenty of local residents and shoppers strolling the streets at all hours every day of the week. It is known as a destination neighborhood, where you would spend an evening walking around and finding a place to eat. If you mention the area to anyone who has explored Seattle, they will say, "Oh, Fremont—I love walking around there!" It has a "sense of place," a phrase that is difficult to define precisely, but includes a distinct, pleasant identity that draws people. Any area where people like to gather has a sense of place. It can be a town square, a neighborhood, or a quiet street. Bellevue, in contrast, has no sense of place. The downtown core consists of a number of office buildings dissected by clamorous, congested multilane streets. Surrounding neighborhoods are generically suburban. Communities that maintain a sense of place are much more active and have more vibrant retail experiences.

The specific location that Blue C Sushi found was on Fremont Avenue, the main north-south street connecting downtown Seattle to the south with another popular neighborhood, Ballard, to the north. The building itself was a new mid-rise, mixed-use complex with underground parking for retail customers. The building design featured a modern, high, glass and steel storefront presentation for the cutting-edge Blue C Sushi concept. Co-tenants in the building included a West Coast-based coffee house, an upscale grocery that was part of an expanding local franchise, and an upscale ice cream franchise that was part of a rapidly expanding national franchise. The overall high level of foot traffic drives a strong lunch and dinner crowd seven days a week. The actual layout of the space required us to make several compromises, but generally, attention to design can overcome most physical limitations of a site, so we did not let physical constraints prevent us from choosing the best location. Finally, we were able to negotiate a few important lease concessions that gave James and Steve an option to sublease the space if the restaurant did not succeed. Always protect your downside when signing a long-term lease, a topic covered in detail in Chapter 15, "Real Estate: Who Needs Who More, When."

Blue C Sushi exemplifies the point that the best way to avoid making mistakes comes through a disciplined approach to locationing. Bryant Keil of Potbelly would rather not go into a market at all than take a secondary location. He knows what site criteria works for his stores to be successful and understands the importance of ensuring that each store is profitable. For your first store especially, keep in mind the imperative of *location, location, location*. If you cannot find a good location to lease in your targeted market, wait until you can. Do not take a lesser location just because it is available. Proper locationing improves the bottom line and more than justifies the added cost over an inferior site. Equally important, every location, particularly the first one, must be treated as an opportunity to establish the brand in the strongest way possible.

CHAPTER 4

Maximizing the Retail Experience Through Design

THIS CHAPTER COULD very well be titled "The Importance of the First Store, Part II." If finding a Grade A location is the initial step in claiming a powerful brand position with the first store, then the proper design of the store completes that process through the physical manifestation of the brand. Finding a designer with the experience and artistic skills to translate a concept into a physical reality can be just as difficult as finding the perfect location, and the process requires the same level of determination and focus. This chapter takes you through the many design considerations, explains the trade-offs between a one-off store design and a design intended for multiple rollouts, and introduces the concept of "Kit of Parts," an approach to produce high-quality equipment and fixtures in high volume and at low prices. To show how design issues play out in actual retail projects, this chapter first examines a design project for a start-up retail venture, and then examines a major redesign project for an existing major retail chain. Together, these examples paint a comprehensive picture of design issues and concerns during the entire life of a retail brand.

Designing for One or Many: The First Decision

After Steve and James of Blue C Sushi found their first location, they set out to engage a design firm that could take their conceptual ideas and create the physical solution to their vision, an environmental design that communicates the concept and establishes the brand's position. I arranged for them to interview three companies that I thought would be able to translate their vision into reality. After a couple of meetings with each firm, they selected Foundation Design in Seattle. David Edelstein, who runs Foundation Design, was instrumental in developing the Tommy Bahama brand. Having traveled to Japan, the design principals knew modern Japanese architecture, technology, pop culture, and music—everything that makes modern Japan fresh and exciting. When James said that he wanted to open a Japanese kaiten sushi restaurant with a "twist," they understood his desire to upgrade the cafeteria feel that is typical of kaiten houses in Japan as well as in the United States. When the passionate entrepreneurs talked about a blend of Japanese and Western culture, the designers recognized the Asian-Northwest visual sensibility they were seeking. It was a good fit because their point of view and personalities meshed with those of the Blue C Sushi founders.

We were close to executing the lease for the first store and needed to finish the concept design, so we met weekly and Foundation Design went through a number of design renditions fairly quickly. In one meeting, James and Steve seemed pleased with the latest work being presented. The conceptual thinking was excellent in many ways, but I grew more and more restive during the presentation. Finally, James picked up on my unease and asked me for a pointed critique of the proposed direction. From our earliest meetings, the two men had discussed their desire to open multiple stores if the concept was successful. "The work has some cool elements," I said, "but I'm not seeing unique materials and cutting-edge combinations of materials that could give us a point of differentiation. I want to see design elements that we can own and can use to roll out a lot of stores." My concern involved a number of things, from material choices to the booth design, to the major graphical elements intended for the walls. The proposed graphic was line art, navy blue and white, showing a series of hands holding chopsticks in different positions, a reproduction of the graphical instructions on the use of chopsticks that are often found on chopstick packaging. The idea was that customers would recognize these elements as instructions and feel welcomed (especially novices to sushi), or that customers would consider the graphic as pop art. I felt that the visual work needed to be richer and more interesting.

Overall, the designers had conceived a beautiful individual restaurant design. However, we were looking for a design that would be applicable to a multiple-store rollout. The first practical consideration for any retailer is whether the design will be for a one-off store or for a rollout of multiple stores. If it is for a single store, the design can maximize the fittings and furnishings for the size and shape of the specific location, but no economies of scale will occur in design or construction. In effect, the retailer will pay a premium for all aspects of the project. For a multiple-store rollout, the imperative is to make the design visually appealing while keeping it modular enough to spread the expense across multiple stores. The cornerstone to a multiple rollout is the idea of the "Kit of Parts," a comprehensive approach to store design and execution. The idea is to integrate all the elements of store design, from cabinets to fixtures to colors to visual imagery, so that they work in harmony to create an impression unique to the concept. Further, all of these parts are engineered to enable a relatively inexpensive rollout to many stores. Because individual components work in so many different combinations, they create an effective total presentation regardless of the size or shape of the space—whether the space is, say, 1,500 square feet or 3,000 square feet. In the Kit of Parts approach, the goal is to make each fixture small enough to fit any store but large enough to be manageable. A cabinet that is 12 feet wide will probably fit in only one out of five stores, whereas one that is 30 inches wide will probably fit in every store.

Each category of retail has different fixture concerns. Apparel sales require larger tables, wall racks, and freestanding racks. Hand goods require smaller tables and wall displays. Restaurants require a variety of cabinets, tables, and chairs. Jewelry stores require large banks of display cases plus sitting areas where sales staff can work with customers. At Banana Republic and other chains, you will notice a standard-size table for clothing. Tables can be broken down to make them smaller or clipped together to create larger displays. Such modular features are called "rollable" elements that can be built or bought in advance, in quantity. This approach enables a company to obtain discounts through the volume of work brought to suppliers and contractors. When the operation is large enough—opening 30 to 50 stores a year—the retailer should generate enough volume to obtain just-in-time delivery of components from critical suppliers.

Regarding the restaurant, my concern with the work of Foundation Design was that I did not see a design theme that Blue C could own and carry to the second, third, or fortieth store or a way to achieve economies of scale with future stores. Fortunately, the designers understood the feedback. Two weeks later they returned with a design concept that was intrinsically different. It had the same aesthetic sensibility as the earlier work but included a material and color palette that could be repeated in a number of ways in different environments. The use of materials was unique enough that we could "own" the elements as part of Blue C Sushi's presentation. Further, in the final design, the physical arrangement provided good flow for both customers and store personnel, and put the main branding element of the restaurant—the sushi chef—front and center. The conveyor belt, which is the centerpiece of the store, was laid out to place the senior sushi chef, who prepares much of the sushi to be served, where he would be visible to everyone in the space. The chef was within eye contact of the front door and was in position to greet entering customers. It would be instantly clear to customers that this is a serious sushi restaurant. Two or three other chefs would also be out front. Surrounding the chefs would be the conveyor belt carrying the sushi. Most of the customers would face the belt, from which they could pull their selections. The food preparation and the people facing inward toward each other would provide the unique theatrical dining/entertainment experience. The down-lights would highlight the sushi on the conveyor and present it like jewels in a display case. The tables would be dark-stained, solid wood providing a nice color contrast to the lighter-colored plates. There would be shoulder-height tile on the walls (an earth color—I vetoed white as being too institutional). Higher tile is special because tile is normally used as wainscoting, set to a lower height of 30 inches above the floor. Higher placement of wall tiles (in this case taken up to four feet, six inches above the floor) creates a powerful visual impact. There would be a large panorama on the back wall depicting the Fremont neighborhood, created by a Japanese and American couple from Los Angeles who specialized in storytelling art. This mural concept could be commissioned to show the neighborhood around every future store, anchoring the restaurant and brand to the community. Large glass windows would open the restaurant to the street, creating an opportunity to excite pedestrians who would be walking by. In general, incorporating as much storefront glass as possible turns a store or restaurant into a stage set and enables the pedestrians passing by to be part of the audience. Large windows also act as a beacon, especially at night when the interior lights are on. This restaurant concept was to be inclusive and inviting. Allowing customers to see in supports the positioning of Bluc C Sushi as a fast-casual dining experience. On the whole, the design was an original avant-garde environment. The feel was an exciting, unique, interactive, and informal dining experience. You would tell your most interesting friends about it and want to take them there to eat.

James and Steve were able to turn both of the space's physical limitations into an advantage. The first problem was that the space included a 700-square-foot mezzanine that the conveyor belt could not reach but for which they still paid rent. Until then the Blue C Sushi economic model did not call for a separate bar for alcohol. Bottled beer and wine were to be served from the kitchen refrigerator. They designed an upper bar area that would generate more revenue and provide a place for people to wait until booths were available downstairs. To best utilize the mezzanine, we designed an open mesh-steel railing for the upper space that made it feel more open and more visually accessible and inviting. The view down from the mezzanine to the eclectic crowd below provided another theatrical element. The second problem was that the 1,600-square-foot main floor did not provide enough space for a kitchen and storage room. We had to build the kitchen in the basement along with offices and restrooms. Overall, we were successful. The final design solution, as the customer sees it, reinforces the brand.

FIGURE 4-1

Blue C Sushi's design creates a unique combination of community, retail theater, and high-quality, inexpensive food—all built around the kaiten sushi-on-conveyor concept and sushi chefs serving from the center. (Photo courtesy of Blue C Sushi)

Using Design to Reinvent Brand

Creating a compelling design and rolling it out inexpensively can be as trying for an existing chain as for an inexperienced start-up. Certainly the process is more complex, although usually the existing retailer has more resources to apply as well. Starbucks faced the problem of an "aging" design in the early 1990s even though the company was relatively new. A little-known secret of Starbucks' success is that the company has had store designers in-house since 1991. The "Main & Main" strategy—locating stores on highly visible corners—required us to develop custom designs to fit spaces of unusual sizes and shapes. When I joined the company in 1992, it was apparent to me that we had to develop our in-house design capability to keep up with projected growth. Starting with a handful of designers, we had more than 150 a decade later. At its business core, however, Starbucks is a concept driven by real estate, so my initial effort as senior vice president was to properly organize and focus our real estate group toward the goal of national expansion. At this time, Starbucks was shifting from opening dozens of new stores a year to hundreds. The company's store designs needed to be reinvented to keep up with our innovative brand positioning, but without good real estate all the leading-edge design in the world does not mean anything. Our original store design concept would take us to 1,000 stores, I told the other senior managers, so give me the time to put the real estate strategy in place and establish our regional real estate offices to enable us to execute rapid and orderly expansion.

At the same time, I knew that our competitors were hot on our heels and our store designs would not be good enough for the next 1,000 stores. Although each Starbucks store was custom designed, we were beginning to hear complaints that our stores had an institutional feel, that they were perhaps even a bit sterile and cookie cutter. For a company that prided itself in creating a personal connection with customers, the criticism stung. In addition, our cost per store was rising as we attempted to be more creative, going as high as $350,000 a store. The design challenge was daunting: create a distinctive, personal look; make that look compatible with each locale; reduce costs; and be able to roll out the design all over the country—and soon, the world. To capture the essence of the "Third Place"—a place where people gather between work and home but without the pressures of either—we had to come up with cutting-edge designs that differentiated Starbucks' brand.

I researched many of the top retail architectural firms in the country. I actually hired one but ended the relationship after several months. Many architects with proven experience in residential, commercial, and institutional projects often claim that they can design and build dynamic store or restaurant environments. But they are not in touch with the retailer's mindset or the retail experience. We are back to that problem again of some designers thinking in two dimensions rather than three, of people seeing only in terms of floor plans rather than the overall customer experience, of not understanding how to create a design that reinforces a brand. In addition, many designers or architects develop a certain "house style." Their designs become predictable. It is likely that your project will look similar to their previous work. This rote approach will not get you a fresh idea. Such architects may design useful space, yet fail to capture the soul of a brand, to create an atmosphere that will connect with the hearts and minds of the customers. They are likely to give you designs that are the retail trend *de jour*, theirs or others, as opposed to designs that are functional and timeless. Did you ever wonder why most clothing retail stores look and feel alike? The Gap feels like J. Crew, which feels like Abercrombie & Fitch, which feels like ... The problem is not with the look of any one of the chains' stores; it is that the chains all look the same. Most architects keep up with retail trends but are not able to take the time to be innovative. Retail is moving so quickly that designers need to be current. In the mid-1990s, for example, bagels became the hot concept. It was expected for this category to mature in three to five years. Instead, it matured in about two years. At Starbucks, we were faced with an onslaught of competitors, both independent coffee shops and regional chains. The coffee may not have been as good, but the environments were comfortable. We had to move fast with designers who "got" what we were about.

To meet our challenges, I decided to take a risk and develop the new store prototypes in-house. We would find the best group of people possible and bring them in house, inculcate them in our coffee culture, our values, and our design philosophy, and then turn them loose to come up with our store of the future. We brought together architects, interior designers, graphic designers, lighting designers, poets, artists, writers, and engineers. Among those willing to sign on was a group of freelance designers, artists, and architects that included a designer named Bill Sleeth. This brash group showed us their portfolios with the attitude of, "Here's what we've done, hire us." We did. That first interview with Bill established a relationship that continues to this day, as becomes clear in Chapter 5, "Seamlessly Connecting Design to Brand While Staying on Budget."

Hidden in a loft space in the Starbucks building in Seattle, the new team functioned as a classic "skunk works," set off on their own with little internal oversight to explore new designs. They reported to Wright Massey, the vice president of design, who reported to me. Wright was an artist as well as an architect. He had retail background as well as resort hotel experience from working for Disney. He knew that good retail design enhanced the retail customer experience. He knew how to use graphical imagery to create a visual language to tell the story of the brand.

Access to the group was limited—only a handful of people even knew the team existed. We invited our in-house design talent to participate as well. CEO Howard Schultz came by to explain his vision for what Starbucks should be. The goal was not to just come up with a new color scheme or style of furniture and fixtures but to dig deep into coffee culture and mythology to capture the essence of the spirit behind our business. The team explored the history of the company, of coffee use and cultivation, of the mythology of the sea (Starbucks was the first mate in *Moby Dick*), of the siren who lured unsuspecting sailors into the rocks. The team kicked around the notion of what the Third Place meant to them. A number of different visual approaches emerged.

Wright worried as to whether he was going to get shot over the transformation he was undertaking. In a lot of companies, unpleasantness flows downhill, but a good manager knows that often his duty is to shield his teams from pressure from above. The design team already felt the weight of responsibility for the company's future. My job was to make sure that they kept their heads in the game. Before a major presentation, I would visit informally with Wright and his team to understand their latest direction and to make sure that they were rolling up all of their individual ideas into a larger business message. One time a couple of the designers were talking to me excitedly about how they could use the maritime theme to create unique visuals. With others listening I asked innocently, "So you're creating an iconography that Starbucks can own?" "Yes!" they replied. These were smart people.

They understood the hint to provide the business justification for the new visuals, which was to help Starbucks maintain an exclusive identity. At the presentation the next day, they couched everything in the context of the brand.

From small victories comes large momentum. Many people do not realize that successful architecture includes the need to sell your client on your point of view. We needed in short order to gain Howard's confidence as well as that of Orin Smith, then chief financial officer and later president and CEO. With their belief in our ability to succeed, we would be granted more funds with which to continue our journey. I made a point of rolling out some of the new visual concepts first in the creation of new kiosks. We presented more than 20 new kiosk-style formats to management for their review and to show them that we were going in the right direction. Out of this first stage came the *breve* bar and the *doppio* (named for a double shot of espresso). The breve bar is designed for a store-in-store display in the lobby of an office building or in the front of a supermarket; the doppio can fit into an even smaller space such as you might find on a college campus or county fair and can be put up or taken down in a few hours. Although prefabricated, both kiosks incorporated the same high-quality materials and finish as used in regular stores. As soon as Howard and the other senior managers developed confidence in the look and feel of the kiosks as proof of our design direction, they authorized us to continue working on the overall new store designs. We had earned another month of work!

Creating Brand Touchstones

Design is a process. Many times when starting out, you establish design parameters and objectives having no idea where you will end up. Out of this process, the designers developed a set of brand "touchstones" built on the alchemy of coffee and the traditional concepts of earth, fire, water, and air. A touchstone is a word, phrase, or image that attempts to capture the essence of the design approach. All future work should refer back to a touchstone in an obvious or sometimes subtle way. Each of the elements related to stages of the coffee bean development, and each of the elements directed us toward a distinctive color palette. *Earth*, which corresponds to *grow*, has shades of green. *Fire*, which corresponds to *roast*, has deep reds and browns. *Water*, which corresponds to *brew*, has blue for water and brown for coffee. *Aroma*, which corresponds to *air*, has light shades of yellow, green, and white.

These new touchstones gave us an organic rather than a commercial look. No Gap-lookalike possibilities here. No use of trendy plastic materials. Hard edges and metallic sheens were eliminated as well. In their place were soft edges, natural materials, and soothing colors. Packaging and iconography were similarly modified to reflect the new motifs. Stores would have wallpaper or hand-painted murals. Round tables would be used exclusively in the seating areas in place of tables with right-angle corners. A single person at a square table looks (and possibly feels) lonely. A round table is less formal, has no "empty" seats, and the lack of right-angle edges makes the person seated at the table feel less isolated. The new designs celebrated the art of custom crafting espresso beverages by using a hand-blown light fixture to spotlight the drinks set on a raised curved wooden handoff platform where the barista presents the beverage to the customer.

From these basic ideas, we created a design playbook containing the four distinct templates, four color palettes, and four distinct formats and describing how they could be mixed and matched for different effects. The design playbook had a rubber cover, a tradition that Wright brought with him from Disney, and became known as the "rubber book." This playbook allowed us to create as many as 12 different store designs, easily varying them from urban to suburban, from high-end neighborhood to funky college area, without having to develop a new creative approach each time from scratch. In Vancouver, B.C., for example, we ended up with two stores diagonally across from each other. One store was in a traditional brick building, the other in a newly erected modern building. Using the new designs, we created two distinctly different visual atmospheres: one that appealed to the general population that frequented the brick building and one that appealed to the hip crowd that frequented the new building to see and be seen.

With the signoff by Howard and others on the new designs, we did not have time to celebrate. Work became the celebration. New designs in hand, we value-engineered each component to lower its costs for mass production, making the overall store construction costs more predictable. Instead of having construction managers trying to save nickels and dimes on a store-by-store basis, we designed and engineered the components in our stores to generate huge savings across the entire chain. This effort came to be known as the "Kit of Parts" approach, the modular component design for flexibility in store layouts. Like quick-serve restaurants, we standardized as many store components as possible—*but we did so without reducing the quality of the components themselves*. We focused on the equipment, fixtures, and cabinetry that every store would need, such as countertops and drawers for coffee beans storage and display racks for pastries. Using computer-aided design software, we were able to lay out the main components of any new store in modular form, using filler panels for any leftover space. Having several different seating possibilities from small tables to long library tables, we were able to develop flexible seating arrangements to match almost any size and shape. Experience taught us that 80 percent or more of every store could be fitted with standard components. Our designers, then, could focus on customizing the remaining 20 percent or so to make it as unique and interesting as possible.

Initially, we were able to prestock standard items at volume discounts of 20 to 30 percent. Later we were able to go to just-in-time delivery for certain components, eliminating the storage costs for many of the modular parts.

All this time, Starbucks had been chugging ahead opening stores. We were now at about 1,250 stores and expanding rapidly. My biggest nightmare was that as we tried to work down our old inventory and begin to work in the new design inventory, the wheels would come off the train. If you are in the middle of opening 85 to 150 stores and all of a sudden the new cabinetry does not show up, store opening dates get pushed back and things will fall apart very fast. If we did not execute properly, either the new stores would fail to open on time or we would be left with hundreds of thousands of dollars of old inventory. But stopping the store-opening engine to make all the changes would also send the company's financials off the track. Three out of four possibilities would jeopardize all of our work, not to mention my job.

This was the one point where I did put pressure on my team. I called special meetings that focused strictly on the execution of our store rollout schedule. Wright was there, along with the director of design, the director of construction—everyone who was on the critical path to delivery. We developed comprehensive timetables and flowcharts on the design, manufacturing, and timing of delivery for hundreds of these items. Remember, we were not creating just a single new design but as many as 12, depending on colors and cabinetry. We identified and tracked every detail, from the dates when the manufacturers needed each shop drawing to whether the manufacturers were in fact producing the necessary units of each component needed to make our commitments. With every decision, I look at the downside. "If this goes wrong," I would ask, "what is the backup?" We identified all the aspects of the designs that could be dovetailed with the new designs if something failed to arrive. We made sure that if we were low on parts in the California warehouse, then we had enough in the New Jersey warehouse to make up the difference, and vice versa. In some cases, there was no way to cover a shortfall. The old floor tile, for instance, did not match the new colors. The complete store tile shipment had to arrive, and on time. These areas received even more diligence.

On reflection, I did not institute any new marvelous management techniques. I did, however, force an extra layer of attention to detail by all the managers for every single item under their control. For every delivery we asked "what if?" What if the manufacturer let us down and failed to produce or deliver the item on time? We were not satisfied until every what-if had a response. We reviewed every article on the flowchart and every delivery milestone. We tracked every item through the system from design to shop drawings to manufacturing, and from shipping to the warehouses to shipping from the warehouses to the stores. The results were gratifying. Customers were giving us positive feedback on the first few new stores completed. Hundreds of people inside and outside the company worked hard to successfully shift to all the new materials and components, but to most people at Starbucks the transition was largely seamless.

This new design and construction approach also required longer-term changes in our organization and in the working relationships of people at headquarters and in the field. Among other things, we organized our design teams into regions so that they would develop an in-depth understanding of the design issues particular to their part of the country. We hired construction managers for each of the major markets to coordinate bids from contractors in the building of multiple stores simultaneously. The payoff for all the changes was a decrease in store construction time from nine to six weeks and a substantial savings in the cost of each store. Before the change, our store costs were inching upward because each and every designer was custom designing each store on a one-off basis. Hundreds of stores were being produced on a one-by-one basis. With the Kit of Parts approach, the key store elements were already designed and the costs estimated before the actual store was designed. The only changes that a designer could make under this system were color palette, wall graphics, and seating layout. Yet to our customers, each store looked and felt different, a result that successfully supported Starbucks' high-quality brand positioning. These benefits were in addition to the cutting-edge new designs that competitors could not successfully copy, because we copyrighted and trademarked our graphics and light fixtures.

We discovered the power of our new designs when we opened the first Starbucks in the fashionable Ginza District in Tokyo. This was our first location outside North America, and our primary objective (besides, of course, selling coffee) was to see whether the Starbucks brand would be meaningful overseas and whether our store design would be understood and accepted by other cultures. Despite heat and humidity that made the neighborhood feel more like Atlanta than Tokyo, the store opened to a full crowd and remained busy all day. Other international stores began to open, each with great success. The store color palettes, the icons, the murals, and high-quality materials—all the treatments came from the same design language we had developed for the North American market. Knowing that every store would have large waves of customers, we planned the stores to have additional cash registers or "points of sale." Early market research also told us to offer baked goods more familiar to the market. We continued to vary each design to match the location any and everywhere in the world, but the final payoff for our revolution in design was that we did not have to create entirely new concepts to succeed outside of our native land.

Developing a Unique Value in Design

Working with a design group to create a unique look for your concept is about more than having a leading-edge storefront or interior space. A unique visual "language" for your concept enables you to establish and differentiate your brand's identity and replicate its most important physical elements while adapting the look to the attributes of each demographic neighborhood and building. A sound strategy for a roll-out design leads to a solution that is standard enough to work in any space but flexible enough to take advantage of the unique features of every location. Using a design playbook and adopting the Kit of Parts methodology enables you to quickly and efficiently roll out the concept in all its glory at minimal cost and with minimal changes. Such techniques enabled Starbucks to place stores in historic banks and railway stations in ways that respected the history of the building, the block, and the community while reflecting the soul of Starbucks—and to build out hundreds of stores a year worldwide without losing control of quality or expenses. All of these factors are important to retail success, but the most crucial reason to invest in a compelling design is that a unique design language is one that you and only you own. It serves to differentiate your brand. It establishes your company as a trendsetter and innovator. Someone once said, "Art is the process of speaking to the heart and soul," and retail design is about connecting with the heart and soul of the consumer.

Lastly, a general "look" can sometimes be duplicated, but a well-executed design that is central to your concept and your values is unique. It cannot be easily translated by competitors into their own designs. When we made incremental changes to our designs, competitors would knock off our ideas—the materials, lighting, etc. Our major redesign, however, thwarted them. One company tried to copy the icons that we had developed, but they made no sense visually within their own store designs. The copied icons were out of place. The artwork simply did not look good. Competitors were unable to translate our images into a meaningful brand statement for themselves. The proper combination of look and *feel*—one integral to your brand—cannot be duplicated and remains a strategic advantage. Store design turns out to be more than a way to create visual appeal for customers. Done properly, design can create a visual look that is recognizable and accepted worldwide. Store design becomes a primary way to ensure that your brand remains unique, readily identifiable, and unassailable against competitive threats and copycat looks: one of the most powerful brand positions a retailer can have.

CHAPTER 5

Seamlessly Connecting Design to Brand While Staying on Budget

GREAT LOCATION IN HAND, the retailer now understands what store design seeks to achieve and how design profoundly impacts the brand positioning. The retailer also understands the need from the earliest stages of the retail concept to think in terms of a Kit of Parts strategy to roll out multiple stores with as little cost as possible, even if that rollout may not happen for some time. Now the retailer needs to grasp the best way to proceed in actually working with a designer, finding a contractor to oversee construction of the design, and dealing with the operational challenges of actually opening the first store. All of these issues require the greatest attention if the first store is to have the necessary brand impact.

Design is not something that happens in the abstract. To obtain maximal results in the shortest amount of time and at the least expense, design requires intense interaction between the retailer and the design firm. Chapter 4, "Maximizing the Retail Experience Through Design," discussed the importance of finding designers whose personality fits with the client and whose sensibility is compatible with the category of the concept. A high degree of trust must exist between the client and designer. The design process is not necessarily linear. It moves forward in circuitous ways. Before any work begins, a good designer will seek to understand the business mission and vision, all of the details of the concept to that point, and the company's financial goals. At the same time, the designer must determine the technical needs and the space requirements for the concept. The designer should know whether the concept is a one-off design or a design that will be used for a series of stores. With this information, the designer will develop a budget for the project.

After the project is approved, the designer's first deliverable should include the brand touchstones as well as preliminary sketches based on those touchstones. The way in which Vizwerks, a design group in Portland, Oregon, has worked with customers illustrates this aspect of the design process. Vizwerks was started by Bill Sleeth and his business partner, Shauna Stinson, several years after working with me at Starbucks. It was Bill and his team who worked on the design concept for Il Fornaio Café and Bakery, mentioned in Chapter 1, "It's About Your Values." Recall that Bill and his team established that the design should be a "Tuscan ideal" around the values and brand touchstones of "authentic," "welcoming," and "fresh." At the same time, Vizwerks also did a visual survey of the look and feel of competitive brands to determine the opportunities for a visual point of distinction—a look that would not only be compelling for Il Fornaio but also one that would be difficult for a competitor to copy. Keeping in mind the business plan and the product mix, Bill's team began to develop the visual framework upon which to present the brand touchstones. The goal was to create a "guard rail" around the design concept so that it would not veer off in the wrong direction. All of this thinking became the basis for the initial drawings, which showed a fairly broad visual presentation of the physical environment. The Tuscan design values showed in the proposed use of the "noble materials"—marble, terracotta, and blown glass, among other beautiful but unadorned materials selected for their durability and utility. The furniture would be modern, with clean lines; the chairs would be formal but comfortable; the eating area would have the tables close enough together to create a communal feel but not so close that customers would feel jammed together. These values served as the "design vocabulary" for the store.

Because initial drawings are sketchy, retailers sometimes do not pay enough attention early on. Psychologically, they are waiting to see a more fully fledged design before they engage. But the first meeting or two, in which the designer presents the brand touchstones, the visual concept, and the preliminary drawings, are critical. The retailer and the designer need to fully agree on the designer's assessment of the brand and the way the designer wants to translate this assessment into what will become a physical reality. Although many things will change during the design process, major changes made early are always the least expensive. Therefore, dedicate concentrated time to the early stages of design.

When the client and designer agree, the design evolves from a broad idea to a specific solution, from drawings that show the general arrangement of different areas of the store to drawings that show the exact size, shape, and placement of each element. The designer solves the operational flow—where different product offerings should be displayed, how the customer traffic should move through the store, where customers should pay, and so on. Selections of material, palette, color, and graphics become more defined. A late drawing for Il Fornaio, for instance, shows that in keeping with the Tuscan ideal the store sign and menu signs would appear to be hand lettered and all metalwork would appear to be the work of a craftsman (as opposed to the work of an artist).

Knowing Your Target Market

Beginning retailers are usually their own target market. This is not surprising because retailers normally engage in something about which they have a special interest and knowledge. Often, just meeting with a would-be retailer helps me understand the likely audience. In any case, the retailer should have early on a good understanding of who the potential customers are. Knowing who you want to speak to translates directly into design work. A concept slanted to women aged 25 to 50 in the suburban market is going to look substantially different from one targeting young males in the inner city who ride skateboards. Having good demographic information enables the designer to begin developing a visual library from which the design can grow. The library should show what the targeted customers wear, what they play with and carry on them (cell phones, Gameboys, both?), what music they listen to, what their rooms look like, and so on.

In addition, before ever engaging a design firm, retailers should flip through magazines and looking for photographs and illustrations that appeal to them. They should file anything that feels right and appropriate about their concept. Often, clients do not have the vocabulary to describe what they want their store to look like, but if they save enough visual material they can provide clues to the designer, who can find and use the common elements in the design.

Along the way, the client must remain involved. The most successful retailers are the ones who sweat the details. This means everyone with a major say in running the store. Probably the biggest design failures are the ones in which the operations side of the business is not sufficiently involved. One company provided Internet access for customers as part of a new design, and then failed to exploit it because the Information Technology staff did not want to open the corporate systems to security problems and electronic viruses. At Starbucks we changed the way the coffee beans were presented in the stores by installing beautiful metal hoppers with large pull handles, much as you might see in an old-fashioned general store. The idea was for customers to think about the freshness of the roasted beans. Customers would stand near the barista (the counter person) while the employee used the mechanism to dispense the beans—an added bit of high-touch. The metal hopper was making a subliminal connection to an in-store coffee bean roaster. We would never place a functioning roaster in a store (fire hazard and dust issues); however, we could mentally connect our customer to the equipment through design. Design is more than surface treatment and fixtures and paint. It must seamlessly connect the brand to the customer experience. Design must be integrated into the brand goals and into the operational and financial plans. Employees must understand and use design elements appropriately. One company I know spent millions of dollars to install a design that encouraged more interaction between the sales staff and customers but never trained the staff to exploit the new way of working with customers. At Starbucks, because operations never embraced the idea, the coffee bean hoppers were never used prominently. They became just a store decoration. The company would have been better off without them, and in fact they were phased out. In the case of Il Fornaio, experienced restaurateurs and operational experts regularly reviewed the developing plans for the new café and bakery. Sometimes they tweaked the plan so much that the designers had to work hard to stay on budget, but too much involvement by the people running the store is better than not enough.

FIGURE 5-1

Early renderings of a retail concept should capture the brand touchstones—important attributes of the physical design such as materials, texture, and color—as well as a layout that will achieve the marketing objectives. For Omaha Steaks, the aesthetic goal was to create a new, warmer, more upscale environment, while the marketing goal was to improve the awareness of the company's complete meal offerings. (Rendering by Don Lange.)

Reviewing Models and Prototypes

Usually, at the end of the process, the designer creates a full-color physical model that is as real as it is possible to make it. The scale is typically one-quarter or one-half inch to the foot, so that most stores can be represented in a model that can fit on a small table. Often, this is the last bit of work before the design is approved and construction begins. However, as we always do when we ideate a new concept and design, we encouraged Il Fornaio to take an extra step. This is why Bill and I met with Mike Hislop, Il Fornaio's president and CEO, and half a dozen of his senior staff in a drafty warehouse one cold winter day in Portland, Oregon. Mike Hislop understood the importance of building a full-sized working model to work through with his operational team.

Before us in the warehouse was by all appearances the new Il Fornaio Café and Bakery, but it was constructed out of particle board. Up front was the station where the pizza maker works dough. This was the emblem of their concept—fresh bread, made daily—and the first thing the customer saw upon entering the store. Close by were the stations for bread, bagels, and pastries, which will offer the customer enticing aromas as well as an enticing view. Farther along was the station for coffee and espresso to complement the pastries. Around the far corner were two large stations for salad preparation. At the far end of the shop was a sandwich and soup bar. If it were not for the fact that we were all bundled up in coats and seeing our own breath in the cold air, we would have been hard pressed to tell this full-sized mockup from the first café and bakery, which would not open for many more months. In addition, we mounted cardboard graphics to test sight lines.

Boeing might be able to design an airliner using nothing but three-dimensional computer-aided design tools in place of a hugely expensive full-scale prototype, but a life-sized mockup is still beneficial for the first store of a potential multiple-store operation. Retail outlets have complex customer traffic flows to orchestrate. The floor layout and the signage need to create customer lines naturally, to "cue the queue." Food-service preparation presents classic problems in time and motion. The space has to enable a smooth progression from ordering to payment to pickup for customers on one side of the counter and provide for a ballet of movement for employees on the other side.

Despite the long hours of work by Vizwerks and Mike's restaurant people and the quality of the brand presentation, the need for changes became apparent as we went through the restaurant station by station. Two counters needed to be narrowed to reduce the chance of spills while servers handed food or drink to customers. Another counter had to be moved to open up a bottleneck for employees. A sink needed to be shifted to provide better access for all the servers in the salad area. The area for to-go orders needed to be made more prominent to remind customers every time they enter the store that the café has a to-go business. These and a few other issues emerged as we mimicked the work of servers and traced the path of customers through the store.

Taking the extra step to build a mockup reduces design mistakes and enables retailers to repair miscalculations before the problems are locked in. Contractors can review the mockup to point out money-saving changes. Sometimes moving a piece of equipment a few feet or cabinets to a different location can save thousands of dollars in engineering costs. Electricians and plumbers can identify similar ways to reduce costs. Because of fewer unknowns, contractors' bids will include lower contingency allowances and fewer cost overruns. Most important, the store can be built faster so that it begins generating revenue sooner.

On the aesthetics side, the mockup enables you to see how the store fits together on both the large and small scale. Although Mike was pleased with the overall look of the café and bakery, he was less happy with the soup-and-sandwich area anchoring the far wall. To hide the workspace behind it, the wooden cabinet was tall, broad, and unadorned. Seen in person, this area was an intimidating fortress of sandwich making that would deter customers from approaching. Mike requested that the designers make the area more approachable by trying different heights for the counters and by adding vertical design elements to relieve the unrelenting horizontal band. On a small scale, the team identified changes to the type sizes of various graphics and to the placement of signs; among them, raising the height of a menu board so that a server's head would not block the sign board on which the "soup of the day" would be highlighted.

Few companies take the step of building a full-scale model. Most owners shy away from the additional cost or believe that their know-how will enable them to avoid significant problems in going directly from a scale model to construction. Computer-aided perspective drawings are great for "seeing" the space and getting a good feel for what the retail experience will be like. No matter how skilled the designer or experienced the retailer, however, some problems can be identified only with a physical walkthrough. A full-scale mockup can cost as little as $10,000. Because the materials are generally inexpensive, much of the cost is in the labor. The prevention of just one substantive design mistake will more than recoup the expense. It is better to fix a problem now than to try to move a sink or resize a counter in the harried days before a store opening, or to experience the chaos and expense of changes after the store has opened. Beyond these benefits is the ability to experience the atmosphere of the store as it actually will be. Giving the direct experience of the full-size vignette mockups of our new design elements to Howard and other senior managers at Starbucks gave us all a comfort level in proceeding that we otherwise could not have obtained.

Keeping Design on Budget

Because of the many variables involved, it is difficult to provide specific budget guidance for design work. A simple one-off concept could be designed for as little as $25,000 to $100,000. A complex new concept design for a national chain could run $250,000 or more depending on the elements requested. Suffice it to say that the design work for many smaller projects can be done for under $150,000, whereas many large projects are produced for well over twice that much. Beyond these numbers, bids from several firms will ensure that the design estimates are realistic and competitive. Unless the designer can explain the differences, be wary of any bid substantially lower or higher than the others. As you narrow down your shortlist, check references with prior clients.

A good working rule of thumb in gauging what a store concept should cost to build out is that the projected established annual revenue should be 2.0 to 2.5 times the estimated construction costs. A store expected to generate $1 million in revenue should be budgeted to cost no more than $400,000 to design and build. Inventory would be extra. Of course, each concept has different costs and margins, and each concept requires a detailed pro forma, discussed in Chapter 10, "Kicking the Economic Model Into Gear." A retailer should think in terms of spending perhaps 15 percent of the construction cost on customizable elements. In addition, the retailer should set aside a minimum of 5 percent, preferably 10 percent, of the total cost for unforeseen contingencies. With a ballpark figure established, the designer will first develop the conceptual construction budget based on the design, material choices, finishes, and so on. After contract documents are drawn, actual construction budgets can be let out for bid. Sometimes the client develops the construction budget or a part of it (for example, the budget for certain equipment). Whoever is responsible, close coordination of all parties is required. A certain amount of push and pull between client and designer occurs before everyone agrees on an acceptable budget.

After the general budget is agreed upon, the client needs to ensure that the client, the designer, and (later) the construction contractor always remain in sync. An apocryphal story in the building trades concerns the client who keeps coming up with changes. "Can we do this?" the client asks, and the contractor says, "Sure." Later, the client asks again, "Can we do this?" and the contractor says, "Sure." Every day the client comes up with more changes, and every day the contractor says sure, they can make them. When the project is done, the contractor hands the client a huge bill for all the change orders. "But I thought you said we could do all these things," the client says. "Sure," the contractor replies. "We can do anything. All it takes is money." Do not agree to a construction change without receiving in writing a firm bid outlining the costs. In fact, before you execute a construction contract, ask the contractor to compile a list of what components may be missing on the contract documents that in his opinion are necessary to complete the store build-out.

Similar kinds of misperceptions can arise during the design phase. Sometimes the client may ask for an unreasonable number of visual approaches or an unreasonable number of changes to a design. Other times, the designer may come up with some wildly creative ideas and simply assume that the client knows that the new approach will be more expensive to design and/or to build. "I thought you knew" is not a phrase you ever want to hear, and especially not in the design and construction process. Although the designer and the contractor should be responsible for advising the client of any budget changes, it is the client who ultimately pays and the client who should regularly remind his team of fiscal realities. At the end of our morning-long review of Il Fornaio's café prototype, we all gathered briefly to summarize the changes that were to be made. The last thing that Mike said to the design team was, "I have only one word for you: cost."

Considering Materials in Terms of Customers

Choice of material and choice of construction have the greatest impact on customer appeal. They also represent the greatest variable in expense. High-quality stone or marble, rounded cabinet fronts, special joint details, special hand-wiped stains—all of these things cost a premium. Put money into materials that the customer will touch and interact with. Select special materials and details for areas that are in the customer's "touch zone," from waist to chest high, and in the customer's line of sight.

When designing your space, consider exciting one's five senses: sight, touch, smell, taste, and hearing. If you are successful in combining responses to the various senses into a design, your customers will have a unique experience that differentiates your brand. At Starbucks, we used the finest materials in countertops and front elevations of cabinets; the pendant light fixtures at the customer handoff area were hand-made. However, as the number of stores Starbucks built accelerated each year, it was important that we established a discipline for controlling costs. I told my designers, "Don't put pencil to paper to redesign anything that will add to our current costs unless you work hand in glove with manufacturing and purchasing to reduce the cost of some other build-out item by an equal amount." For example, the back bar, which customers do not interact with, was inexpensive, dark-colored plastic laminate. I scratch my head when I see expensive tile placed behind the bar where it is out of the customers' view. Never pay extra for materials in such places. Whenever possible, balance every expensive exotic material in view with affordable materials out of view.

Ceiling design and installation work has probably caused designers more grief than almost any other part of the store. It is important to define the overhead plane. Installing drop ceilings with required earthquake bracing above it is very expensive, yet the result is a typical bland lay-in acoustical tile ceiling. At Starbucks, we altered the design to leave the ceiling area exposed. We spray-painted the upper area dark colors, including the ductwork, to let the ceiling "die" away. We used other design elements to direct the customer's attention elsewhere and to keep the customer's eye fixed on a plane eight feet and below. The upper area simply vanished to the customer's view. The savings from this change paid for the continued use of high-quality materials and hardwood cabinetry where we wanted them—where the customer came in contact with them. Another area of a store that can save money is the flooring. We used exposed colored concrete floors with a few areas of carpeting wherever possible to save money. Because the store arrangements were so compelling, the concrete "disappeared" below the customer's view. We started doing this in 1996, well before it became popular in the industry.

It is possible to go overboard with low-cost materials. To save money, some architects have used MDF, a plain and inexpensive paneled building board, as a flooring material. By the time they have stained the MDF tiles a custom color, installed them, and sealed them (MDF is not durable), the floor—although beautiful—costs more than marble. It is important to carefully consider initial construction costs; however, always project and value-engineer usability and the life of the materials. If the material wears out faster and needs to be replaced more often, costs over time will be higher. Where durability and maintenance are an issue, be willing to spend what it takes in the initial investment.

Managing Store Construction

Having approved the design and moved into the construction phase, a retailer is likely to be engulfed as the project races to conclusion. If you have ever built or renovated a house, you will have some idea, although a store build-out is an order of magnitude more exacting and complex. In particular you will not believe how busy you will be, especially during the last 30 days before opening.

As in the selection process for design firms, the retailer should interview several contractors. Because building a store or restaurant requires different experience than building an office building or residences, experience in retail construction is a prerequisite. Blue C Sushi, for example, evaluated several contractors, each of which had different strengths and varied levels of experience. Eventually, Blue C Sushi requested three firms to bid on the construction of the project based on the final designs. We reviewed the bids and asked hard questions about how each contractor would approach the work. For example, the Blue C Sushi design called for the installation of laminated sheets of bamboo lining the staircase. How would the contractor handle the edges, or would the contractor recommend another material on the wall leading up to the mezzanine? Would the contractor request multiple subcontractor bids for the electrical, mechanical, and framing work? The issue is whether the contractor would be a true partner, study the plans carefully to determine what costs might not be evident from the architect's drawings, help proactively solve other problems before they occurred during construction, and offer other recommendations to help ensure that the store would open on time and under budget.

James and Steve ultimately chose the contractor who had provided the greatest level of detail in its estimate and who also had some experience building restaurants. They checked the contractor's references personally with three prior clients and visited his completed projects. Because finished carpentry and installation work represent the greatest potential variance in build-out cost, Blue C Sushi worked with the design firm and the contractor to ensure that multiple bids were obtained for just about every special item. Blue C Sushi promoted the use of the "coolest" material in each category but also requested to see two or three less-expensive alternatives. Probably the best example of teamwork was in the creation of a stainless steel curve located at floor level at the base of the conveyor belt stub wall. Foundation Design laid out the design, the contractor modified it for code compliance, and an engineering company did the final fabrication drawings and the actual work.

When building a store, plan for Murphy's law ("whatever can go wrong, will") times three. In Blue C Sushi's case, Murphy's law came into play the week that the kitchen equipment was supposed to be installed. The kitchen designer, who had laid out and ordered the equipment, went AWOL—never to be seen again—while Steve and James coped with a rash of errors in the equipment orders they discovered in her absence.

As work progressed and opening day approached, every little detail mattered. We discussed whether the corners of tables should be square or rounded. We argued over the booth seat height. We debated the texture and durability of materials. Many times when James and Steve were close to completing a phase of the construction, they discovered something new that was not quite right. A problem with the location of a floor sink held up equipment installation in the kitchen for a couple of days. When they went through the restaurant trying to determine the sight lines from all the seats, we discovered that when the door to the pantry was open, customers could see the servers preparing miso soup or pouring soft drinks in the back room. In food service, food preparation can be planned to be part of the presentation, or it should take place out of sight. The only solution was to train the staff to always close the door as they passed through. Hiring and training of staff came during the busiest of those last few crazy weeks. The Blue C Sushi founders spent hours with state and federal employment-related paperwork while trying to get the construction punch list completed before opening.

Of course, from the beginning we were working on naming the sushi concept. Naming a one-off restaurant is one matter. Selecting a distinctive name that works for a planned rollout of multiple units is another. Blue C Sushi considered more than 250 names, trying to find a word or phrase that would capture the essence of quality and fun. Steve and James pondered some of the great brands and tried to understand what made the names memorable. Usually, it was not the name itself but the value created behind it. They ruled out Japanese names as being too typical of a sushi restaurant, although one of the finalists was "Moto Sushi"—it sounded vaguely Japanese while also connoting the motorized conveyer system. "Blue C" had been a strong candidate since it made a late appearance on their naming board. It moved to the fore when the logos were developed for the final candidate names. The Blue C Sushi logo, a big fading blue letter C that resembled a wave, fit the natural spirit and feel of what they wanted. The C is a strong Western symbol, while the stylized calligraphic brush stroke gave a nod to Japan. "Blue C" was a homophone for "Blue Sea," source of their fresh fish, and the big blue character C could also stand for conveyor (the core concept) and for creativity and community, two elements the restaurant sought and that have since become the restaurant's watchwords. Some people found the name difficult to say; others enjoyed the tongue-twister (say "Blue C Sushi" three times fast). Eventually, they decided that the name captured the spirit of fun they wanted to convey. What will the brand mean in 10 years? Too early to tell. As with the major brands they studied, it is up to the entrepreneurs to create a great restaurant experience in each and every unit that will imbue the brand with significance.

At last, on August 21, 2003, Blue C Sushi opened in the Fremont neighborhood of Seattle. This was preview night, the equivalent of the dress rehearsal for a major play. A preview should be controlled to give the restaurateurs a chance to fine-tune staff training and to hear feedback from the initial diners. Being new to the game, James and Steve booked a "full conveyor belt" of family and friends for the entire evening. A few people brought uninvited friends; other people just showed up; many people stayed longer than the planned 45 minutes between seatings. The restaurant got behind early and never caught up that evening. For the owners and staff, the first night was, in Steve's words, "like drinking from a fire hose."

In fact, the restaurant has been running "all out" ever since. "Like George Jetson on the treadmill," Steve says—an interesting image from a guy who serves food on a conveyor. The good news is that Blue C Sushi was profitable within a few months. The bad news is that they did not have time to ramp up and work out the operational kinks. All the learning has occurred on the fly. For example, they had not thought through the mechanics of takeout food requests. At first, they planned to accept telephone orders. Then they realized that there was no reason. Customers could come in and pick up whatever they wanted directly from the belt. However, the floor plan did not take into account the fact that takeout customers would be blocking the main walkway while waiting for their orders to be rung up. Blue C Sushi added a line of counter tables along the front window. Now diners could simply step across the aisle to the belt to select their sushi and return to the standup counters. It is not a major inconvenience, and the setup provides faster service whenever the booths are full. The bar area could drive more revenue, so they added a happy hour to increase sales on slower days of the week.

Other changes were not as dramatic but were equally important to achieving profitability. In Japan, the food plates are uncovered as they move along the conveyor belt. In the United States, the plates need to be covered. The original clear plastic lids were about 15 times more expensive than disposable lids. The sturdier lids lasted about a month but required a tremendous amount of labor to wash. Disposable lids lasted only a day, but did not require the additional labor to wash. The question of which to use vexed them for more than six months before they changed to disposable (but recyclable) lids to reduce labor and to provide greater visibility for the product beneath the lid.

Blue C Sushi's founders understood the importance of getting their first store right. They did not start with a poorly defined concept and hope to eventually stumble upon the right formula. Rarely does such serendipity occur. A few mistakes are inevitable, but imagine how much more difficult and expensive the opening would have been if the founders had lacked the discipline to systematically find the right the location, create the proper store design and brand connection, or find the right contractor. Doing everything right also means you are more likely to start with a bang. Solid preparation will keep you from being overwhelmed after opening. Getting the most important early decisions right greatly increases the odds of success. Getting the early decisions right also creates value in the brand from the start and makes successive stores far easier to open and less speculative financially. The first Blue C Sushi restaurant has proven the aesthetic appeal and economic viability of the concept, incorporating a unique design palette and look that can be reproduced. Working out operational kinks is an ongoing task. Achieving operational perfection is a lofty goal. The entrepreneurs know that to successfully operate a multi-unit concept they must complete the operations manuals to ensure rollout success.

When learning to walk, toddlers put all their energy into getting the first step right. Soon they are tearing around the house. After the first step, it is a matter of repetition and variation. The same thing is true in retail. If you put all your effort into getting the first store to be as good as it can be, you too will soon be off and running.

Understanding Cost Versus Brand

Many times, Starbucks spent far more than the average projected store construction costs necessary to build out a store in a retail space, so it may sound contradictory to assert that most people spend too much money on their retail build-out. "Too much" is difficult to quantify. "How much is appropriate" is a question that must be asked in terms of how the spending establishes the brand. Design and build-out costs must always have an eye toward the goal of brand building as well as operational efficiency. A retailer who does not understand the concepts described in this and the previous chapter is likely to spend "too much" because the retailer will not know what to look for or how to both enable and control the design and construction process. A retailer who fails to make the substantial time investment working with a designer early will spend "too much" because of a failure of the design to meet brand goals or because the design creates operational problems. A retailer will spend "too much" by failing to bid out the construction and failing to monitor the work in progress. A retailer will also spend "too much" when the designer rather than the retailer drives the process and the result is a design for design's sake rather than a design that increases sales; or a design that is so expensive to implement that it devastates the return on investment. New retailers tend to over-invest without considering the value of the investment or accurately projecting the return on investment.

It is crucial to know what kind of return on investment the improvements will bring, either in sales or brand building. For example, Starbucks' strategy was to open a highly visible flagship store within the first year of entering a market. Preferably the flagship store, located on a major intersection in a downtown commercial core area, would be the first store to open in the market. This was to introduce the brand with a bang, to build awareness, and start the marketing "buzz." Usually, we opened stores in urban neighborhoods and surrounding suburbs only after the flagship urban stores opened. Customers would visit the flagship store during their work week and see it as they drove to and from work every work day. Having had a quality experience in a downtown store, customers would visit their neighborhood stores over the weekend. The suburban stores, although a consistent high-quality design, did not usually require the kind of investment in the store build-out as the flagship store. As sales volumes grew enough to justify additional stores, we opened additional stores in the downtown central business districts. These store designs generally matched the company's average store construction cost.

A first store, or a flagship store, merits the additional investment of design and build-out dollars because it establishes the brand for an entire market through a design that projects your brand properly and powerfully. Whenever Starbucks restored a building to its original grandeur or added additional design features to properly integrate our store into its surroundings, the company had a strategic reason related to brand building. We not only created a place where customers wanted to come (and spend their money), we also kept a careful eye on the connection of a store's locationing elements to the brand's overall presentation to the customer and the brand's strategic positioning. Think in terms of "cost containment" for design and construction elements that customers do not see or that otherwise do not impact brand. Think in terms of "spend what it takes" to achieve the brand positioning you seek. Superior brand positioning will justify the cost through increased sales and an increased return on investment.

CHAPTER 6

Merchandising: Maximizing Your Profits

A DISCUSSION OF MERCHANDISING usually begins with some of the basic principles: Have clear sight lines; that is, arrange the furnishings so that customers can see all of the main displays, all the way through the store. Make it easy for customers to move from one shopping area ("grazing area" in retail parlance) to another. Provide a visual attraction, focal point, or a necessity at the back of the store to draw customers farther in past more products. Provide a smooth, obvious route through the space and an efficient checkout process so the customer leaves with a positive impression. All of these rules are important, but they are presumptuous. They presuppose that the customer is already inside the store and prepped to buy.

The first step in the art of merchandising is to get the customer to notice you and take the first step ... *into the store*! As Chapter 5, "Seamlessly Connecting Design to Brand While Staying on Budget," showed, the retailer has to create a sense of place, a place where the customer wants to be. A sense of place begins with locationing, the aesthetics of the building and environs, and continues with the company logo and the supporting iconography—the visual images that the customer connects with your brand—displayed in a manner that is tastefully aligned with the brand positioning. If the iconography is sufficiently strong and the brand has developed familiar visual touchstones, the store name itself does not have to be screamed out. Abercrombie & Fitch uses giant, high-quality wood-framed posters of attractive models wearing A&F clothes as a signature element to depict the store's business. The posters, prominently placed at the store's entry, leave little doubt as to what A&F sells. Similarly, Starbucks developed such a strong visual language that the green Starbucks disk, a large, clean glass storefront, and custom glass globe lighting fixtures in the window were all we needed to communicate "great coffee here." In a few cities where we had already achieved brand awareness with densely packed stores and where consumer acceptance for our products was high, we toyed with the idea of dispensing entirely with the large signage identifying the company on the storefront.

The suggestion is not that you treat your store like those hard-to-find nightspots in major cities that deliberately omit signs as a mark of being hip. Rather, the merchandising must be tied to your sense of place and to the customer experience, and the sense of place begins with a unified, consistently executed visual representation of your brand. The logo and iconography identify the brand; the overall visual presentation saturates the customer with the brand's characteristics and sensibility. The storefront must attract the customer's attention and romance the customer into the establishment—hence the treatment of the storefront as stage set and the people inside as actors in the drama. For most concepts, this means maximum fenestration—all the glass possible out front. Large window spaces create more opportunities for creative displays and brand presentation. Large windows enable people to see into your store, piquing their curiosity and interest to what is going on in there. Guess what—people draw more people!

About the only business that prospers with a closed-up storefront is a bar. The purpose of the "dark front" is to protect the privacy of everyone inside enjoying a drink. The retail outlets of a company called Illuminations have closed storefronts, evidently to create some sort of allure that will draw customers in. But most people do not even know that Illuminations is a candle company. Its storefront should *illuminate*. The windows should have warm displays that engage people with the most interesting candles, using the inherent visual appeal of the product to invite the customers inside to investigate the wares. Illuminations filed for bankruptcy in early 2004 with the characteristic explanation of overly rapid expansion. I am convinced that its repressed storefronts did not help in attracting customers.

One of the biggest names in fashion retailing, Tiffany's, also has a closed storefront. The company relies on its reputation and on tiny window vignettes to highlight the exclusivity of its unique jewelry products. The small displays, however, mean that the marketing potential of its varied and gorgeous product line goes largely unrealized. The reason for small windows is theft, the same reason that a number of consumer electronics companies have storefronts that are totally "blank." Retailers are afraid of "smash-and-grab" thieves who bust a window and make off with whatever merchandise they can carry. But by minimizing their exposure to the street, they are minimizing their exposure to customers! Other ways exist to prevent theft. Roll-down steel gates are the most obvious, because most smash-and-grabs occur after hours. This is why department stores invented full-size window displays. The lifelike scenes depict the store's products in visually appealing lifestyle settings without exposing the store's most valuable merchandise to robbery. Barneys of New York, to name just one store, is famous for its unconventional window treatments. Window decoration is so integrated with the brand that customers come to the store just to see the changeovers, especially at holidays. However you manage it, you need to let people see the play that is unfolding inside your store.

Engaging the Senses, Inducing Emotions

From the moment the brand registers or connects with the customer, the store itself must strive to engage all five human senses. Drawing the customer into the store and engaging the customer's senses might be termed *meta-merchandising*: the things a retailer must do above and beyond the placement of product in the store. Meta-merchandising consists of all the elements that engage a customer's senses and establishes an atmosphere that encourages sales. It is the most overlooked aspect of retail sales. Touch, taste, smell, vision, and hearing all create powerful visceral reactions. Smell is the most powerful sense because it triggers memory and emotion, and smart retailers take advantage. Bakeries put their vents to the sidewalk to engage the sense of smell and market their products. A huge store, Costco, recognized the power of smell and put in bakeries to take advantage of the human connection between baking and comfort. Sam Goody's, the music store, experiments with burning incense. If the scent of leather goods does not permeate the air of a clothing store, you can be sure that a good clothier will have potpourri to engage the sense of smell. Illuminations greet customers with a whiff of aromatic candles. Artistic glazing on the door windows appeal to sight; the style and the door handle design can appeal to touch. Entering, the customer should be drawn to a visual focal point. In Oakley stores, large-screen televisions display sports scenes showing the company gear in action. Clothing stores use music that appeals to target customers. The louder the music, the younger the customer. Make sure, by the way, that the music is geared to the customer, not the staff. The music selection of some stores is far too young for the target audience and can be explained only in terms of entertaining the employees during slack times. (Note to mom-and-pops: Having a TV turned on in a retail store detracts from the customer's experience.)

Another way to appeal to the senses is through the "theater of retail experience," engaging the customer in some activity that enriches or enlivens the buying experience. Employees handing out food samples or perfume samples are good theater. So are aestheticians who do makeovers at cosmetics counters. In Johnny Rocket restaurants, a 1950s hamburger and milk shake concept, when a particular song comes on the juke box, the employees break into a line dance for the crowd. The employees at restaurants who sing and bang drums to celebrate birthdays are also theater, although too often you wish they were mimes. Theater can involve customers as well. Children's slides and similar entertainments at fast-food restaurants are theater as well as a way to give parents a few moments to enjoy a meal in peace. Karaoke is a concept entirely based on theater. Some athletic stores allow customers to jog up and down the street in front of the store to test the fit of new running shoes. Practical theater. An afternoon at a Disney theme park with its colorful array of characters and its variety of entertainments illustrates the degree to which the concept of theater can transform an ordinary experience into something magical.

Theater must not only be well designed, but also well acted. I was eating in a fast-casual Italian restaurant not too long ago. The layout places the chefs out front, in the line of sight of most of the customers, so the cooking of meals is intended to be part of the customer experience. The chefs, however, seemed to think that they were behind a wall. Neither man had shaved. Their white frocks were dirty from the evening's exertions. One wore a chef's hat, the other a hair net. They both had worn-out sneakers. One wore fuzzy gray pants, the other a pair of low-rider pants favored by some young men, complete with chains. (Customers watched in suspense to see whether the pants would stay up, probably not the theater intended.) Imagine the impression for customers if instead of dressing like short-order cooks in a cheap diner, the two men both wore crisp black pants, black shoes, and white frocks and chef hats (changed hourly to remain spotlessly white). Imagine the enjoyment by the diners if the chefs made a display of preparing the dishes, if they had snappy little routines and crisp gestures, if they bantered with the servers coming to retrieve the dishes. The customers had no choice but to watch the chefs, but the chefs failed to act as if they were on display. I do not know what offended me more: their slovenly dress or their failure to put on a show. Your store is a stage set, your employees are the actors, and the customers are the audience. They are always watching!

Whether you are aware of it or not, everything you do or do not do in a store works to establish a mood and atmosphere. Lighting can establish a mood faster than almost any other feature of a store; but many retailers use two-by-two-foot or two-by-four-foot, generic drop-in fluorescent ceiling fixtures throughout. This kind of lighting is cheap and monotonous. The mood it creates is uniform dullness. Intensifying lighting in certain areas gives the store's interior space a sculptured look and highlights your nicest products. In addition, different incandescent and fluorescent bulbs produce light in different parts of the color spectrum, affecting presentation in subtle ways. Bulbs that glow on the bluish-green side of the color scale make people look pale and unhealthy and are particularly unsuited to dressing rooms. Bulbs on the warm (red) side of the spectrum should be used to highlight food, especially meat. Dressing rooms require good overall lighting with few shadows; bulbs on the red side of the spectrum make customers look healthier as they try on clothes. (Actors know that pink light makes them look younger.) The healthier the customers' skin looks, the better they feel about the product. By all means, explore energy-efficient lighting, but be willing to spend a bit more to obtain a more natural lighting spectrum where it matters.

All of the other materials you choose should convey a distinctive feeling: expansive or intimate, luxury or value. The most important factor in design and merchandising is how well the materials and layout fit with the brand values to create an overall customer experience. For Apple, the choice of wood surfaces and bright track lighting conveys a high-quality, if precious, feel to its stores. The company also presents each product individually, as Oakley does with its sunglass displays. A product that "demands its own space" creates a sense of exclusiveness, like two or three fine pieces of jewelry in a window. Costco, on the other hand, would never put in expensive fixtures, which would conflict with its "lowest-cost" message, and most product is stacked in boxes, one atop the other. The large, plain, open shelves reinforce the notion of "stack 'em high, let 'em fly." Not only does this approach make it easy for customers to get what they want—to "grab it and go"—but it also makes the product look like it is a great bargain. Target has perfected the balance between promotional pricing and higher-quality brand positioning without spending a fortune on store furnishings. Using slightly more expensive materials and more varied colors for paint and floor finishes, the company has a more tasteful and coordinated interior design than other price-value stores. In addition, Target changes the traffic flow and aisle layout and orientation to more clearly delineate its offerings; it feels more like a traditional department store than a Wal-Mart. As a result, the Target customer is perfectly happy to buy a $3 hand towel or an expensive teapot from a well-known designer.

Paper and related products can be sold as an "office supply" concept or as a luxury fashion item. Mass retailers have large, open stores with high steel shelves full of paper by the box and ream, a very businesslike atmosphere. At the Kate's Paperie stores in Manhattan, however, individual stationery items are uniquely presented on inviting fixtures and shelves of a variety of natural woods and wood stains, elevating the product from functional provisions to personal fashion. The owner, Leonard Flax, knows how to present paper as a fashion item.

This is a very important concept. In a world of commodities, try to find a way to present your wares as "fashion."

Whether you are selling tacos, tires, or Tiffany lamps, the design and layout must communicate the brand intrinsically. Restaurants typically invest a lot of money into their interior design to create a mood that complements the dining experience. My favorite restaurant in New York City is named Il Mulino. The intimate eatery could easily add ten more seats to its dining room. Instead, the owners use a lot of the space near the entry for a colorful display of fresh fruit and anti-pasto piled high. It is a vivid signal that you are going to dine on incredible, fresh, high-quality food there. The fast-casual and much less expensive Pei Wei restaurant chain has also done an awesome job of paying attention to mood-setting details throughout their stores. Rooted in a richly lacquered, glossy red motif, the restaurants tap into the design of traditional Chinese restaurants. The restaurants have one major icon in their space: an antique wood food carrier about three feet tall that is prominently displayed between the ordering line and the dining room. For me, Pei Wei's best and smartest features are the wood shutters installed inside the typical anodized aluminum and glass window storefront. The shutters create a more intimate and upscale atmosphere than a customer would expect in the strip shopping centers where the restaurants are usually located. Few customers notice the shutters as being the defining point of differentiation, but all customers notice the feel of a quality dining experience.

Losing the mood means losing much of what makes a concept special. The rise and fall of bagel stores speaks volumes on this point. Bagel stores originally were a specialized bakery, vibrant community eateries serving freshly baked breads. The best bagel stores understand this history and place the bagel counter at the front of the store, where the sight and smell of bagels stimulate the customer's appetite. But as the concept became popular about a decade ago, several rapidly expanding chains ended up homogenizing what had made the bagel concept special. To differentiate themselves, they added more food products. To centralize food preparation and the point-of-sale (POS) registers, they moved both to the rear. In an evident effort to try to draw customers into the store, they put the bagel counters in the back. They also showed a lack of imagination in general food service design

Adding coffee beverages and power bars homogenized their positioning. They lost their ownership position of the bagel category. The result is that they morphed into just another generic eatery. What they gained in efficiencies they lost in excitement and intimacy. They distanced customers from the one product whose sight and smell had drawn them in to begin with. They lost the feel of the neighborhood bakery and did not replace it with anything nearly as unique and interesting. They started to fail long before the low-carb wave.

Mood is a quality that is difficult to achieve, but it is as important in general retail as in food service. Everything about the experience must be aligned with your brand values. In my neighborhood in Seattle, a lingerie boutique does a fantastic job of creating a sense of intimacy in line with its products and services. The store is small and cozy, with several unobtrusive mirrors, placed in private dressing areas. Victoria's Secret uses similar design techniques even though the stores are much larger. They use merchandise and other elements to break the store into small, intimate spaces within the larger environment. You get a completely different feeling upon entering a Crate & Barrel store. The light woods and large open windows create a monolithic, clean, stylized atmosphere that showcases the furniture and house wares in a simple, elegant manner. Abercrombie & Fitch creates a lively environment for its target audience of preteens and teenagers, as well as the parents who take them there. The stores feature a great mix of clothes on racks and tables that invite shoppers to browse, touch, and pick up. Notice the difference between their hanger stock and the T-shirts piled up on floating tables. A message is being sent. Nicer, more expensive shirts and blouses are on hangers. The clothes require a little more care, and someone buying one of these will take a little more time. Inexpensive T-shirts are folded on the feature tables. The clothes are low care, and a customer can "grab and go." On a table like this, products become convenience items, even impulse items. People are always looking for a nice, low-priced T-shirt to kick around in.

Each of these stores has a different manner of visually displaying its wares according to its brand values. The visual merchandising of Abercrombie & Fitch mimics the untidy, laissez faire attitude of its 20-something target market, with well-crafted but decidedly informal arrangements. The displays emphasize the lifestyle and the clothing

itself. The visual merchandising of Victoria's Secret, in contrast, focuses on *her*, the well-educated woman who looks beautifully and sensually fit—or who wants to look that way. Product is secondary to the lush, expensive photographic displays that emphasize a well-sculpted woman in her 20s or 30s.

Financial resources also come into play. The small retailer does not have the money to design and produce the elaborate photography of Victoria's Secret. The local lingerie retailer must rely upon visual artwork supplied by the manufacturer. Unable to target the specific demographic, the small retailer must find ways to appeal to all potential customers regardless of age. The displays are more generic, emphasizing the availability of the merchandise across all potential customer groups.

To succeed in this situation—a local retailer competing against the brand and marketing capabilities of a national chain—you have to be a great merchandiser. Sometimes a retailer is a great merchant and sometimes the retailer is a great operator. Seldom is a retailer both. The merchant figures out what is going to sell in a retail setting—what to lead and follow with in sales, what to stock and how to present it, and how moving a mannequin two feet to the left can increase sales 37 percent. Everything the merchant does revolves around creating the right space to enhance the shopping environment. An operator is the one who figures out how the sales machine functions. The operator is real estate, facilities management, the planning, space management, and education and training—all the nuts and bolts. Merchandising deals with everything that goes on in front of the curtain. Operations cover everything that goes on behind the curtain. Merchandising at the local level requires an analytic eye, a designer sensibility that understands color and composition, a willingness to exceed customer expectation, and impeccable attention to detail. The small retailer in particular must know how to promote the buying pattern, for example by being certain to display a mannequin with three or four layers of color-coordinated clothing, accessories, and shoes. By showing all the possibilities, the retailer maximizes the sales potential. In the case of lingerie, which generally cannot be showcased with other clothes—other clothes usually hide the lingerie—the retailer must focus on the intimacy of the sales experience, on the quality of the fitting process, and the personal attention.

Providing Chairs, Mirrors, and Other Comforts

In addition, the centrally located chairs in Abercrombie & Fitch make it easy for customers (or parents) to hang out comfortably and watch "the show." People like to sit and relax, regardless of the nature of the retail establishment. For the life of me, I cannot understand why most clothing retailers fail to provide more seating where male companions can wait while their wives or daughters shop. Fashionable shops have some seating, but often it is for design instead of comfort. A few retailers are getting it right. On a recent trip to Napa Valley, my wife and I visited a shoe store called Foot Candy. Not only does it have a great brand name, but the owners have a seating area in the back of the store, in the middle of the men's shoe department, that has seating with a television and an Internet computer. (The owners figured out that men would either be accompanying their female companions or they would finish their shoe shopping long before the women did.) Seeing me entertained back there surfing the Internet, my wife decided not to disturb me. She left the store to continue her shopping down the street!

Design has also gotten ahead of functionality in terms of wall graphics. Clothing stores have slowly but surely taken mirrors out of the general part of the store, limiting them to the dressing rooms. Why? To use the space for more merchandise displays or to install trendy graphics. Often, a person just wants to hold up a blouse or dress or shirt to a mirror to get a general sense of style, color, and fit. The customer should not have to traipse all the way back to a dressing room and check in with security. Besides, people like to look at themselves. It is part of the fun of shopping. A single great wall graphic, properly executed, has more effect than dozens of smaller graphics placed without any relation to the brand. Graphics should provide a focal point, not just fill up wall space. Leave the mirrors on the walls for customers.

Another aspect of the shopping experience is the bathroom. The design and maintenance of a bathroom is a direct indicator of the operational standards of a company. The cleanliness and gentility of the restroom show, up close and personal, your attention to detail and consideration for the customer. Yet it is the first place that people try to cut costs. Many retail restrooms look barely more finished than a garage, and far too many are less than scrupulously clean. Rigorous hourly maintenance by store personnel is, of course, imperative. The store manager should make spot inspections and have the restroom cleaned more often as needed. Cleanliness in and of itself is an operational issue, but retailers need to go beyond spotless. You should think of every operational issue as an opportunity to improve the customer experience and further delineate the company's brand position. In many establishments, the customers' restroom has morphed into a storage room. Among some obvious pointers:

- Never leave cleansers, plungers, or store supplies in view of the customer.
- Make the bathroom more than four bare walls and a glaring light. Put in flooring that is a cut above the typical vinyl or institutional tile. Paint the room in the same colors as the rest of your establishment, install a nice light fixture (in a "warm" tone, remember).
- Add at least one design element that is unique to your store and brand—the wainscoting, wall tile, a graphic.

The bathroom should reinforce the brand by being as inviting as the rest of your store, not a place to be tolerated while nature calls.

Spit and polish extends to the store as a whole. Some small retailers have excellent products but terrible presentation. No one is minding the store from the customer's perspective. One juice bar, for example, has created a cultlike clientele in the local university community and takes pride in its "authentic" down-home environment. What I saw, however, was carelessness. It is one thing to have cracks in the old wood floor. It is another thing to have visible crumbs and dirt in the cracks. It is one thing to have old window sashes that do not hang straight. It is another to have dead insects on the windowsill. In my view, the owners were coasting. No matter how good their product is, it will never connect with me. Even retailers who do not care about the potential for expansion should have more pride in their presentation and their work. For someone who owns a single store, the store is that person's home. It should be well cared for.

Every aspect of presentation must come together to create a special experience. At Potbelly Sandwich Works, it is the smell of toasted bread and the diverse antique furnishings and materials, the interesting knobs on the counter drawers. It is the queuing line that is easy to understand, the easy-to-read, hand-painted menu board. It is the simplicity of the sandwich choices. It is the absence of plastic. During lunchtime, musicians play to the crowd from a mezzanine. The live music, a "surprise gift" to guests featuring tunes from different eras, is theater that distinguishes Potbelly from competitors. If you went to a cheesy fast-food restaurant, you would not feel cool about seeing your high school girlfriend there. Unless you were there escorting a child under ten, you would both feel a bit embarrassed. But you would be okay running into her at a Potbelly because it is a cool place to be. This is a subtle little thing, but it is important to people.

Executing on the Science of Merchandising

Finally we reach the part that most people consider "merchandising." Of the basic concepts, the two most important are establishing view corridors and providing a visual attraction in the back to draw customers well into the store. To create a view corridor, tables, display cases, and racks should form clear visual and physical paths into the store. Usually the rows are straight, but slight curves work nicely, too. The store should not feel crowded or in disarray. The difference between a junk store and an antique store is the care with which the product is laid out. A jumble of products marks the junk store, whereas a well-merchandised antique store uses line-of-sight techniques to draw customers toward its "hidden" treasures. Most department stores lay out merchandise crisply, but during busy seasons they can sometimes fall short. Last Christmas season, one retailer jammed so many racks of clothes into the children's department that not only was there no view corridor but the aisles were also too narrow for shopping carts. For most retail operations, clutter is death.

Related to clear corridors is the idea of "wayfinding." The layout of the store, the lines of sight, the signage, and the location of the POS systems should enable customers to easily navigate a store and also should pull them through along a desired path. Retailers can almost always improve wayfinding. If you have ever been unable to tell whether you are supposed to line up on the left or right at a deli or fast-food counter, or if you have ever entered a clothing or furniture store and suddenly became unsure as to which way to go, you have experienced examples of wayward wayfinding. A majority of people have a tendency to turn right upon entering a store. One retail store had a column and an escalator that constricted customers' ability to turn right comfortably. Customers were confused without knowing why, and a surprising number of them turned away. A redesign of the entrance was required. Always reinforce consumer behavior!

Wayfinding should ensure that customers easily find the products they want, but along a trajectory that you want them to follow. Omaha Steaks' new design, for instance, has displays that draw the customer to the areas that feature complete meals. The display *conveys the store message* that Omaha Steaks provides complete, nutritional meals to consumers, an upgrade to the brand positioning. Omaha Steaks is already well known for its individual meat, poultry, and seafood products, which are well displayed farther inside. If the customer wants a frozen cut of ribeye, the customer can get to it pronto. But in passing the whole-meal counter, the customer may pause and decide on the handiness of a prepared meal tonight. The customer has an opportunity for added convenience, and Omaha Steaks has a chance to improve its bottom line.

Small retailers often miss the concept of conveying the store's message. They do not know whether to highlight the slow-selling big-ticket items or the low-margin but high-volume T-shirts and socks that serve as their bread and butter. So they try to push both. They try to display and sell so many products that they water down their message. Every concept has to stand for something. You have about a minute to show the customer visually that you are the expert in that *something*. Major merchandising displays, therefore, play a dual role. From a brand standpoint, the role is to establish your expertise. From a financial standpoint, the role is to highlight those goods with the highest margins, which are usually the "brand-imprinting" products that establish this expertise. Think of merchandising this way: If your store simply vanished overnight, what would you be remembered for? The answer should be immediate and definitive.

- "They had the best cinnamon rolls in town."
- "They knew everything about cross-country skis."
- "They had the finest silk dresses you could imagine."
- "They could fix any appliance ever made."

If a customer cannot come into your store and quickly determine what you stand for, then your merchandising strategy has failed. So the retailer's predicament is not really a predicament. The "branding" products should achieve the most prominence. Other products should support these displays. A combination of layout, flow, and add-on selling (which requires trained personnel) will ensure that you will sell the mix of products you need without diluting the message impact of merchandising.

For example, the "branding" products should be presented on mannequins in conjunction with related products or on the most visible tables and racks. Windows displays should be complete, showing three or four related products, but not jammed with every possible accessory. Tables close to the window displays should have related merchandise. "Lifestyle" displays should show a major product surrounded by related accessories. Whatever the final arrangement of the store, you should create maximum brand impact and maximize sales of high-margin products by placing products together to create an integrated visual presentation—color-coordinated shirt, pants, sweater all together—and place the less-glamorous but high-volume products nearby, grouped with similar-style merchandise. Even though customers seldom need to replenish their supplies of skis, snowboards, bikes, ATVs, televisions, or other long-lasting products, a single visual presentation—with the "big-ticket" item at the top of the psychological pyramid—makes it far more likely that the customer will consider you the expert in that area and return for *your* big-ticket item when the time comes.

Placing Merchandise in the Store

On the most functional level, merchandising is where the customer sees what, when. Merchandising is how all the products tie together versus the customer "hunting and pecking" through the store to find the goods. In general, the newest goods should be generally toward the front of the store, displayed in the windows and on tables, racks, and other fixtures that can be seen from outside or upon immediate entry. The front displays should be freshened weekly to attract repeat customers. This is important so that the customer is pleasantly surprised to see and learn about new products. Fresh displays also tell customers that you are innovative and that they should look forward to stopping here on their next visit. The center of the store is the primary selling space, where the sales staff interacts with customers. If the center area is divided into more than one space, a salesperson should be available for each one. The back of the store should be reserved for the oldest and least-profitable merchandise. The slowest-moving merchandise should also be toward the back, unless it consists of higher-margin goods that you *want* to sell. (With some experience, you will learn which products sell poorly because of poor placement and which products sell poorly because of low demand.) Many variations on these basic themes relate to the size and shape of the store and the number of different departments or groupings of products that a retail concept has. Grocers and drugstores place milk and juice and promotional items in the back of the store hoping you will pick up a few more items as you walk through.

Products should also be arranged vertically according to value. "Elbow to eye" is the strike zone for retailers, and the most profitable items should be at eye level for maximum exposure. Less-profitable items should be placed lower, and nothing except storage should be below the knee. Anything below the knee diminishes the product. (This is similar to not having customers go down steps; nobody wants to go or look down.) Place something high, above six feet, only if the goal is to create a visual appeal from a distance. In general, anything above seven feet is a waste, although occasionally goods can be displayed up high in a way that creates a graphic effect. Good examples are sweatshirts, T-shirts, or hats displayed on a wall. In most stores, customers need to be able to see their way through the store ahead of time. That is why Costco has merchandise on low tables at the entry and in the middle. High racks line the perimeter of the store.

Some retailers are in the habit of putting their sales merchandise up front so that passers-by will see the goods (or see the people going through the goods) and stop in. However, this approach has the perverse effect of concentrating attention on your oldest and most heavily discounted wares. Advertising the sale at the front of the store with signs and banners makes sense, but crowds jamming the sales racks can impede entry into the store, and sales areas also tend to be messy. A rare "sidewalk sale" is fine, but in general neither a congested entry

FIGURE 6-1

A merchandising display must have visual appeal that draws customers as well as prominently display the high-margin items that the retailer wants to sell. The closer an item is to eye level, the more likely a customer is to consider purchasing the product.

nor a pile of pawed-through goods is likely to be the best way to promote your brand. Putting sales racks in back is another way to draw customers through the store. Conversely, you could put a sales rack in each shopping area according to product type in order to pull customers through different departments. Notice how high-end retailers put their sale merchandise off to the side so as not to diminish their other products.

Location of the POS systems and cashiers requires some thought. Fast-food and fast-casual restaurants usually have the cashiers toward the back because they need to form manageable queues of customers and have food production at hand for delivery. Starbucks uses an L-shaped queue to minimize the distance of the cashiers and baristas from the customer. The POS for clothing stores is often in the middle, where the salespeople are most active and where customers do not have too far to go from changing rooms. The POS is also sometimes located in the front to discourage shoplifting. Grocery stores, discount stores, and the like have the POS at the front for the ease of customers with shopping carts or heavy bags, as well as for security. Unless a concept requires a particular position for the POS, I prefer to set it to the side so that the customer has the full impact of the visual heart of the store upon entering.

Merchandising culminates in the way your store bids farewell to the customer. Whether you sell doughnuts, gifts, coffee, clothing, cars, or candles, you need to develop an overall strategy, a psychology, to highlight the product at the end of the sales transaction. At Starbucks we specifically designed a beverage handoff counter at eye level, highlighted by a stylish overhead glass globe light, upon which to present the coffee drink to the customer. Directly lit from above, the drink is presented as a custom-crafted piece of sculpture. Other competitors have provided a shelf on which to place the coffee but do not really understand what we were doing from a brand standpoint. Tiffany's wraps its products in signature boxes and bags, all light blue. The Europeans and Japanese put tremendous care into wrapping a product. It is a sensual delight to watch a salesperson wrap a product in fine paper and ribbon as if he or she is preparing a special gift for the customer. It takes just an extra minute or two to make the product *feel* special to the customer and to make the customer feel special for buying it here. It is such a simple thing, but it is your way of saying thank you and goodbye. *A finely wrapped product means you care about how your product is presented when someone takes your brand away with them!* Customers want to have something to take away with them. Pay as much attention to this part of the transaction as to everything else. When customers unwrap the package, they once again think about their store experience and your brand. You have successfully reconnected with them!

Finding the Right 20 Percent of Goods

It is not enough for merchandising strategies to increase sales. They must also maximize the sales of products with the highest margins. One way to increase margins, of course, is to lower your costs. Because of its volume, Wal-Mart can drive down the cost of its goods. Most of these savings pass through to the consumer, and the customer benefit drives more volume. But volume retailers have already driven their costs so low it is unlikely that they will see any more breakthroughs there, and most retailers are not volume retailers anyway. The solution is for retail stores to use merchandising *management* to sell products with higher margins. Stores, therefore, need to be designed to the economics of the concept. At Starbucks, our core product was pretty much the highest-margin product. We maximized the throughput at the barista area to produce as many coffee drinks as possible and focused on being as efficient as possible in the counter area. Other merchandise is limited to 15 or 20 lineal feet, all supporting the sales of our core offerings. These products had generally good margins with lower volumes of sales.

Often, however, it is not the core product that provides the greatest profit. In every retail concept, the "80/20 rule" applies: 80 percent of the sales come from 20 percent of the product. Yet too often retailers fail to determine what those 20 percent are. Too often people just stock what they stock and sell whatever of that stock they can. Analyzing sales and trends at the level of stock keeping units (SKUs, the basic pricing unit in retail) implies high-quality financial systems. Such systems are well within the reach of small retailers today. Retailers also have to have a senior manager or managers focused on such analysis. For small stores, that is probably the owner. But the results can be spectacular. Costco spends a lot of time figuring out the 4,000 or so SKUs the company stocks. Some stores that are a quarter of Costco's size carry 35,000 to 40,000 SKUs. Costco buyers are excellent at figuring out what to stock. They turn over their merchandise something like a dozen times a year. Most stores would be happy with half a dozen, and small retailers with two or three. Normally, a retailer pays for stock 45 to 60 days after the stock arrives. If stock sells rapidly, the retailer has the use of the money for some period of time before paying the bill. If stock sells slowly, the retailer has to pay for the merchandise before receiving any revenue. Fast turnover enables a retailer to "live on the float," a process that can dramatically improve cash flow. Consider the advantage to Costco with turnover every 30 days or so and payment due every 45 days. So determine the best-selling SKUs and stock primarily those. Everything else is stage setting. You want a sufficient number of supporting products and accessories to flesh out the concept, but not so many as to drive up the costs of inventory and logistics and drive down the overall return.

You can be certain that Costco's analysis is not just of those products that sell the most, but of those products that make the most profit. The retailer's profit rule should be "x transactions including these high-margin items," and merchandising should follow suit. A food concept might offer a 10 percent discount if a customer buys two pounds of lobster or might offer a pound of hamburger free if the customer buys a minimum of $15 worth of steak. Prescriptions used to be high-margin items, but competition, Medicare, health maintenance organizations, and other factors have driven down the margins for pharmacists. If a drugstore makes 18 percent on prescriptions and 50 percent on ice coolers, then the retailer needs to promote ice coolers, using the merchandising policies outlined here. Look around your chain drugstore during the summer months. You will see coolers displayed everywhere. Now you know why.

In this context, merchandising is not a matter of physically attractive product placement, but a strategy to sell higher-margin goods. "Value meals" offer a good deal for customers but also increase the margins of fast-food restaurants because customers buy more items than they would otherwise. Super-sizing, now falling out of favor because of dietary concerns, is the same idea. Fast-feeders love to sell an extra nickel's worth of French fries and charge another 19 cents. Every "bundle" works on the principle that the combined sale, whether it is for a computer system or a set of furniture, increases margins despite a lower price because it increases the number of items per transaction. Formal bundles—two or more items at a combined price—are common in some concepts and rare in others. Clothiers seldom have a bundled price for coordinated separates, but they display shirts, sweaters, and trousers together to create a presumption that a customer should buy them all.

Recently, my company found margin problems in an analysis of the product mix of one retailer. Of about 200 SKUs, 89 percent of them had less than 1 percent of sales each. Only 6 SKUs—less than half of 1 percent—had more than 2 percent in sales. Worse, the top-selling items had gross margins that were 7.5 percent *lower* than other products. We recommended that the client develop a line of bundled products to increase the number of items sold per transaction. We also recommended that the company develop a new line of products to capture the latest trend in that category. This proposal was not a matter of jumping on the latest fad but a natural extension of its business, which already featured a core product that was substantially on trend. By proper marketing of the new products and proper merchandising of them in stores—this would also require training of the sales staff to promote these products—the company will be able to increase sales of high-margin items and reduce the number of unprofitable SKUs.

Perfecting the Art and Science of Merchandising

While implementing your merchandising strategy, evaluate the way in which similar retailers display their wares and learn what you can from what they do. Also observe closely to understand their weaknesses and to learn where they either fail to be smart about merchandising or have fallen into a static "cookie cutter" approach. Let your creative talents loose; however, keep in mind that the ultimate goal is not to please your aesthetic sensibility (or that of your designer) but to please the customer and make it easier for the customer to buy.

Nike's concept store in downtown Seattle, one of half a dozen the company uses as a flagship presentation and to develop its merchandising strategy, is a good example of learning. In this case, it was the company learning from itself. Finding the right merchandising presentation is not easy, even for a billion-dollar company. Initially Nike arranged the product by sport—running shoes with running clothes, soccer shoes with soccer clothes, and so on. The arrangement made sense according to most merchandising theory, putting all lifestyle elements together. The approach, however, proved problematic in practice. Each of the shoe areas was small and crowded. Nike used a "shoe elevator" to bring up stock in the proper sizes when the customer was ready to try on shoes. Runners—in this context, employees going to get the shoes, although many of them were runners in the track sense—came from all directions to get the shoes from the elevator. The small crowded aisles and constant hurry created a jumbled feel. The pounding street music added to the sense of noise and congestion.

After a while, Nike moved all the shoes together into a large open circle in the middle of the store. Shoes are still grouped by sport, but the central placement and the wide aisles invite customers to come inside and take a look. New, lifelike mannequins in a variety of body styles stand behind the shoe area, modeling the clothes related to each category of shoes and creating a softer feel for the entire display area. Instead of head-banging music, the music has a lighter sound—not quite soft rock, but no longer edgy urban. The beat makes you want to tap your toes—or take off down the street in your new pair of Nikes. When I first saw the changes, I commented to an employee that the store was much quieter now that they had removed that clattering shoe elevator. Puzzled, the employee said that they were still using the elevator—in fact, here came a load of shoes at that moment. The changes in presentation and music had *totally* altered the sensory experience of the store. So apply the basic principles, but change them as needed to meet your customers' needs.

Too many retailers simply put out their goods and see what sells. This approach is no more than warehousing with price tags. It leaves to customers the responsibility of finding what they need rather than the retailer leading them to it. Merchandising, which is both an art and a science, requires you to think big (another example of making no little plans). The art involves the creation of a seamless connection of the physical experience to the brand positioning. The art involves establishing a sense of place, inviting customers in and making them feel at home, and treating them so well that they feel glad they stopped by whether they buy a lot, a little, or nothing at all. A customer treated well is a customer who returns and who tells friends about the experience. The science represents the operational side of the business. Too often, it seems, operations is treated as being one discrete part of retailing, whereas marketing and brand building are treated as another. Excellent retailers, however, recognize that even the most mundane aspect of operations touches upon the customer experience in some way. Therefore, the POS system is not merely a means of expediting transactions, but a way to create a pleasurable customer experience; the presentation of the store bathrooms, along with every other part of the store design and presentation, is a way to reinforce the brand positioning. The science also involves organizing the products not only to maximize sales through proper placement and promotion of products, through queuing and the flow of customers through the premises, but also to maximize the sales of the products with the *highest margins*.

Merchandising, then, begins with the presentation of the brand from the outside. The storefront must be visually interesting enough to register with the customer. The iconography outside must present the brand positively. The window displays must be attractive enough to draw the customer into the store. Upon entering, the customer must be engaged by all five senses. The format of the displays must match the concept, and everything about the experience must be compatible with the brand values and must come together to create a unique experience. Before the traditional steps of merchandising begin, meta-merchandising connects with the customer in subtle and sometimes subliminal ways. By solidly establishing the store message—what the store stands for—meta-merchandising sets up the traditional elements of merchandising. These traditional elements then draw customers through the store, steering them toward higher-margin merchandise while encouraging cross-selling to increase the overall margin.

Retailers who put a lot of thought into merchandising learn to integrate both the fine art and the practical science. They convey a single store message—the brand position and the products that most support it—and see the greatest success.

DETAILING THE RETAILING

Although the following guidelines apply particularly to soft goods, the underlying principles apply to any kind of retail merchandise. The proper display of goods in a store embodies the principle that retail is detail.

- Shirts, jackets, blouses, and so on should be hung straight so that all the collars line up, to create a clean line.
- Price tags and size tags should be visible so customers do not have to unfold items or pull them off of hangers to check.
- Mannequins should wear a full inventory of product, from T-shirt to shirt to jacket to pants to shoes.
- Change mannequins weekly, before the start of the weekend or whatever is your busiest time.
- Do not overload tables. Put representative product on the table and stack the rest of the product on shelves or hang it on the wall.
- Shelves should be evenly spaced. Leave several inches between the top of the merchandise and the shelf above.
- Use unusual but neat folds for clothing on tables.
- Put related items only on a single table or in groupings along the wall (for instance, golf-related clothing and accessories).
- If you have logo items, all the logos should be visible, and all should line up.
- Group impulse items, whether inexpensive consumables or discounted best-selling books, near checkout counters. But please—do not dangle candy in front of babies just because Mom is trapped at the checkout line.
- Provide conversion charts for international sizes.

CHAPTER 7

Customizing Customer Service

IF THE PRECEDING CHAPTER sounds as though merchandising is a matter of clever placement of high-margin goods ... well, much of it is. But the human element ultimately dominates merchandising. The way a store treats customers on a personal level will do more to keep customers in—or run them out—faster than any other aspect of a store. A rude clerk can negate the benefits of knowledgeable merchandising. A helpful clerk can overcome poor merchandising, at least after the customer enters the store. In an effort to prevent mistakes and to ensure consistency, however, too many of the rules regarding employee behavior seem geared to produce robots instead of pleasant store personnel.

My son worked for a shoe store that required an employee to acknowledge every customer within 60 seconds of the customer entering the store. My son hated the policy. Some customers make it clear by their body language that they do not want to be approached. They bristled when he followed company policy and drew near. Another retailer requires its employees to stay within three feet of customers as they meander through the store. But few, if any, customers want a salesperson hovering over them constantly. Gap employees used to have a reputation for "pouncing" on customers as they entered, a behavior that the company has begun to rectify. Instead, the company is giving customers more help in the fitting rooms, where the attention is appreciated. For several years, Staples cashiers would ask every customer at the register, "Did you find everything you need?" Clearly some executive created this policy to make the customers feel attended to. But the right time to ask this question is when customers are shopping in the aisles, by employees circulating specifically to help. After a while, cashiers asked the prefab question with a noticeable lack of enthusiasm. The rare time a customer said something like, "No, I couldn't find the bond paper," then the entire checkout line shut down, inconveniencing other customers, while the cashier called someone to retrieve the product. Never ask questions you do not mean. And ask them when you are most capable of responding to them quickly. The last time I was in Staples, I could not find a certain kind of printer cartridge. After my second time down the aisle, an alert employee noticed and came out of his way to help me find what I needed. This was service at its best: unobtrusive, friendly, and genuinely helpful.

Customer service has a simple underlying premise: Put yourself in the customers' position. Begin by respecting their personal space. Customers let you know how they want to be approached. Someone with a specific need—a certain size of shoe in a particular color and style, say—comes directly to an employee and asks, or searches an aisle intently. Customers who are "just looking" do just that—idly working their way up and down the aisles. Customers who are interested in buying need a few minutes to make a preliminary mental sort of the merchandise. Suppose, for example, that a man is looking for a comfortable dress shoe. When he first enters the store, he requires a few seconds to orient himself to see where the dress shoes are. If he moves toward that area, employees should let him go unaccosted. If he looks lost, employees should spring forward to help. Once in the area of the dress shoes, the customer picks up several different styles, looking for the right combination of dress style, weight, and comfortable insole. Mentally, the customer picks out two or three pairs of shoes that he likes. At some point, he has questions, or he is ready to try on some

shoes. When he turns to locate someone, an employee should material-
ize at his side, prepared to assist. If no employee is free at that instant,
the nearest one should acknowledge him with eye contact and a smile,
indicating with or without words that someone will be with him right
away. Attentiveness is the order of the day, not stalking.

Employees at high-fashion shops linger over customers more, and
employees at discount stores are few and far between. Customers understand these tradeoffs. A person who buys a $2,000 suit expects a
cup of coffee and a lot of personal attention along with the suit,
whereas a person who buys a $200 suit expects nothing but a suit (al-
though a cup of coffee wouldn't hurt). In general, however, the timing
and degree of interaction between employees and customers depend as
much on the employee's instincts and basic courtesy as on the retail
concept. Yes, eventually the browsers need to be acknowledged, but retailers should not send employees charging off to greet each and every
person when they could focus on the people who show by attitude and
interest that they are likely to buy or they need help now. Too often,
customers feel besieged by employees when they do not want them and
cannot find employees when they need them. The classic example is the
grocery shopper who cannot find the last item or two on the shopping
list. Grocery stores have express lanes to save customers a minute or
two in the checkout line, but they never notice the increasingly frustrated shopper wandering their store for 20 minutes looking for the
frozen orange juice.

If a suggestion of additional service personnel seems extravagant,
consider the business advantage. The Westfield Shoppingtown family
of malls offers valet parking, special parking for expectant mothers,
package carryout for customers, and even concierges who seek out
customers to assist with shopping. The Westfield Group considers customer service to be its primary differentiator in competing with other
malls both for customers and high-quality tenants.

Courtesy is the first but not the only step toward great customer
service. The greatest service that an employee can provide a customer is
solid facts about products and services. This is also the greatest service
the employee can provide to the retailer, because timely and personable
delivery of meaningful information drives sales. Waiters should know
not only the restaurant's specials for the night but also the unusual ingredients and how they compare with common ones. Employees of

clothing stores should know the difference between knit and woven fabric, know that 100-ply thread is smaller than an 80-ply thread (resulting in a finer weave in a shirt or blouse), know any special care instructions for every piece of apparel the store sells, and know other details of the clothes-making art.

Whether the concept is outdoor sports or interior furnishings, the salesperson should use the customer's needs, usage, and abilities to sell the appropriate product—not just the customer's price point. I am fond of asking salespeople whether buying the most expensive product means I am paying for the best product or just a fancy label. I phrase the question so that they know that I am depending on their honest recommendation. What, I ask, is the difference between the high-priced item and the medium-priced item? At one athletic shoe store, the employee looked at me like I was an idiot and said, "Well, this one here is more expensive." At another athletic shoe store, the employee launched into a description of the superior outer sole support, inner sole comfort, and overall resistance to wear of the more expensive shoes. Guess where I bought the shoes, and guess which pair?

Instead of insisting that employees use superficial actions or words intended to fake a concern that is not there, hire and train individuals who like their jobs and respond to genuine customer needs, and give them permission to make good business decisions. Customers know the difference. Residents of the Northwest are familiar with Les Schwab Tire Centers. When you pull into a Schwab dealership, customer service personnel come a-running—literally. Even the company's ads feature employees on the run. Les provides all kinds of free services, such as rotation, swapping of summer and winter tires, and repair of flat tires, but it is the attitude that brings customers back. His employees are just *not* going to send you on your way unless you are happy.

Contrast this approach with an experience my wife and I had returning on Delta Airlines from the East Coast. We had had a long and tiring trip, so I tried to upgrade to first class for the five-hour return trip home. The ticket agent checked our tickets and said, "I'm sorry, we can't do that. Special fares can't be upgraded." I asked, "Is first class full?" "No, sir." I offered to pay the difference between our discount tickets and regular coach tickets and then purchase the upgrade on top of that, so that Delta would receive all the revenue it should have. He could not do it, he said. I went to a supervisor, who gave me the same story. "These are *discount* tickets," he said, as if certain fares were purchased only by undesirables. "Let me get this straight," I said. "You have empty seats in first class and a customer willing to pay the full value for the difference between our tickets and first class, and you can't do it?" "No, sir." At this point I was pretty steamed. "Name your price," I said. He again declined. The tickets were not upgradeable, period. The flight departed with four vacant seats in first class, a full coach section, and some standby passengers left at the terminal.

Passengers who have paid less than other fares should have a lower priority for seating or upgrades than other passengers, and upgrade prices should be adjusted for any differences in fares. But in this instance we were the only ones who wanted the better seats, and we were willing to pay the full value to trade up. The airline turns down revenue while infuriating a customer. The business logic escapes me. Perhaps this scenario helps explain why Delta was teetering on bankruptcy. The one action that would have benefited both the company and the customer, the employees were "not allowed to do."

Customer service starts at the top, in one of two ways. The first involves process, the idea of "insert Tab A into Slot B" quickly and efficiently. A company must put in place the systems to have the right products in the stores, to ship products quickly as needed to customers, to make exchanges painlessly, and to repair or replace products—all the things that keep a business humming. In Delta's case, the problem with the upgrade could have been a computer system that was too inflexible. No doubt the employees lacked a special code for this unusual transaction. But that lack of capability demonstrated an underlying attitude that upper management, at a great remove, should make all decisions involving customers. This attitude makes sense on issues involving flight safety and security, but not for pleasing customers at the gate.

Rather than enforcing rigid rules, retailers must enable their employees to make smart business decisions, especially decisions involving customer service. Then retailers should hire good people, train them to think, and insist that they use their own good judgment in dealing with people.

The second aspect of great customer service is the attitude of management toward its own people. One retailer understands inventory management and financials, but he will never create a great retail service organization because he is a commander instead of a team builder. Another retailer is a rah-rah people person. His staff loves him; his operation runs like a happy family. However, he has absolutely no knack for the operational and technical systems necessary to grow his few stores into a major chain. As you probably learned in a psychology or business management class, most people tend to be like these two individuals, either task oriented or people oriented. Studies show that the best leaders score in the middle on personality tests, reasonably good at both. (And some chains now give personality tests to prospective managers to determine their leadership traits.)

Growth of a field organization requires managers who have focus, who understand systems, and who can impart enthusiasm for doing the routine well. But great service also requires managers who create an environment in which people matter, which means listening to their ideas and feedback and folding their concerns into company decisions. People in the field also have to understand that in most retail organizations promotions often come from building teams that "love" you. When a job becomes open, store employees, store operators, field-service people—all are eager to tell management who they would like to see in that role. How do these issues relate to customer service? The attitude that managers show toward customers becomes ingrained in the corporate culture, and employees treat customers exactly the way managers treat them. One of my colleagues once worked two jobs to support her family. After struggling for some time, she went to her boss and asked to work fewer hours to better meet her responsibilities at home. Although the company frowned on it, the manager agreed. The manager's thoughtfulness made my colleague, in her words, "want to be the best salesperson on the floor." The company benefited, the employee benefited—the customer benefited.

If such considerations seem a touch too warm and fuzzy, they have a direct bearing on the bottom line. One national chain examined the relationship between store financial performance and management turnover. The chain discovered that every time a store manager changed, store revenues dropped an average of three percent, and it took a year for the store to recover. The same thing happened with an *entire region* when the regional manager changed. Store sales related directly to customer service, and customer service related directly to the attitude, enthusiasm, and experience of the leader.

The following Chapters, 8, "Blueprint for Execution," and 9, "Taking Your Organization Long," explain the ways to build systems and develop the human side of the retail organization to achieve customer satisfaction.

Serving Customers with a Smile— Remember That?

Good customer service is the hallmark of specialty retailers and lifestyle retailers, but good service is actually a more profound differentiator in concepts where people *don't* necessarily expect good service, as opposed to the high-end concepts where good service is a given. Too many fast-food servers seem afflicted with glazed eyes and a fervent wish to be somewhere, anywhere else. When employees at a quick-serve restaurant go out of their way to help customers, customers respond. At Potbelly, customers have come in and asked for Pepsi to drink. Potbelly serves Coca-Cola, but more than once, an employee has run next door to get the customer a Pepsi. There is no rule about this. Potbelly has not prescribed spontaneity (a contradiction in terms). It has, however, encouraged its employees to be real to people. Often, being real is nothing more than a smile or a greeting, but the smile or greeting is genuine.

Larger chains can also benefit from this kind of employee hustle. The Subway Sandwich franchise on the north side of Bend, Oregon, is an average store by any superficial appraisal. It has a decent but not great location. The interior design has not yet been updated to the newest Subway standards. Access is problematic during busy times, especially left turns in and out of the parking lot. Yet this franchise ranks anywhere from first to sixth in sales in the state of Oregon, depending on the season. The franchisee, Jeff Moore, greets regulars by name. He knows the preferred sandwich and condiments for dozens of people. Whatever needs to be done, whether organizing things in the back or preparing sandwiches behind the counter or cleaning tables out front, he does with a smile and often a joke. When he cleans tables, he visits with customers—those who want to be visited with. None of this is a put-on. It is who he really is. Jeff hires people like himself and pays them a little better than the going rate. By temperament, training, and imprinting from Jeff, they display the same positive attitude. The pay-off comes in return visits. Many customers eat there two or three times a week.

The idea of "high touch," introduced previously, relates closely to good customer service. High touch means that you treat the customer as a close friend; not with false intimacy but with courtesy, consideration, and respect. High touch creates a personal connection and a memorable experience. It registers with customers when they are treated well. The personal touch strongly increases the odds that the customer will become the most valued customer of all, the one who makes repeat visits.

Can you say, positively, that the attitude and behavior of your employees is an inducement for customers to return? If so, you have a great base for your merchandising strategy. If not, here is an area in which focused effort will yield substantial dividends in customer relations and sales.

For the retailer, customer service is the "softer side" of business, but it requires the same kind of hard-nosed thinking that any other aspect of the business requires. You need to examine closely what it takes to provide good customer service in your category. You need to understand what part of customer service drives sales, and what operational support you require to achieve that service. For consumables, the service that drives business is at the point of sales. For other categories, the service may rest on a sophisticated distribution system. For another, the differentiating factor may be parts and repairs. For another, phone or Internet support may be crucial. (If you use technology directly for customer service, the technology must always work—no "infinite holds" on the phone or hard-to-navigate Web sites.) Once again, operations should not be viewed as a set of "back-room" activities, but as a driving force for customer satisfaction. The level of satisfaction directly impacts brand building.

Good customer service is fundamental to delivering a special retail experience, and much of that service rests in the state of mind and culture of the organization. But because it means *delivering results*, customer service must be a defining factor in strategic planning, particularly with regard to organizational development and structure, the subject of the next chapter.

PART TWO

Go Long

There are two ways of going on offense. You can become very conservative, or you can go the other direction. I like using the whole field. Just attack. You eliminate the "what-ifs" by getting good players, coaching all the details, and then just letting them play. Don't play conservatively. Put the pedal to the metal and just let your guys go.

—Mike Martz, head coach of the St. Louis Rams

CHAPTER 8

Blueprint for Execution

THEORETICALLY, A RETAILER SHOULD WRITE the strategic plan for the business before ever breaking ground on the first store. Realistically, the first store often precedes the plan. Often a retailer opens a store because she's an expert on lingerie or has a great pizza recipe and only later considers broader possibilities. Or, like Potbelly's Bryant, the retailer may buy a store when the opportunity arises, knowing that a plan for expansion is to come. Or, like Blue C Sushi, the owners might want to understand the totality of the commitment required for one or two stores before considering regional or national expansion. Ultimately, what matters is that the strategic plan is in place before a retailer undertakes significant growth. When you start down the slope of expansion, the work and the money issues snowball. Too late, you may find your growth creating an avalanche that buries you in unforeseen problems. Several times a year, the business press writes about a company that failed because it "grew too fast." The underlying tale is that the company overreached because it lacked a solid plan.

Writing the strategic plan is part of the creation phase. This is seldom the most exciting part of the retail experience, but when beginning to outline the plan, do not think of producing a tome. Develop the plan in bullet points so that you can focus on the issues rather than struggle with the verbiage. Structure the plan as a PowerPoint presentation designed to prove (to yourself and others) the practical and financial feasibility of the concept. Each section of the plan should be no more than four to six slides. (You can write up a formal plan when you are finished.) As you develop the plan, force yourself to confront the hard questions. Put yourself in the position of being approached to invest in the concept. Ask yourself what information you would need to be convinced. Anticipate all the difficult questions and make sure the plan answers them all.

Section one of the plan should begin with your core values, mission statement, three-word mantra, and an analysis of your competitive differentiation. The section should also describe the most important difference between your concept and others. Compare yourself to mom-and-pop shops or local boutiques that may already have a loyal following. Compare yourself to national chains that have far greater marketing clout. If you can cogently and precisely differentiate your concept from others, you stand a great chance of convincing skeptical investors of the opportunity ahead. Unfortunately, the converse is also true. Pay particular attention to how the idea itself, the store design, and the product offerings together will create a new concept or bring new life to an old one. Be honest. Ask yourself: Does the world really need another dry cleaner—or whatever your concept may be? Ask yourself: How will my customer service be better than that of others'?

The first section should then describe the opportunity in broad terms (for example, the number of markets you could reach in two to three years and the demographics that support such an expansion). Young businesses can realistically plan only one to two years out. A more mature business should plan three to five years out. This section should describe external risks, such as major competitors or economic conditions that might affect success. The hospitality market, for instance, is highly vulnerable to recession or war. Food service is affected by the latest diet to sweep the land (to carb or not to carb?). If no major direct competitor exists today, identify the closest one and examine the impact of that competitor moving into the category or niche. Ask and answer the question of how you would compete if a category killer moved into town.

Section two of the plan should outline the strategic initiatives and strategic objectives. Strategic initiatives would include such things as "define new product lines," "identify largest markets," "expand retail locations," "create exciting new store environment," and "develop portfolio of high-quality real estate." Strategic objectives would identify particular actions for each initiative along with a defined timeline. A strategic objective might be to "open four stores in the next 12 months" or to "create a new store design by X date at no more than Y dollars." Supporting objectives might be to "maintain current return on investment to fund expansion" or to "create a training department to support hiring for new stores." The particulars depend on the current state of your own organization. Again, evaluate how customer service will drive sales and what systems are needed to support that service. Be certain that your plans address what you need to do organizationally to achieve those service goals.

Section three should describe a store development plan that implements the strategic objectives. To establish a baseline, the first slide should summarize the performance for any existing stores today. If you have not yet opened your first store, the data should be based on comparable performance by competitors. Store development should list the specific metropolitan areas to be sought for expansion, define the target customer and the number of planned stores in each area, and document the human and financial resources required. The section should also include all key assumptions, such as the number of stores to be opened in a year and the expected financial contribution of all the stores if they open on the scheduled dates. The section should also identify critical issues, anything that could materially impact progress on the plan. These might be the need to create or revamp the sourcing and distribution system, or the need to develop new information technology to track sales, inventory, and real estate/construction costs across a broad region, or the need to create a human resources department to manage the large increase in staffing. External risks were identified previously; internal risks should be identified here—such things as conflict between retail and wholesale channels or possible cannibalization of sales if new stores split a market rather than help grow it.

STRATEGIC PLANNING PROCESS

PERFORMANCE REVIEW
- Progress vs. Budget
- Up-to-date Performance Analysis
- Actions to Address Problems

BUDGET
- P & L budget
- Capital Budget
- Anticipated Results
- Measurements

OPERATING PLAN
- Strategic Goals & Objectives
- Specific Tactics
- Milestones
- 1 - Year Budgeting & Projections

STRATEGIC PLAN
- Strategic Analysis
- Strategic Goals & Objectives
- 1 - 3 Year Projection
- Financial Plan, Specific Metric (e.g., EPS)

ANNUAL REVIEW

FIGURE 8-1

The foundation of every solid retail concept is the strategic plan, which must clearly delineate the strategic issues, competitive threats, and financial projections, and which must establish firm metrics for desired results such as earnings per share (EPS). From that plan comes the annual operating plan, which includes all of the goals and tactics for the next year. The operating plan drives the budget. An annual perform-ance review forces the company to examine what is working and what is not and to adjust the business plan accordingly. The original strategic plan does not have to be wordy—the shorter, the better—but it must be thorough, rigorous, and painfully honest.

Finally, the strategic plan should review the financial results of the planned expansion, broken down by best, average, and worst case. The best case would assume that all stores open on schedule and on budget and generate the projected revenue. The average case might assume that two-thirds of the stores open as scheduled at 10 percent over cost and generate the current store average. The worst case might assume that only one-third of the stores open on time and perform no better than the worst-performing store you have today. The particular scenario for average or worst case will vary with the situation. Opening three new stores in the same town, using the same contractor, will be much easier than opening three stores in another city in the region; and opening three stores within the region will be much easier than opening five stores on the other side of the country. The plan should demonstrate that in the worst case you can remain viable (if not prosperous) while you straighten out the problems that have hamstrung the expansion—or you determine to pull back. The average case should provide a decent return on investment. The best case should blow an investor's socks off. One planning strategy is to use the average case as the basis for expending all hard costs and to accelerate spending only after revenue consistently exceeds expectations.

A strategic plan should not drown the retailer or a potential investor in paperwork. Nor should it, like too many plans, be put up on a shelf and forgotten by either of you. The strategic plan must always be the touch point for major decisions after the plan is under way, but its most significant value is to force the retailer to do a deep and exhaustive analysis up front. Done properly, it tests every working hypothesis about the distinctiveness and achievability of a concept. Sometimes the plan contains information that is little better than an educated guess, but the point is that the guess is educated. Another point is not to be afraid of the weaknesses exposed by the plan. Use the plan to learn, and use the learning to improve the plan. I have seen strategic plans that were poorly thought out, and I have seen retailers unable to defend plans with data when asked pointed questions. The impression is that some businesspeople are afraid to look at their ideas in depth for fear of finding a fatal flaw that would prevent their dreams from proceeding. The unspoken assumption is that they will solve the problems as they go. Believe me, there are plenty of problems to solve as you go without bringing along problems from the start. The sooner that you can identify weaknesses, the sooner that corporate brain-power can be brought to bear to minimize or eliminate them. Always plan for the downside of an investment. At one company, whenever a junior executive is about to present to a senior executive, the peers of the junior executive serve as a preliminary audience. Their role is to shoot holes in the proposal before it goes any further. The feedback invariably causes the junior executive to stay up most of the night refining the presentation. And it is always much improved for the effort.

Retailers should take a similar approach with their own strategic plans. You should be its harshest critic, not the investor who first notices that the data does not support the financial projections or that you promise to open ten stores next year even though you have barely got your first store running now. Careful analysis may show that the concept will scale to multiple stores if you can develop products that have higher margins, or increase store volume by 10 percent, or reduce construction costs by 5 percent. Any of these or similar things being the case, you now know which problems to solve. At the same time, a good retail concept with a strong unit economic model can expand on an almost exponential basis: three new stores this year, ten next year, 30 the year after that—soon, 100 or more. Working through the implications of such growth on infrastructure and human resources is mandatory before you get pulled into an ever accelerating cycle of growth.

I speak from experience. When I joined Starbucks, the company had about 100 stores. In what seemed like the blink of an eye, we had added a couple of hundred additional stores and grown to about $300 million in annual revenue. We were starting to position ourselves to get to $1 billion annually. But every manager and employee was in an all-out sprint. Each of us was able to meet the individual challenges before us, but the company was growing and changing so fast—both in the number of new people and in the shifting of responsibilities and other organizational changes—that it was difficult to maintain an effective and cohesive team.

DECIDING WHEN TO "GO LONG"

After you have the proper organizational structure and management team in place—even if the team is small—you can begin to plan for growth. Have realistic goals and set both conservative and aggressive growth targets. Begin execution against the conservative target. Evaluate the process against all aspects of the business: finance, operations, management, staffing, locationing. When you are able to execute successfully against the conservative goal so that each new store becomes a "no brainer," shift to the aggressive plan. Constantly evaluate results; slow down if your organization shows any sign of imploding from the additional effort.

Before "going long" with your retail concept ask yourself:

- Have you written a three-year strategic plan that includes a strong competitive analysis, a store development plan, a profit-and-loss statement, and a clear outline of the capital required?
- Are you thinking ahead about the infrastructure and person power you will need to fuel your growth?
- Do you have a well-developed new store concept ready?
- Do you have an experienced store development team in place?
- Do you have a well-defined conservative rollout plan and a well-defined aggressive plan in place, with metrics determining which plan to follow?
- What is the ramp-up time for the conservative approach?
- What is the ramp-up time for the aggressive approach, if you switch to it?
- Do you have a pipeline of target trade areas and potential site locations that can be leveraged? If not, how long will it take to develop these locations? Real estate leads other aspects of growth by 12 to 18 months.
- Are all organizational resources prepared and aligned to support dramatic growth? In addition to a solid infrastructure, do you have the ability to recruit, hire, and train the people you will need at all levels?

To help us get a grip on our future before we too ran the risk of succumbing to rapid expansion woes, Orin Smith brought in Eric Flamholtz of UCLA as a consultant to executive management. Eric had a history of working with companies transitioning from entrepreneurial start-ups to "real companies," and he had recently updated his book *Growing Pains* on that subject. Eric outlined for us a concept of the "pyramid of organizational development," which helps young companies frame the many steps needed to shift from the seat-of-the-pants entrepreneurial approach to professional management. The base of the pyramid corresponds to a beginning business: identifying and defining a market. The next layer up involves developing products and services. Successive stacks in the pyramid call for acquiring resources, developing operational systems, and developing managerial systems. The apex of the pyramid is managing corporate culture. These are things that companies need to execute over time, but they need to be planning for them from the start. (*See Figure 8-2.*)

My "a-ha!" came in recognizing that Starbucks was strong at the bottom (finding a niche market and developing products) and at the apex (managing corporate culture), but all of us were weak in the middle, in the area of developing management and operational systems. By this time, Starbucks had a reasonably elaborate management structure and many of the financial and operational systems we needed to grow successfully. None of us would claim, however, that as an organization we were functioning efficiently at full productivity. Eric's particular value was to provide a methodology by which we could relate "key result areas" to our actual teams. The management principle is simple. For every key result you want from your organization, you need to have a functioning leader and unit wholly responsible for that one result. In a smaller organization, or for a smaller task, the responsible "unit" might be a particular person. But always, a one-to-one relationship must exist between the organizational structure and the organizational goals and objectives. In the melee engendered by growth, however, new duties and areas of responsibilities pile up rapidly. Often they are assigned or assumed haphazardly. Functions become confused by ad hoc decisions required to handle the latest crisis (for example, the arbitrary assignment of a new role to whoever happens to be standing there when an emergency erupts). Other new functions evolve and do not get covered at all.

REAL ESTATE / STORE DEVELOPMENT PYRAMID

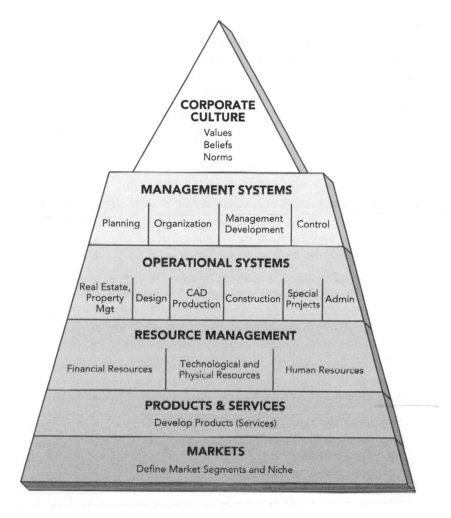

FIGURE 8-2

To make the shift from start-up to professionally managed organization, every company must develop multiple layers of capabilities, and every company is invariably weak at one level or another. An analysis of Starbucks' real estate operations identified an overlap of responsibilities. Development of this chart, specific to real estate-driven retail concepts, helped identify and correct internal problems by putting each "key result area" wholly under a particular team. The methodology was developed by Eric Flamholtz of UCLA, and the pyramid design is based on his model.

Eric did not give us specific answers to our operational problems, but his insight caused me, for the first time, to focus intently on the division of functions in the areas under my responsibility. By concentrating on the key result areas against actual team responsibilities, I saw fairly quickly why we were struggling despite a lot of "above-and-beyond" effort by individuals. In these areas—real estate, design, construction, and special projects—many functions had overlapping responsibilities. With that realization, I was able to pinpoint which senior manager needed to be accountable for each objective. I could eliminate the bleed-over of responsibilities between teams that resulted in nobody owning a result. When everybody is responsible, nobody is responsible. From that point, it was relatively easy to put together objectives and the name of the person responsible for getting results for each item. Most critically, we developed the ability to put down a specific date by which vital issues needed to be handled. Fairly quickly, my team began to get traction. The new approach proved especially valuable when we launched the store redesign project soon afterward.

CONSOLIDATING FUNCTIONS SPURS GROWTH

In 1991, when I was the company's independent real estate broker for northern California, Howard Shultz invited me to join Starbucks as head of real estate development. I had known Howard since 1978, and we had enjoyed working together to establish Starbucks in the Bay Area. I knew he was building a company that would be exciting to grow with. But the real estate position did not appeal to me. "You know what?" I told him. "The store operators berate the construction department for not turning over a store on time, the construction group tells the operators to stop whining, and they both blame the real estate folks for picking a bad site in poor condition with little or no tenant improvement dollars in the deal. I don't want to deal with the internal battles."

In most retail organizations, real estate, construction, and operations all report to the senior vice president or president of retail, someone who usually comes up through operations. Operators are conservative and have relatively little understanding of the concept of locationing. Because real estate drives everything else, I had long since come to believe that real estate drives every expanding retail company. Whereas operators understand property as little more than a space for build-out and sales, real estate people have to be forward thinking and creative in their vision for a location. They need to be much more aggressive than a typical operator to get the right properties well ahead of the need.

I came back to Howard, Orin Smith, and Howard Behar, president of retail, with a proposal for a different organizational alignment: a senior vice president responsible for store development including real estate, design, construction, and asset management. The position would be at the same level as the senior vice president of operations. The new organization would enable Starbucks to develop a holistic approach to all of the issues related to finding Grade A locations and creating the brand position, in-store design, and building the stores on them with quality, efficiency, and speed. The new integrated team would be better able to meet the needs of operations, with less interdepartmental conflict. This unified structure also meant that real estate would be specifically responsible for executing the rapid growth plans outlined by the corporation's strategic plan and have an equal opportunity with Howard and Orin to garner the human and financial resources it needed to get the job done. Whether they hired me or not, I told them, this was the right approach to help the company succeed with its meteoric growth plans.

They listened politely, but I did not leave that meeting very optimistic that they would accept my ideas. After all, they were still fairly new to the game. They had a powerful board that had told them to "find a real estate executive." It was hard to listen to an outsider (even one with a modest stake in the company) telling them how to reorganize their management. After several meetings over four months, Starbucks agreed to my structure. I was hired.

Although few other retail companies follow this organizational model, I am convinced that the consolidation of real estate, design, construction, and asset management into one organization was a major reason for the company's capability to roll out 100s of stores a year while maintaining the high brand standards.

Creating Systems to Deliver the Brand

Part of the strategic plan should be devoted specifically to organizational development, which means the structure of the organization as it grows and the systems that it needs to expand. For an existing chain, the organizational issues can probably be covered in sections two and three, in support of growth objectives. For a new retailer, the organizational issues may be worth a section of their own. Delivering what the customer wants is the purpose, ultimately, of organizational development. Traditional brand building is all too often concerned with logos, marketing, and advertising, the superficial images that a company projects. Enduring brands go far deeper to the capabilities needed to deliver on the promise. Their ability to deliver sends roots deep down into the hearts and minds of their targeted customers. These customers become, in turn, disciples of the brand, and spread the word. Customers seldom think about the robust set of capabilities that deliver differentiated service. Nor should they. Customers should not wonder how lumber arrives at their favorite hardware store or fresh beef to their favorite restaurant or fresh flowers to their favorite florist. Subconsciously, however, customers recognize that the freshest food or the latest product is always in stock, and they return because of the implicit brand promise that the company will have the product they want, when they need it, at the right price.

Organizational infrastructure, at its most robust, can become the very essence of the brand. Since Michael Dell began selling refurbished personal computers while a college student, Dell Computers has built its reputation on great products, fast delivery, and good pricing. Long before the phrase "eliminate the middleman" became current, Dell Computers sold direct, investing in ever-more-sophisticated inventory management systems until today the company can custom build and deliver PCs within days while turning inventory more than 80 times a year. It may seem strange that a book on retail highlights a company that has shunned most traditional retail outlets, but Dell has blown away its retail competitors because of its systems, which include not only inventory management but also unrivaled customer support for both large and small customers. Its systems strength has enabled it to win on pricing, which is why only a highly customer-oriented lifestyle retailer will be able to compete successfully, delivering the face-to-face presence that Dell has so far chosen to bypass.

Infrastructure can also be so visible as to become retail theater. Despite some financial problems, Krispy Kreme has won loyal customers by producing uniform doughnuts in more than 400 stores throughout the country. The company's manufacturing process has become its brand presentation. The scale, building materials, and proportions of the Krispy Kreme company stores are designed to emphasize the creation and delivery of doughnuts. The buildings convey a retro look that adults associate with their childhood, when doughnut bakeries were relatively common and hot, fresh doughnuts were a mouth-watering treat. The panelized design, down to the flat roofs, sends an image of solid, unassuming charm. The stores do not overdo the entertainment factor. They stick to a relatively minimalist approach that keeps attention focused on the doughnuts, which customers view through the large plate-glass windows as the product rolls though an elaborate baking and glazing system.

For most companies, however, the infrastructure consists of all the invisible things that deliver the visible brand. A good example is the Toyota Motor Company, the world's leading automobile manufacturer. Toyota's vaunted lean manufacturing system provides its major competitive advantage, but other companies have tried to replicate this system without achieving the same results. The reason goes back to mission and values, so this example serves a double duty. Toyota's explicit mission is contributing to society through high-quality products and service. The company will say that the values, beliefs, and business methods based on its core principles are the real source of competitive advantage. Its production systems, and the efforts that employees make to continually improve them, are the result of its principles, not the reason for its success.

Few people think of Toyota as being a retailer, but of course automobile manufacturers are vertically integrated retailers. More and more retailers are likely to become vertically integrated in the future. Going forward, there just is not enough revenue to support a profit margin for both a wholesaler and a retailer. As more companies look further upstream to improve margins, they need to consider the Toyota lesson. "Retail is detail" applies to every aspect of the business, every step in product design and development, every step in production, every step in store design and branding, all the time. Continuous improvement needs to be at the heart of retail systems as it is at the heart of heavy industry. Americans have a great deal to learn from older cultures about taking a long-term view and improving our processes and our work every single day. At Toyota, the fable of the tortoise and the hare is part of the culture. Without losing the energy of the hare, U.S. retailers need also to think and act more like the tortoise, combining creativity with steady execution and regular improvement of every system of every kind.

Supporting All Aspects of Business

Organizational systems cover every aspect of business. Management systems include planning, organizational structure, personnel development, and control. Operational systems include all the systems required to produce or acquire the product and deliver it. For retail, a parallel set of systems involves the development and management of real estate. Financial systems include all the procedures, software, and personnel required to collect and analyze financial and sales data. By showing trends promptly, good financial systems enable a company to become proactive to market conditions. It is beyond the scope of this book to describe all of these systems in detail, but the point is to begin to plan for them early in organizational life.

In my experience, the two system areas that cause the most problems are financial/inventory and real estate expansion management and control. For its 30-plus retail stores, Oakley today has a sophisticated computerized inventory system that automatically reorders whenever store inventories drop to certain levels; when the company opened its first retail store, however, the manager ordered and replenished supplies manually. The company had quite an exciting time before it upgraded from pencil and paper to computers. Oakley investigated a number of software packages to handle finance and inventory, seeking a system that would be affordable for its fledgling retail operation and would also grow with the company's needs. Because Oakley already had an inventory program from SAP for its longstanding wholesale operation, the company eventually settled on additional SAP packages that plugged into its existing systems. Oakley's experience, however, is instructive. The company found packages in the range of $150,000 to

$200,000 that would have done the job. The most elaborate financial packages were $600,000 or more.

Even $150,000 is a lot of money for start-ups, and less expensive systems are available. However, at the minimum, you want to be able to do inventory tracking and evening polling of sales. You want to avoid cheap point-of-sale systems that can handle only a small set of transactions or that are not easily networked to roll up results from multiple stores. The initial system should grow with you. You do not want to have to throw out your financial system just as you hit your most rapid growth. The most expensive system components, you will find, are the computerized cash registers for the point-of-sale systems, which can run $7,000 or more each. If you pick a less expensive financial system that will not scale beyond a certain point, make sure that its data can be easily exported to potential replacement systems down the line. As an example of a pragmatic approach, Blue C Sushi chose a nationally known vendor of restaurant software, neither the most nor least expensive. The product is designed to scale to numerous stores, but Blue C Sushi's owners did not yet commit to licenses for multiple stores so that if the product does not work as expected, they will not have washed money down the drain. And they may test another product in the second store.

On the subject of financial management, make sure that while you are a small company (before you can afford your own controller or chief financial officer), you have good accounting support from outside the company and an objective review of all financial transactions. Unless it is the owner, no one person should handle all of the money and financial paperwork. For example, one person should make out deposit slips and review the bank receipts that come back, while another person should make the actual deposits. No one person should be writing checks and reconciling accounts. Sad to say, many small retail concerns are robbed by employees who have regular access to cash, checks, and deposits.

Rapid real estate expansion creates another set of problems. Tracking progress on store development is particularly hard for retail establishments because the retailer is usually focused on running the current set of stores and pushing sales. Real estate is like "over-the-horizon" radar. It must constantly scan well beyond today's needs. Property-related issues—finding a location, executing a lease, managing the construction process—can reach a crisis long before other kinds of problems normally manifest themselves. Real estate is easy to ignore until the last moment, but real estate problems can set you back weeks and months. They can ruin the financials for an entire quarter, if not the year.

Retailers need to be adept at tracking progress on the real estate front. World-class retailers use a limited set of store development tools to manage key property-related processes. These programs, which are effectively project management software tailored to real estate development and property management, are divided into three general groups: those that track lease terms and property information, audit payables, and reconcile payments; those that manage activities from acquisition through closure, capture key store attributes, and speed the approval process; and geo-mapping software that enables the analysis of demographics as described later. You should begin researching store development tools from about five stores on; the systems should be in place by the time you reach 30 stores.

Such sophisticated software tends to be used by larger chains, although large and small chains alike can use consultants for these services. None of the programs are as comprehensive as they should be, and most of them are too expensive for a beginning retailer. However, even if the effort is manual early on, retailers must establish store tracking reports, monitoring progress against defined milestones in everything from the identification of locations to lease signings to delivery of construction inventory. A simple electronic spreadsheet with a list of all deliverables and associated dates will do for starters, provided that the owner assiduously tracks progress. Otherwise, the odds are very high that a major delay will occur somewhere along the way in the opening of your next store, or your next set of stores. To find the right systems, do thorough research, go to trade shows, get detailed briefings from product vendors, ask around among other small retailers and among other retailers who have gone through growth spurts. Find something with the best mix of value and features according to your financial capabilities (or limitations). The guiding principle is to get good information before deciding and to take a longer-term view in acquiring the systems that you need.

Using Internal Strengths to Create External Results

An important part of the blueprint for growth is creating a workable strategic plan that lays out not only the business and financial goals but also the management and operational systems to be implemented at each stage of development, appropriate for the company's size. I cannot emphasize enough the importance of always being one step ahead in terms of developing the right organization and hiring the right people to run the organization. Discipline is required on both counts. The first discipline is to create the systems early. The second discipline, covered in the next chapter, is to hire only the best people and well ahead of your needs. Understanding in advance that your organization not only will change but that it must change at various points in its life cycle—including the end, when it needs to reinvent itself—will help get your head around organizational issues from the start. Having an approach in place to handle organizational and financial systems, human, and systems from the earliest days of operation can result in the greatest source of savings—that which is never spent on costly mistakes! Getting people, money, and a strategic plan in place can save millions of dollars as well as help guarantee the success of the concept. Without such a blueprint, your concept will probably stumble or—worse—self-destruct during the initial stage under the pressures of getting started. For retailers who already have several stores or a sizable chain of stores, a hard-core review of management strength, investor involvement, and strategic plan will likely pinpoint critical weaknesses and lead to changes that can restimulate growth. Completing this blueprint and working through it several times is the last step in the process of creation for your retail concept.

Executing on the blueprint will become an unseen strength that will separate you from competitors over time. Other retailers can enter your category; they can copy your products; they can try to mimic your look and feel; they can try to outflank you with better store locations. But the top three levels of the organizational pyramid—a strong corporate culture supported by professional management systems and operational systems—are as unique as fingerprints. They are virtually impossible to reproduce. As the external attributes of the brand differentiate you in the mind of the consumer, these unique internal attributes represent the only manner in which you can develop the long-term staying power necessary to establish any great brand.

A CHECKLIST OF QUESTIONS TO ASK

☐ Are you fully committed to bringing this concept to fruition?

☐ Do you have the proper experience in this category? Who should you target to bring on board?

☐ Do you have sufficient personal resources to survive until the business becomes profitable? To get through down times, you will always need more money than you think you do.

☐ Do you have sufficient emotional support to help you through the grueling process of starting and growing a business? Make sure personal relationships are secure.

☐ Do you have enough points of differentiation to compete head to head with a category killer?

☐ Do you have the right management team to handle local or regional growth without disrupting operations or profits in existing stores?

CHAPTER 9

Taking Your Organization Long

I N THE SAME WAY that a head football coach brings aboard coordinators for offense, defense, and special teams, the founder of a retail brand has to bring aboard seasoned professionals who can help the team "go long." In retail, people in senior positions need to have backgrounds in a wide variety of areas: brand, marketing, operations, merchandising, finance, real estate, design, and customer intelligence. You would be surprised at how few companies have the spread of talent to cover all these areas. Many companies have three or four senior people with tremendous talent in one area—usually merchandising or operations—and none whatsoever in the other critical areas, such as real estate selection or design. (Entire categories sometimes have the issue of focused expertise. Banks, for instance, are very good at operations and poor at concept development and design.) Even if you personally have all the skills necessary to serve as a coach for every position, you will not have the time, bandwidth, or inclination to cover them all. The personal span of management for an entire retail business will not extend beyond three to five stores at most. The sooner you establish veterans in each of these areas of expertise, the faster your concept can move in synchronized fashion downfield. Do not forget the psychological issues mentioned before. If you are a good task person, make sure you have a good people person aboard; if you are a good people person, make sure you have a good task person aboard.

Other skill areas are specific to the business category. In the grocery industry, you need expertise in finances, vendor-supplier relationships, and merchandising. In clothing you need a good (no, a great) merchant. A great merchant is someone who understands merchandising trends, loves face-to-face selling, and has expertise in sourcing. In pharmaceuticals, you need experience in drugstore management, general merchandising, and retail sales. In food service, you need substantial background in food preparation and operations. In all categories, be sure to obtain any specialized knowledge that you lack. James of Blue C Sushi had been an operations manager at Microsoft and Go2Net, but he had never run a restaurant. So Blue C Sushi recruited Shinichi Miura from Sushiland. Shinichi's 20-plus years of experience in Japanese restaurant management provided, among many other things, knowledge about specialized cooking equipment and about sourcing fresh fish.

If you have rounded out the management team with as diverse a skill set as possible and still lack a critical intellectual asset, budget to bring in that expertise well in advance of when you need it so that you are not scrambling to find the talent at a crucial moment. At certain phases of development, you may want to bring in consultants to provide an outside perspective and reality check as well as to fill in any knowledge gaps.

Bryant Keil was a "team of one" when he bought the first Potbelly Sandwich store in 1996. After he opened his third store, he began to build a meaningful organization. His goal was to find "smart, honest, good people" who knew how to take businesses to the next level—and not necessarily just restaurant people. His chief financial officer came from a high-growth, public real estate company. His operations chief had run a small restaurant chain as well as having worked for a large one. His marketing chief was the former head of marketing at Sears and (Bryant learned) a Potbelly fan since 1982. When Oakley began its retail expansion after 20-plus years as a wholesaler, the company brought in real estate experience in the form of an outside broker. Next the company found a top-notch merchandiser and someone who understood buying, inventory management, and forecasting. Soon after came a financial analyst. The order may vary according to your own experience and who you find, but generally finance and operations are the first two senior positions to fill.

A retail concept with expansion in mind should have a dedicated senior resource for real estate early on, but this can be an outside position, in the form of a consultant or other trusted outside broker. Other outsiders who can bring industry knowledge and provide considerable business guidance are venture capitalists and other investors. Investors, discussed later in this chapter, should be evaluated according to the same guidelines as you would evaluate any other important member of your organization, because the fit is as important with investors as employees and because many investors become de facto working partners with the retailers that they fund.

Initially the head of operations is responsible for most hires, but by the time you reach 4 or 5 stores (or 50 to 60 people) you should have a head of human resources to develop consistent hiring and personnel practices and deal with government paperwork. Real estate and design expertise can remain out of house for some period, although larger chains eventually build large departments because of the demands that fast growth puts on this specialty. (At Starbucks I had 14 people working with me at the 100-store level and more than 500 specialists by the time we reached 4,000 stores, when we were opening an average of 3 stores per day annually.) At approximately 15 stores, you should have a full-time merchandiser. At roughly 35 stores, a full-time marketing person should be aboard. In an expanding chain, each of these important hires will soon require staff of his or her own. As always, the retailer has to budget additional personnel against competing needs and the overall percentage of corporate overhead to revenue.

Searching for Heart, Not Pedigree

Always hire your replacement. The truism of hiring people with the skills to grow begins with the initial senior people you hire and extends to every level of the organization. An organizational schema is only as good as the people who inhabit the roles. In a growing business, people not only wear a lot of hats, they also must be able to quickly wear bigger and bigger hats. Expanding beyond a handful of stores is possible only if your original team can step up and run the existing stores for you. Becoming a major regional or national chain is possible only if your senior staff can each manage a number of stores each. At every level, people must have the capability to step up to the duties of the next level above. The same capacity for growth is required for every other aspect of the business, from real estate to finance to human resources. This means you need to be as careful in hiring a cashier as you are in hiring the head of operations.

Entrepreneurs have difficulty making the shift to a professionally managed company, or making the shift without becoming bogged down in bureaucracy. Sometimes the difficulty comes when the founder/owner is unwilling or unable to "let go" when the organization becomes too large for the entrepreneur to run directly. Sometimes the entrepreneur brings in people who have experience managing a larger company but not one in the throes of transition. Even if the owner/founder and the original management team understand their organizational problem and can take step back from the fires of daily business, they seldom have the expertise to plan the development of their organization. They plunge ahead, working harder and harder, until organizational friction and personal burnout bring the organization to a grinding halt. Be ready to shift from "doer" to "delegater," and be sure to plan ahead for the structure that you will need to manage a far-flung organization. Psychologically, by establishing the idea early that "everybody moves up, everybody grows," you are less likely to cling to old responsibilities when you should be taking on new ones.

Have the confidence as well to hire people who bring skills you do not have and who are good enough to challenge you, your initial management team, and your assumptions as the business and organization evolves. Insecure leaders cover up their own sense of inadequacy by requiring sovereignty over the people they hire. They do not want anyone to show them up. Executives who are defending or hiding their vulnerabilities frequently fire employees. The initial result is constant turnover, which brings its own set of problems. Eventually, these executives succeed in surrounding themselves with people whose skills and temperament make them comfortable, the proverbial but still extant "yes men." Having the skills to placate the boss is not the same thing as the skills to grow the company, which is what ought to actually please the boss. Hire people who are smarter than you. They will make you look good by exceeding expectations as a team.

Of course, identifying and then being able to hire high-quality people for your company is a challenge. Most executives focus on the wrong things. It is like your best friend asking you to find him a date. Your friend gives you a long list of preferred qualifications, but it really comes down to the men wanting a gorgeous babe and the women wanting a good-looking hunk. The same holds true with companies seeking job candidates. The company always has a long list of abilities that the candidate should embody, but in the end they want ... Cindy Crawford or Richard Gere. (Who, as I recall, did not do well as a team.) In other words, companies tend to want the best presentation, the candidate who is the most impressive, rather than the one who is most capable of filling the position. Without intending to, they treat the external or "cosmetic" features of candidates as the primary criteria. Hey, this guy went to an Ivy League school. Hey, that gal worked for a Fortune 500 company. Employees with these kinds of credentials earn the hiring manager and the senior management team bragging rights. The hire feels safe. The subconscious belief is, "If they don't work out, don't blame me." Yet "resumés," as I call highly credentialed people, often do not work out. They may look good on paper, but paper does not tell you what is in the heart.

An education from a fine school and work experience in a major corporation are assuredly good things, but ask hard questions: Why is the person from a Fortune 500 company available? Is a senior person from a major company the right profile anyway? What if the individual expects the kind of resources and support available to a Fortune 500 company when you are struggling to make your first million dollars? Different companies have different needs depending on who they are and where they are in their stages of growth. Your candidate might be perfect if he or she has a small company background as well as a large company or is free of the rigor mortis that sometimes comes from corporate work. Some individuals become so entrenched in their old ways of doing business that they continue to do whatever they have done up to this point to move up the corporate ladder. They just do not comprehend the change in work context or speed that comes with the environment of a smaller firm. They may want to accept your company's working circumstances and its values, but they just cannot. I know of a great "strategy" guy who joined a company that also needed him to execute tactics. He never engaged. He actually said, "Tactics are beneath me." To me, this was his insecurity speaking, not his superior abilities. He did not last long.

Making the right hire is not about resumés or pedigree. It is about the personal values and abilities of the person. It is about finding a person whose values, abilities, and goals are aligned to the right job and to the brand, values, culture, actual job requirements, and growth plans of the company. You need individuals who are sufficiently in touch with themselves that they are open to accepting the culture and the values and beliefs of your company. If you find a person who has the combination of terrific experience and humanity (an ability to listen, to be open to learning, to participating in your culture), then you have picked the right person to complement your management team. You should look hard for evidence that this person is a team player, someone who can work within a structure and is happy to use conventional approaches when they work. Tradition is a good thing when it represents the distillation of hard-earned experience about how to get things done. At the same time, your hire needs to be irreverent enough to challenge the status quo—a dish breaker but not an anarchist. It does not hurt to have at least one of your core team with experience in high-growth enterprises, either. When you hire good people, you will find that they are harder on themselves than you are on them.

Two instances from the major expansion of Starbucks in the Southeast illustrate the importance of hiring heart over resumé. One hire was a senior real estate person who had extensive corporate background with a major retail chain. He knew real estate strategy, he understood the problems related to opening stores promptly, he had a good grasp of financials, and he presented well in the interview. We soon learned that he was very good at quantitative analysis: Put numbers in front of him and he could pick the right site in an instant. However, he could not do a qualitative evaluation. He had trouble developing a feeling for the romance of the Starbucks brand positioning and how it related to selecting new store locations. Faced with evaluating the aesthetic attributes of competing locations, he looped into analysis paralysis. He could not make a decision. In contrast, another individual who came aboard at the same time had little corporate experience. However, he had worked on the brokerage side for several retail rollouts throughout the Southeast. Brokers have to get deals done in order for them to get paid, and I wanted to build our real estate group with such aggressive personalities. This person's natural sensitivity to Starbucks brand positioning led him to rapidly find prime locations that properly presented the company to the public. This person, a perfect example of hiring attitude over experience, remains one of the best hiring decisions I ever made.

Also, the most effective people are not hot dogs. Jim Collins's latest book, *Good to Great*, identifies 11 companies in a variety of industries that have gone from average to great by objective financial measures. Collins discovered a number of common traits among these highly successful firms. One of the traits is that not a single company of the 11 had "rock star" leaders, larger-than-life characters who enjoyed the limelight. The finding should not be surprising. If company attention is focused on boosting the CEO or other senior managers, it takes attention off the customer. The same rule applies to every team at every level in the company. Ask yourself, "Did this person become a star at the expense of others or to the detriment of his or her team, or did this person become a star because of the great team he or she created?" The most effective people at every level focus on the results at hand, and they make those around them look better.

Personal interviews represent the best opportunity to find out what really matters about someone, but most experienced businesspeople are well prepared for interviews. They offer crisp, compelling, credible answers to all the toughest questions. To really learn about the person, you need to talk about less formal matters. My friend Mark Jaffe likes to say that a candidate interview is like the first session with a psychotherapist, with one difference: You get important personal information from them, but do not have the responsibility to make them feel better! As I do with potential clients, I ask prospective employees about their family, their parents, who they were in high school, what books matter to them. None of this data is particularly important in isolation. What matters is your listening to the voice when people talk about unrehearsed things. Their response to questions that have "feeling content"—about family, for instance—often reveal the most. Note that "reveal" means the person's values and psychological state, not marital or parental status or other personal matters that are inappropriate, as well as illegal, to ask applicants.

MATCHING MOTIVATION WITH VALUES

A simple test can help uncover the values of a job candidate, whether that individual is motivated by the external trappings of a job or the job itself, and whether the person's values align with those of the retailer. Ask the individual to rate the following items about the job and the firm in the order of importance:

- Money: Compensation, both cash and noncash items
- Prestige: Brand cachet of the company as perceived from the outside
- Status: The person's rank in the new job in company's internal pecking order
- Culture: Camaraderie, values, shared ethos with the company's principals
- Autonomy: Degree to which the person may define his or her own goals and objectives
- "Wow" factor: The ability of the person to do or participate in something hugely innovative, unprecedented, or not possible elsewhere

Source: Wyatt & Jaffe

Looking for the heart of a person is not the same thing as hiring only with the heart. My biggest hiring error came when a classmate from grade school connected with me again in a job application. I was so enthralled to be hooked up with a childhood friend that I hired him quickly. He was qualified for the job, but I did not do enough due diligence as to whether he was the right fit with my team. His ultimate termination was painful for both of us. The learning from that experience is that I should have first determined objectively whether by training and experience my friend was the right candidate before allowing myself to respond on an emotional level, or I should have let others in the company do more of the initial evaluation and screening about his fit with our team and the company before I became involved.

As a strategic plan defines success for market penetration or sales growth and a personnel review defines success in terms of the person's necessary achievements, the job description for new positions should describe not just the responsibilities but the results you require. Defining success will help crystallize the type of person you really need. Who has done this thing before and what does this "thing" mean? What kinds of skills do people in this role really need to be successful? A company that is struggling may not need someone with experience in the same industry. The company may need an expert in turnarounds. When IBM went outside the company—and outside the technical field—to hire Lou Gerstner in the 1990s, a lot of people wondered about the move. Yet Gerstner knew how to work the organization from the inside and how to instill confidence in customers on the outside. He led the technology company to a major rebound within just a few years of taking the helm. Before joining Musicland, Eric Weisman was CEO of Alliance Entertainment Corporation (AEC), a provider of business-to-business infrastructure services for home entertainment products. Paul Pressler, who led the resurgence of Gap Inc.'s brands (the Gap, Banana Republic, and Old Navy), had a 15-year career at Disney, where his major responsibility was running the company's theme parks (although he did have charge of Disney stores at the end).

Certain skills and qualities transcend particular industries, and it is often these traits that establish the right fit. Judging talent requires you develop with an eye toward promise and potential as much as to past performance. Personally, I have not always been the most qualified person for a job—at least on paper—so perhaps that is why I look for other attributes when I am in a position to hire. But I have always had related work experiences that other applicants have not had, and I try to bring a lot of energy and leadership to the game. For these reasons, I tend to look for focused energy and for what I call "utility players"—a sports term meaning athletes who can play a number of positions. Given the choice between a person with a good but single set of skills and a person with a variety of skills and the right kind of attitude, I will almost always go for the person with the widest range of talent. Such people have already demonstrated the greater potential for learning new skills. Looking to hire the person with the best skill set rather than the person who best matches the job description is another way of getting beyond the resume and evaluating the person's fundamental temperament and abilities.

Consider an example involving store operators, the heart and soul of a retail company. Suppose that you have found a person who by all appearances has the skills to manage your newest store. Through personal interviews and reference checks, you learn that the person has shown consistently good results, has been diligent in merchandising, and has shown a solid tactical understanding of financial matters. At the same time, you come to realize that the person has not shown any kind of creative flair for merchandising, does not have a great grasp of the strategic implications of finance, and has a reputation for being so hands-on that subordinates demonstrate little growth of their own. Another applicant for the job is an assistant manager who has worked in several related fields, shows a gift for marketing, and has great personal financial and personal skills, a definite "up-and-comer."

If the opening is for a store that has suffered from inconsistent leadership, then the first candidate, someone who is great at blocking and tackling and will likely be around for a long time, may be the correct hire. This choice of hiring the best "position player" becomes clearer if there will be few opportunities for other management positions and candidate Number Two might ultimately feel stifled in that position. If, on the other hand, you see this hire as being a linchpin in your future growth, as someone who will rapidly rise from managing a store to managing other store operators, or who will be able to jump into any number of other roles—then candidate Number Two is the better hire, unquestionably.

Part of the evaluation process, then, is to match a person's talents and achievements with his or her ability to work effectively in a new context. This is more than switching from chocolate to strawberry. This is about tapping into what your new hires will be able to do next in their careers.

Telling the Company's Story

Of course, evaluating people is a very tricky thing. Some executives acquire a talent for it and some do not. Finding the right candidate has less to do with identifying ideal criteria than with the hiring executive developing a high degree of self-awareness, an ability to take careful stock and inventory of what you as an executive and the organization as a whole have to offer. The best way to recruit high-caliber people is to have a compelling story to tell about your company. Try to understand why the perfect person wants to do this particular job for you. Granted, telling the story is not easy. Hiring top executives by yourself is like doing psychology on yourself. Most people do not have the right discipline or honest self-image to realistically articulate what they have to offer. They cannot provide an honest and compelling argument for why a high-caliber player would want to work for them. If you are finding it difficult to locate the right person or have had a string of poor hires, consider hiring a third party, an executive recruiter, to assist. A good headhunter will help you identify your assets, help you find real as opposed to ideal candidates, and ensure that you articulate your story credibly.

With recruitment, take as much time as humanly possible. Do more than check references. Your potential hire has worked for somebody. Somebody has worked for him or her. Find someone who actually knows the person. (What clinched the decision for the great hire in the Southeast were the glowing recommendations from colleagues who knew him.) No matter how desperate, do not hire just to fill a slot. No manager has ever ended up happy after "settling" for someone to hire. A poor employee will cost you far more energy and pain than you will ever spend covering an open position.

Once hired, new employees need to be inculcated into the core values and beliefs of the company. This is an important principle I learned from Howard at Starbucks. He called it "imprinting people with our DNA." Every hire, at every level, went through extensive training about the company's mindset as well as about its processes. Every hire, at every level, served as a barista working in a store to experience the nature of the company's customer service. Toyota has a similar indoctrination process engineers and managers are expected to get their hands dirty learning about cars—and also talks about imprinting people with corporate DNA. I am shocked at how little attention some retailers pay to the importance of instilling their culture into new employees. More than once I have talked with a company that is about to open a new store and have inquired about training for the new manager. "Oh, we hired a great person from the Gap," the owner will say. "She has a lot of experience. We believe in her. She'll start at the new store."

"You're going to bring in someone to manage your new store who has never been in either of your first two stores? Someone who has not been with the company long enough to know its history?"

"I'll spend half my time over there the first couple of weeks," the owner will invariably respond. "It will be fine."

If the manager is good, it may be fine from an efficiency standpoint, at least in the short term. But what about values, beliefs, mission, attitude toward customers, attitude toward employees? How will the manager, out there by herself, ever feel a personal connection to or loyalty with the rest of the company? If she has no feel for the people in senior management and how they make decisions, how will she have any sense of what decisions to make on her own and what decisions to refer to headquarters?

Investing Wisely in Investors

Although some people mortgage their houses or drain their life savings to start a business, this is rarely the best approach. You will invest a lot of your money regardless and contribute a great deal more in "sweat equity," but putting all of the risk on yourself and your family is too stressful a way to begin. A good concept should find support from some kind of investor, even if it takes time to identify the right one. Therefore the right investor group is very nearly as important as the right management team.

Individual investors may include friends and family. The primary investor in Blue C Sushi is a longtime friend and former colleague of James and Steve. Friends and family are often the most patient investors but can also be the least likely to understand the word "risk" if the investment fails completely. "Angel investors" are individuals who invest either individually or collectively in a company in its very earliest stages. Another source of funds is known affectionately among fund raisers as "DDM," or "dumb doctor money." It comes from private wealthy individuals—doctors, lawyers, software moguls, and other professionals—who invest to diversify their portfolios. DDM investors are likely to be interested in your idea but bring no real expertise, whereas angel investors will usually offer business expertise and expect to have a seat on the board. Individual investors were the source for investment money when Howard Schultz was first trying to create a retail coffee business. He found them by going to his friends and to every financially successful person he could find in greater Seattle. Of the 242 people he asked to invest, 217 said no. But the 25 who said yes were enough to launch him on his way. (I was one of the 25, a very modest investor.)

Best known among institutional investors are venture capitalists (VCs), who usually come in once a company has proven its concept and needs money to rapidly expand. VCs normally want one or more board seats and expect to see a return on their investment in three to five years. As opposed to DDMs, VCs take an active role in guiding and growing the company. VCs see their return when the company goes public or when the company sells for a profit to another company or investment group. VCs can be aggressive to the point of ruthlessness, or they can be the best partners a company could ever want. Other institutional investors prefer to be silent partners, relying on the expertise of the founders for the business to succeed. Other institutional investors are more comfortable with mid-term investments, when the company is well on the way and relatively low risk; for example, when you fund your second round of expansion rather than your first. Institutional investors include a number of merger and acquisition (M&A) funds active in the United States at any moment. Some specialize in certain categories such as food service; others are involved in a variety of retail businesses. Investment bankers are another source of capital; they may not invest directly but their business is putting together deals among interested parties. The original Potbelly Sandwich stores were so successful that Bryant Keil had institutional investors knocking on his door. One of the companies was Maveron, a venture capital firm whose principals are Dan Levitan, a former investment banker, and Howard Schultz. This was 20 years after Howard's first foray into the investment world, and now he was dispensing funds rather than soliciting them. Bryant funded his first outside round primarily through Maveron and a second round through Maveron, Oak Investments, and Benchmark Capital, all nationally recognized venture firms.

At the local or national level, you will find that the investment community is relatively close knit. Many of the players have done deals together in the past, and they talk all the time. Sometimes the conversation is on the order of, "I found this. Are you interested and do you want to take a portion of the round?" Other times, the conversation is more along the lines of, "If you're interested, I might jump in, too." An "angel network" is expressly designed to engage a variety of individual investors. Potential investors are easy to find. Ask your banker or investment advisor or friends in the financial community. Read the local and national business journals. Find out who is investing in what kinds of enterprises. An Internet search on the names of any of the VC firms listed here will lead you to dozens of Web sites related to venture capital and investments, including Hoover's Online and InsiderVC.com, both of which offer information about venture companies. (Hoover and InsiderVC offer some analysis free and some for a fee.) Eventually, you will find a connection that will enable you to work through the proper investor network, local or national, individual or institutional.

Entering into a relationship with an investor has the same potential for happiness or disappointment that any other marriage has. However much you need an infusion of cash, do not fall for the first sweet-talking suitor. Investors have their own goals and objectives—not to mention personal agendas—that may or may not align with yours. Howard's sweep of the Seattle financial community almost cost him Starbucks before he had even bought it when one of his own investors tried to maneuver the deal out from under him. (The ploy failed.) Stealing a deal from someone else at the eleventh hour is called "gazumping" in England. I like the word because "gazumped" expresses the feeling of having the wind knocked out of you. Getting "gazumped" happens more often in business than you might imagine. Recently I sought to invest in a company, which brought in a consultant to review my offer in light of the company's somewhat tangled financial situation. The consultant ended up lending the company money, a bit at a time, until he had effectively cornered the remaining security available to a new investor.

While a potential investor is doing due diligence on your company, you should be doing due diligence on the investor. Generally, a retail start-up needs a long-term investor. Do not sign up with a VC who specializes in "quick flips" and then be outraged when he wants to take his money and run in 2 to 3 years.

Just as you would with potential employees, determine whether your values and mission resonate with investors, or whether their eyes glaze over when you talk about anything except the bottom line. Evaluate what they bring beyond their money. They should have contacts in the vendor community or be able to bring in other investors or recommend potential senior management members. Do not overlook the human element. Can you enjoy time spent with the investors over coffee or a beer? Do they laugh at your jokes? If you were in town and did not have business with them, would you call them just to say hello? Business is hard enough without a clash of personal styles. Find people you like to work with. Most important, try to assess whether the investor is the kind of person that you can make money with—the kind of person who will be happy for you and your success. There are many people with lots of money who, deep down, do not want to see other people be successful. Unless you can find the right person, you are better off scratching along by yourself.

Due diligence into potential investors includes an evaluation of their previous deals. Deals that failed are more important to understand than deals that succeeded. Did a deal fail because of bad luck, unfortunate timing, or a disparity of goals? Did recipients of previous investments find the experience to be a good one? It is fun to be an investor when times are good. You put money in, more money comes back. The test is when times are bad. In doing his research, Bryant's good feeling about one institutional investor was confirmed when he learned that during a particularly bad time for another company, one of the investors had dug into his own personal pockets to save the business, which ultimately became very successful. That action speaks to a human commitment as well as to an alignment of business objectives.

Avoiding Mismatches in Mindset, Goals

A mismatch between the mindsets of the founders and the investors, on the other hand, can lead to catastrophe. I once sat on the board of a fast-casual restaurant. Two VCs were eager to get on the bandwagon for one of the hottest new food concepts of the year. Needing more funds for expansion, the founders went several times to the VCs, who eventually took control of the board. One by one the founders were asked to leave. To placate the VCs on various issues, the management team had to divert more and more time and energy away from the business. Based on a pledge by one VC to invest more money in the next round of financing, management made commitments on leases and construction to continue expanding. When it came time for the VC to deposit his funds, he backed out. The dot-com industry was in a steep dive, and losses in that industry forced him to reassess all his investments. In short, he lost confidence. His need to reduce his own risk led to the company being dumped at fire-sale prices—despite having a good chance to achieve profitability in the near term.

This example demonstrates that the structure of any deal should leave the retailer in control of the company. Unless it is a last resort, be in position to control your own destiny. Moreover, be sure to raise enough money in the first round of financing to sustain the company for a reasonable time. Think in terms of enough money to operate one store for several years or to open several stores within a reasonable period of time. The last thing anyone needs when starting up a company is to worry whether the money will last long enough to get off the ground! Investors should support this goal. Do not let anyone talk you into starting out with less money than you need. (Most beginning retailers underestimate their cash needs, sometimes by as much as half.) The only reason for investors to offer less than the minimum is to ensure that you will come back later when your needs are more critical and your leverage is diminished and they can foist terms upon you that are more advantageous to them. To state the obvious, this is a poor way to start a new relationship.

Many times potential investors will have experience investing in a variety of retail businesses. Their background here is one of the values they bring. However, beware of someone with an investment in a direct competitor. As above, the investor may make choices in favor of their other investment. Although most investors are professional enough to "compartmentalize" competitive information, in the worst case they might glean the sweet spot from your new concept and attempt to knock it off.

Finally, the investment documents should adequately describe the next steps financially if the business does not meet its financial goals. The contract should describe under what circumstances and under what terms one party can buy out the other. The document should describe the disposition of assets in case of dissolution. There are myriad control mechanisms that you could put in an agreement. Seek legal advice.

Investors come in many shapes and sizes. You need to find one that is a perfect fit for you. The best way is to ensure that their motivations are totally aligned with yours; that is, that both of you are building for the long term or both of you agree on a goal of selling in an agreed upon number of years. Make sure the human connection is there. In Asian cultures, it takes a long time to reach agreement on a contract. The reason is that both parties want to get to know one another. In America, we tend to rush into contractual relationships, assuming that the written word will protect us and we will develop the relationship as we go. Take the time to develop a personal bond with your partners. A contract should ratify the relationship. It should not *be* the relationship.

Last but by no means least, if you ever get a funny feeling about a potential investor, run for the hills. If your gut instinct tells you that something does not feel right, *listen to it!*

Making the right decision about the senior management team and investors is an example of what software designers call "early binding decisions"—decisions that determine many of the characteristics of the system, such as its fundamental organization and logic flow. The quality of the initial management team directly relates to a company's ability to race ahead in the market. Sometimes retail start-ups err by spending the wrong kind of money ahead of the curve—ahead of the actual need. Retailers do this when they obtain more office space than needed or fill too many staff positions before the revenue can justify the positions. To go long, however, you must always hire ahead of the curve when it comes to the people who will make the decisions that will drive growth. They will have the background to make the right decisions about when and where to invest money and when and where not to. Unless they are "silent" by contractual agreement, investors should also bring business experience and business contacts that flesh out your organization. Good early hires and good investment partners can help a fledgling retailer eliminate costly mistakes of all kinds. Eradicating even a single error of omission or commission in the first phase of a company's life can save many months of time and millions of dollars later on. More than eliminating mistakes, having the right management team and critical partners in place from the start propels the company positively into the market and provides the best way in which to establish the retail brand. Having a comprehensive set of the proper skills provides the company with the best opportunity to succeed in its retail category. In addition, creating a leadership team that shares the same personal and corporate values and is strongly committed to the corporate mission ensures that the right corporate DNA will take hold in the organization as it grows and evolves. The combination of skills and values will lead to a culture that perpetuates and extends the company values as the business grows. Establishing the human framework, as described in this chapter, will enable your company to score big by giving it the personnel and mindset to "go long."

INVESTING IN OTHER WAYS

A lot of start-ups overlook another way to obtain investment or its equivalent. One possibility is best described as an "in kind" or "sweat equity" investor. Consultants, designers, landlords, and others may agree to take an equity stake in lieu of some or all cash payment. In addition, service providers such as attorneys, accountants, printers, and other vendors may accept long-term payment plans for immediate work or immediate inventory. In these situations, do not lock yourself into their services just because they are willing to finance you. That is, do not end up with a broker only because the broker is willing to take his fee as equity; make sure the broker is the best person to find the real estate you need. Do not end up with a landlord willing to take equity in lieu of rent unless the property is the property you actually want. And so forth.

Another investment device involves a vendor supplying inventory on a "consignment" basis, billing only for what is actually sold each month. The "consignment" inventory is not practical for perishable goods, but it has been used in fields ranging from clothing to shrink-wrap software. Vendors keep clear title to the inventory in case the business fails, and the monthly audit of sales gives the vendor a window into whether the business is succeeding.

These various steps reduce the business's initial cash flow and financing requirements. In essence, the retailer's business associates take on some of the risk in the expectation of creating future business for themselves. (One issue, if you plan to seek bank financing, is security precedence for all parties, a detail that can usually be worked out.) Arrangements involving special payment normally end after the first year, when the new retailer has established a sustainable cash flow. Like any other investments, an equity position for suppliers should spell out the terms under which the parties will ultimately be paid.

Needless to say, suppliers are under no obligation to accept anything but standard payment for their services. Much will depend on the overall scope of your plans, the potential for growth, your personal and business relationship with the other parties, and the level of risk that they already have in their business. An outside firm may not be able to defer payment, or may have other "in lieu" equity positions and cannot do more right away. Many landlords in Silicon Valley were badly burned by accepting stock in dot-com companies rather than rent and are unlikely to do similar deals anytime soon. Special arrangements are worth pursuing, however. They can dramatically ease the financial strain of the first year, and they may also involve you with people who prove to be good partners in the long term.

CHAPTER 10

Kicking the Economic Model Into Gear

A CONCEPT'S ECONOMIC MODEL is the engine under the hood. You do not see it, but it makes the enterprise go. Without a good economic model, your concept will just spin its wheels. The degree to which entrepreneurs understand the economic model and the related financials varies with their sophistication. Some people understand a few components of a profit-and-loss (P&L) statement but do not understand the ultimate profitability. Some people understand what the numbers mean financially but do not understand how the numbers directly relate to the physical operation of a store. A few people, usually CEOs and senior executives of successful chains, understand the intimate bond between the operations and financials and how to connect the one to the other. Their understanding of the unit economic model is a major reason for their success.

Other people may think they "know" the model because they have been in general business or some part of retail for a long time. However, a new concept can have a different expense or income structure than what people are used to. Other people who should understand the financials in broad terms—the real estate people, design staff, contractors, and new store managers—seldom have a good grasp of the P&L. Suffice it to say that there are very few true connoisseurs of the economics of a concept. This chapter highlights the most important aspects of the financial statements with a focus on two points: 1.) how to develop a meaningful financial model and how that model can help you evaluate the performance of the underlying model; and 2.) how a successful economic model can fuel growth. Minimize your downside, and maximize your upside. That is the goal of the financial analysis of every decision you make in creating and executing on a concept. Whether ensuring that a new concept is on a solid economic footing or recalibrating the economics of an existing concept, the financial analysis enables you to establish the economic viability of the business and set the stage for expansion. Proving the economic model is a large part of proving the concept.

The economic model has to be robust enough to generate excess cash that can power expansion. Every store must be treated as an investment geared to generate cash. This requirement means that the primary numbers that a retailer needs to focus on are gross margin and net income. There is no other way to proceed but by jumping into finance terminology. Gross margin is revenue minus the cost of goods sold (COGS). More simply, gross margin is what you have in your pocket after you have paid for your goods but before you have paid for your operating expenses, which are often collectively called the cost of selling. Assuming a similar product mix across the chain, the gross margin for each store is roughly equivalent to the chain's gross margin as a whole, and so one number can stand for both. Net income (described in detail in this chapter) is gross margin minus operating expenses and depreciation. It is what is left in your pocket after you have accounted for the rest of your costs. A chain rolls up net income from each store and deducts corporate general and administrative costs (G&A) to return the chain's overall net income. An individual store's net income, then, will be 6 to 10 percent higher than the company's overall net income because of corporate G&A expenses that come after the money goes to headquarters. This chapter focuses on the net income for each store. For small retailers, corporate G&A is minor, and for chains big and small, store net income is the primary engine of growth.

A healthy gross margin is needed to provide oxygen to survive and grow, because things go wrong all the time in operations. Construction delays cause you to open late and miss your high season. You have a problem with store personnel and sales sag. The sidewalk gets torn up and sales drop for a week. Your computer or phone system goes on the blink. A snow or ice storm closes you during a peak holiday weekend. A hurricane strikes. In retail, Murphy's law prevails, and many of the things that go wrong are out of your control. A retailer needs every possible hedge against the downside, against unexpected increases in rent or labor and other unforeseen expenses. High gross margins (or, correspondingly, high volumes) give you more ability to adapt to the unforeseen and to deal with problems and mistakes and still have a decent net income. Thus, while your concept may not have inherently high gross margins, you need to know what others in the category average and ensure that your concept does not fall into the bottom of the range. Buying in small volumes through jobbers and distributors, new retailers seldom get the best deals. New retailers do not always recognize how thin their margins can be, and how little cash they will have to pay for the unexpected.

If your gross margin is below the industry norm, you should examine the COGS and reevaluate the economic model. One step, discussed in detail in Chapter 6, "Merchandising: Maximizing Your Profits," is to change the product mix to achieve higher margins. Another is to exploit competition between suppliers. Perhaps you plan to sell a certain brand of shoe but another supplier has a comparable offering at lower cost to you. Restaurants can reduce costs by buying raw ingredients and preparing dishes instead of buying, say, prepared soups and bread. Because chefs or food preparers will be working on other dishes anyway, a few additional "homemade" items will not necessarily add to labor costs. Being careful about COGS does not mean to go with cut-rate products unless that in fact is your niche. Being careful simply means that retailers should wring every possible penny out of COGS.

A labor-intensive concept, such as food service, needs a higher gross margin to cover the still-to-be-paid labor costs, whereas a less-labor-intensive concept, such as an automated car wash, can get by with a lower gross margin and still return a good net income. Happy is the retailer who can set arbitrarily high gross margins, but the "invisible hand" of the market creates limits. A gross margin that results in an item being overpriced will result in few if any sales; overall, a loss is likely. Competition also drives down prices (read "gross margins") to the "correct" level for each concept. If the automated car wash overcharges for a wash and wax to obtain a high gross margin, then one day a competitor will open a similar car wash that charges considerably less for the same service. To stay in business, the first operator has to cut prices to match the competitor. The only way either operator can then maintain a price differential is to offer special services, such as hand waxing.

Over time, consumer habits and competition create a natural level for pricing and margins that only differentiation can lift. In fact, one can draw a general rule that gross margins track differentiation. The more specialized the product, the higher the gross margins. The more a product approaches commoditization, the lower the gross margin, and the more that volume is required to compensate. Thus a new retailer has to carefully ask: Is my offering unique, or am I selling essentially the same thing as my high-volume competitor down the street? If the latter, how will I compete?

Broadly speaking, retailing falls into four financial groupings:

1. Food concepts, where gross margins often run 65 to 70 percent and sometimes as high as 73 percent, and where labor costs are high

2. Specialty retailing and targeted lifestyle retailing, where gross margins can be as high as 70 percent and almost all concepts are above 50 percent and labor costs are low

3. Traditional retailing, where gross margins have declined and now hover around 30 percent and where sales volumes and labor costs are moderate

4. Groceries and other high-volume businesses, where gross margins tend to be in the mid to high 20 percent range and where high labor costs result in low net margins (but high cash production)

Specialty and traditional retailing are more of a spectrum than separate groupings, with gross margins starting high for hand-made, one-of-a-kind items and declining as the products become mainstream. The following table, Table 10-1, of fiscal year-end results as of early 2004, shows the gross margins, corporate net income, and estimated store net income for a representative sampling of retail companies in different categories and at different degrees of differentiation. Most companies target corporate G&A at between 6 and 10 percent. However, the actual net income of individual stores is difficult to estimate across concepts because some companies and some industries are more efficient than others. In addition, some franchises hide corporate costs through additional mark-ups in the price of product and equipment to franchisees. Thus, corporate overhead can be as high as 12 percent. In Table 10-1 the corporate net income comes from company annual reports; the store net income is estimated from that number. For purposes of illustration only, corporate overhead is assumed to be 10 percent.

Company	Category	Gross Margins (Percent)	Corporate Net Income (Percent)	Estimated Store Net Income (Percent)
Luxottica	Eyewear, accessories	72	12	22
Starbucks	Food service	65	13	23
McDonald's	Food service	75	9	19
Chico's	Women's apparel	61	13	23
Oakley	Performance wear	56	7	17
Dillard's	Department store	32	0.1	10.1
Whole Foods Market	Grocery	34.5	3.5	13.5
Kroger	Grocery	28	0.6	10.6
Safeway	Grocery	30	−0.5	9.5
Best Buy	Consumer electronics	26	3	13

TABLE 10-1

Gross margins, Net Income, and Estimated Store Income for a Variety of Concepts

Gross margins and net income generally track the differentiation of the brand. Specialty or lifestyle brands have the highest margins, whereas less-differentiated brands have lower margins. For example (see Table 10-1), the gross margins of Whole Foods Market, which is highly differentiated, is higher than that for undifferentiated super-markets Kroger and Safeway. The difference ultimately translates in net income that is three percent higher for Whole Foods—a huge disparity in a high-volume category. A corollary is that as any concept approaches a commodity, it becomes difficult for the retailer to maintain gross margins or net income, and the strategy must shift either to differentiation or to generating high volumes. Food service requires high gross margins to cover labor costs, so differentiation shows up in the net margins, where a high-quality brand will be in double digits and a quick-serve brand will be in single digits. The most important lesson for new retailers: You need double-digit net income from each store to produce an overall profit for a chain of any size.

Winning with Net Income

Net store income, which equates to the profit contribution by each store unit, is the "end of story" for every concept. Some people say store net income of 10 to 12 percent for each store is pretty good. In my view, the "go" or "no go" number should be a net income of at least 12 to 15 percent for each store. I will not even look at a "four-wall contribution" (as store net income is also called) of less than 15 percent. For a growth concept, the number needs to be higher, 20 to 25 percent. Why take all the risk of opening a retail business and expend all the energy for years to make it succeed if you cannot get a 15 percent return for each store? Because you still have corporate over-head to deduct, leaving a final return of 10 percent or less, you are better off investing your money in something else—say for an 8 percent return and low risk. A low net income also makes it hard to support growth and cover the overhead of expansion.

From an entrepreneurial standpoint, store net income represents the fuel for growth. After you have a successful economic model, each store becomes a cash-generating machine. With net income of 15 percent, a store generating $1 million in revenue yields $150,000 in cash.

Seven new stores generate another $1 million in net income. Become successful enough to open 100 stores a year, and net income increases by $15 million. At this point, you can hear the cash registers chiming all over the country. "Ka-ching, ka-ching—sending the money home." In terms of cash to fund expansion, the net income generated by a concept is at least as important as the return on investment (ROI). A store returning 12 percent on $1 million in sales generates $120,000 in cash, whereas a store returning 15 percent on $600,000 in sales generates $90,000 in cash. The $30,000 may be the difference between being able to expand this year or next. For this reason, employees should receive incentives for the cash generated as well as for ROI. (Of course, you would also try to figure out why the smaller store is doing better on a percentage basis and try to replicate its success in the bigger store.) A few high-volume businesses such as grocery stores, drugstores, and gasoline service stations have net income in the range of 3 to 5 percent or lower, because fierce competition has suppressed pricing. However, high volume enables them to generate the necessary cash from the business. Kroger, the supermarket chain, returned only 0.6 percent corporate-wide net income for its most recent fiscal year, but that generated $314.6 million in cash, enough to build 30 more stores, assuming all the cash was used for this purpose. On a much lower base than Kroger, Whole Foods Market generated $137 million cash.

A healthy net income requires a solid financial model. The first step is the creation of the pro forma financial statement. This is not, as its name implies, "a formality," but rather the best financial model you can create of the new business. The model, a typical U.S. financial framework, will work for any locale once variations in taxes and accounting methods are taken into consideration. Its main purpose is to enable an analysis of the business in detail, and in advance. The following overview assumes a working knowledge of accounting, which new retailers should have before proceeding too far with their concept. Business classes at local colleges can provide such expertise, and a search on "financial statements" at online bookstores will turn up a number of books on the topic. In particular, three good books in descending order of sophistication are *Financial and Business Statements (2d Edition)* by George Thomas Friedlob and Franklin James Plewa, which emphasizes daily operations, analysis of business details, and problem solving for people starting or managing a small- to medium-sized business; *Balance Sheet Basics: Financial Management for Non-Financial Managers* by Ronald C. Spurga; and *Keeping the Books: Basic Record Keeping and Accounting for the Successful Small Business* by Linda Pinson.

A look at the pro forma for a new retail store begins with a few assumptions. First, we will use $1 million as the estimate for annual sales. Many different kinds of retail outlets can generate this level of revenues, and $1 million makes a nice round number. In this example, COGS are 50 percent, which means that the gross margin is also 50 percent. From gross margin you subtract major operating expenses such as 10 percent for labor, 10 percent for advertising/marketing, and 8 to 12 percent for occupancy costs—all reasonable numbers for non-food retailing. Subtracting controllable costs and general and administrative costs for the store leaves earnings before interest, taxes, depreciation, and amortization (EBIDTA, a standard metric in the United States). In this example, EBIDTA comes in close to 20 percent. From EBIDTA you subtract depreciation, which depends on the number of stores being built and their cost. In this example, depreciation is 5 percent, so net income turns out to be 15 percent—a very attractive store return.

The pro forma should include other numbers such as the revenue you need to break even. (Breakeven is the cost of COGS plus the cost of sales and G&A.) Most retail concepts also want to know the gross margin per square foot to determine the effective use of space. Food concepts, in which a large portion of space is set aside for consumption rather than sales, often track hourly transactions, the number of transactions per day, and the revenue per transaction. Starbucks tracks sales revenue versus rental cost to determine whether the real estate is returning a good value. Be sure to find out any other important metrics in your category.

Now you do a reality check against these numbers to determine their validity.

For a new concept, it can be difficult to come up with exact numbers. Even established businesses sometimes don't know what they don't know about their operations and costs. You can get detailed financial analyses of a company or industry from a stockbroker. You can purchase detailed industry trend analyses from market analysts who specialize in different fields. Dun & Bradstreet, Hoover's Online, and other services provide research on tens of thousands of businesses. Marketresearch.com provides in-depth research on industries and various retail categories. Bizminer.com provides research structured according to your use (marketing plan, business plan, business valuation, and so on) and has a special section for startups. Some reports are free. Most require a fee, and some of the fees can be hefty. Bizstats.com has a variety of detailed financial data on various retail categories. The Small Business Administration has a Web site with much useful information for start-ups and small firms. Scouring the Internet for articles on your industry will turn up interesting tidbits. Call a consultant who is an expert in your field. Some will provide a solid but fairly general analysis; the really good ones will provide a high level of detail. Organizations exist that provide coaching for start-up companies; identify someone with a strong background in retail finance. If you cannot afford a consultant, check with the local chamber of commerce. Many communities have retired business executives who provide business guidance to start-ups for little or no cost. SCORE, a nonprofit association, has both retired and working executives who provide entrepreneurs with free, confidential business counseling either face to face or via e-mail. You may also want to build an advisory board consisting of experienced retailers.

Online

For further reference, the book's Web site, www.builtforgrowth.com, contains a number of documents pertaining to this chapter: sample pro forma statements, links to related Web sites, and other supplementary information.

Perhaps the best place to begin is with annual reports of public companies in the same category. Pay special attention to "management's discussion and analysis" of company performance. Sometimes the analysis is perfunctory, there to meet minimum reporting standards, whereas at other times the analysis serves as an insightful "state of the industry" for that category. A review of Kroger's and Safeway's annual reports would tell you, among other things, that price pressures from super-centers and other discounters have substantially hurt gross margins of both chains. A would-be grocer would need either to factor in declining margins or to find a specialty niche insulated from the industry-wide price storms.

From these various sources, you begin to develop realistic numbers for your particular concept. You should be able to find the average sales volume per store. You can probably gauge the sales per square foot for your type of business, but you have to be careful. Staples has three formats and store sizes, and sales are not broken down by each one, for example. Kroger lists $53.8 billion in sales in 2,532 grocery stores and department stores, or $21.2 million per store. Revenue also includes convenience stores and fuel operations, so the big stores probably do $20 million annually. Store square footage is listed at 560 million square feet, which works out to a suspiciously low $98 per square foot, but Kroger's 42 manufacturing plants, plus distribution and office space, figure into the square footage, so you would investigate further to get average sales per square foot. One way would be to simply walk off the length and width of a typical store, compute the square footage, and divide that into $20 million. Whole Foods Market, on the other hand, lists its sales per square foot, $786, at the start of a recent annual report. Walgreens also proudly states that its drugstores average $7.4 million in annual sales and $677 in sales per square foot, so a drug-store concept has a ready comparison against the industry leader.

Further, major retailers, which are always looking for new locations, typically broadcast the size of stores they seek. You can check in retail trade magazines or talk to your real estate broker and quickly find what kinds of concepts are seeking what kinds of space. Claritas provides the number of employees and sales estimates of many companies so you can estimate the average revenue per employee. It is critical that you build the numbers from the ground up and benchmark yourself against competitors.

Sometimes the annual reports themselves have virtually all the information you need. Let's assume that you want to start a clothing concept that appeals to urban women older than 30, with moderate to high income. In its annual report, Chico's FAS, Inc., a chain selling to a comparable demographic, provided a chart showing that its net sales per net selling square foot were about $900. Separate figures showed that 426 company stores generated $738 million in revenue, or roughly $1.73 million per store. Divide $1.73 million in sales by $900 per square foot and you end up with stores that average a little more than 1,900 square feet of selling space, or probably a little over 2,000 square feet total space. Other charts and figures corroborate the estimates of per-store revenues and square footage in the low-2,000 range. The annual report of another women's apparel chain, Coldwater Creek, describes the two formats of its planned stores, 3,000 to 4,000 square feet and 5,000 to 6,000 square feet, as well as the expected sales per square foot, of $600 and $500 respectively. Multiplying revenue per square foot times store size, you end up with revenues of between $1.8 million and $2.4 million for the smaller format and $2.5 million to $3.0 million for the larger format. Taking the information from the companies together, you can make two important surmises. First, 2,000 square feet is probably a good workable size for high-quality women's apparel. Second, an established shop could generate as much as $1.7 million in sales in that format. Recognize, however, that it could take several years to reach that sales volume. Many chains use three years as a default assumption for a store meeting its full retail potential. Food concepts expect to reach full sales after 12 months.

Finding good numbers for high-end fashion concepts is more difficult because many of the leading companies are not public. You may have to pay for research on out-of-area markets, but you can use unobtrusive measures to establish how retail establishments in your area are doing during the different day parts and use this information to calculate total daily sales. For a restaurant, you can track approximate sales volume by pricing a typical meal and multiplying that number by the number of customers. In large retail stores, you can hang out by the cash registers to see what people normally buy and how much they spend in typical transactions. You can see what add-on purchases customers regularly select. In stores where loitering is not possible, you can guesstimate sales volume from the street by tallying the total traffic, the number and size of shopping bags people carry out of the stores, and the price of common merchandise. (It's not hard to tell that one shopping bag contains a pair of shoes and another has a couple of shirts or blouses.) Some retailers still track the daily number of transactions on their sales receipts. If you buy a couple of items from them a few hours apart, you probably will be able to calculate their numbers. Seek to estimate volume by the hour for all the major day parts along with the value of the average sales transaction. With public companies, you can use annual sales to estimate daily sales. More than 95 percent of all the data you need to construct a believable pro forma is available somewhere.

If a 15 percent return is the norm in your category and your projections show only a 12 percent return, it is imperative that you determine what costs must come down or what products (or product mixes) with higher margins are needed to increase revenue. You have to keep digging and refining your model until the numbers work. This approach will keep you disciplined—disciplined in getting to the right economic model and disciplined in your approach to site selection, another critical issue for revenue generation, as we will see.

Let's assume, then, that you have done your homework. You find that one similar concept averages more than $1 million per store. You find other data that shows that the category average is $500 revenue per square foot and that typical store size is 2,000 square feet. These figures reinforce your estimate of $1 million in sales. Glean every bit of relevant data and factor it in. Determine whether the norm is based on a five-, six-, or seven-day work week. Do you plan to be open the same number of hours per day as the companies on which you are basing the estimates? Some downtown locations have too little business to stay open on weekends, whereas others thrive. Which applies to your area? On $1 million in revenue, the difference between a seven-day week and a six-day week is roughly $140,000 in revenue annually—your hoped-for net profit! You would have to sell another $450 in merchandise a day to make up the difference.

As we saw with women's apparel, it is important to correlate your store size with the typical size for the industry. If the industry average income is $500 per square foot and the typical store size is 2,000 square feet, and you plan a 1,600-square-foot store, then your store must do $625 per square foot in sales to reach equivalent revenue. Depending on the number of days the store is open, this is a difference of $500 to $600 a day. If you are selling designer dresses, the differential may not be meaningful, perhaps one sale per day. But if you are selling $5 sandwiches, you would need 120 more sales per day. Is that volume reasonable? Could you physically serve the extra customers you would require (and remember they probably would come during rush periods)? Would there be sufficient parking? If you cannot increase the number of transactions, see whether you can change the product mix to increase the average price of each transaction. By increasing the average transaction by $1.25, from $5 to $6.25, the sandwich shop would make up the difference in daily sales for the smaller format.

Putting Expenses to the Test

After you have satisfactory figures for income, it should be relatively easy to match those numbers against associated expenses, which should be proportional to sales. Compare every line of your pro forma against whatever data you can unearth. Chico's gross margin in 2003 was 61 percent, and Coldwater Creek's was 39 percent. You would want to dig further to understand the discrepancy in cost of goods, which is also reflected in corporate net income of 13 and 2.4 percent, respectively. You would examine the results of other retailers in the category to ascertain conservative numbers that would most likely apply to you. (For simplicity, these examples show one or two comparisons, but you should do half a dozen or more. If you are in clothing, for example, you should be able to say about financials, "The Gap does this, Banana Republic does that.") Selling and G&A expenses for Chico's and Coldwater Creek are similar, 37.6 percent and 35.1 percent respectively, so you could probably use 37 percent as a reasonable estimate for yourself.

Carefully review each of the line items involved in the cost of sales. Be sure to understand whether labor costs are high in your category, as is true for grocery stores and restaurants and similar service related stores. In addition to price pressures, Kroger and Safeway faced increased health and pension costs that were also major factors in employee strikes in 2003 that further hurt the bottom line. Will you face similar expenses, or labor problems? Know whether your state has more restrictive laws on overtime, higher worker's compensation payments, or a higher minimum wage, all of which drive up labor costs. Most states require a minimum shift of four hours for each employee, which may increase the number of labor hours you need to plan for. Major shopping centers require stores to be open for fixed periods, something like 9:30 a.m. to 9:30 p.m. Monday through Saturday and 10:30 a.m. to 7 p.m. on Sunday, and levy fines for each hour you fail to be open. Your analysis must include the number of employees you will require for each day and each hour that you are open.

Occupancy costs can run 6 to 12 percent. Therefore, if you are certain that your other costs are in line, then you know that the 8 percent figure for occupancy costs in the above example is the maximum you can afford. If your occupancy costs are much lower, look carefully to see whether you have a location that will be good enough to support your sales projections. Maybe you are lucky and you have found a bargain, or maybe the rental price is telling you something about the ability of the space to deliver sales. Again, benchmark yourself against established retailers in the category. The others have been through the wars. They know what they can afford to pay to generate the foot traffic they need. If the occupancy costs are too high, either your income projections are too low or your proposed rent is too high. Use your calculations to negotiate with the landlord.

An exhaustive review of your projections against category averages and common sense should give you confidence that your projections are honest and defensible. The more each of your metrics lines up against established numbers from your category, the more likely it is that your overall projections are accurate. This same kind of analysis should be done regularly for existing stores to determine how to optimize operations. One of our clients had gross margins of 50 percent but the net income was quite low, and there were no obvious reasons. In our analysis, we discovered that the retailer had classed certain expenses as a manufacturer would rather than as a retailer. Once adjusted, the retailer's COGS were too high as a percentage of sales and gross margins were actually closer to 42 percent. Knowing this, we could analyze the COGS more closely. When further analysis showed that the COGS were in line, we could proceed to an analysis of other expenses. When these turned out to be within reason, then we could surmise that the real problem was that the stores needed to generate more revenue rather than just cut expenses. But until we could clear up the question of COGS, we could not successfully work through the rest of the problem.

Another aspect of analysis involves timing. Seasonality can make or break a store's ability to generate enough cash flow to survive in its early days. I have seen ski/snowboard shops open in July and close before the first snowfall. To last long enough for your financial projections to mean anything, you have to open your store as the category is coming out of the low season, taking out the worst two or three months of sales during your startup cycle. Whatever you do, open before the start of the high season to capture the best sales and establish the brand to help build momentum for the next year. Geography and weather determine much retail traffic. Resort areas have well-defined tourist seasons, sometimes two. In urban areas with cold winters, the summer is the high time for quick-serve and fast-casual restaurants and other retail concepts that benefit from "walking around" traffic. Mall concepts and white-tablecloth restaurants, on the other hand, show less seasonality. Both presume that people will be indoors. Spring and summer are the high season for automotive concepts. The more a concept depends on people being outside, the more the concept has to contend with seasonality. The high and low seasons are often obvious. The Christmas season is the high for soft goods and various gift products. Greeting cards sell well from Thanksgiving to Valentine's Day. Gardening equipment sells well in early spring. Chocolate eggs sell at Easter ... And so on ... At the national level you can check annual reports for comparable concepts to see which quarters have the lowest and highest sales. Using that data as a base, adjust for the seasonal patterns in your area that might apply.

Analysis of the pro formas of existing chains in my experience turns up three consistent problems:

1. Rent. Under the pressure to grow, it is hard to be a tough negotiator and keep occupancy costs down. Also, most concepts expand first to the bigger markets where competition and rents are highest. Plus, all chains, including the best, have a few nonperforming locations that fail to deliver revenue so the relative cost of rent to sales is high. In recent years the Gap closed 85 underperforming stores; Kroger had 74 underperforming stores and closed 44; and McDonald's closed about 650 stores.

2. Costs. It is tough for new concepts to duplicate their success when they get out of their home market. Most retailers need time under their belt to make their operational systems super-tight. As a result, labor as a percentage of sales increases. Also, money can always be saved in operational expenses, whether this is utility bills or excess use of copy machines.

3. Product mix. There is seldom a real model to attain a product mix that will generate the gross margins that are necessary for success. Most companies can quickly understand how to control costs but they do not always see the potential to generate more revenue by changing their mix of product lines. Retailers need to be aware of the uniqueness of each market and be very aware of the need to adjust product mix to meet local demands.

After you have put together an accurate pro forma, the numbers drive operational decisions. Depending on the detail, you can end up with 5 to 15 line items that serve as the metrics for each of your organizational teams. All the people in your company should understand your corporate goal for each line on the pro forma and their role in achieving those corporate financial objectives. If you are trying to achieve $667 per square feet in sales in a 1,500-square-foot store for $1,000,000 in revenue, and your pro forma shows that labor will cost 30 percent of revenue, then Bob, the head of operations, has to figure out how to hire and schedule staff over a year so that labor does not exceed $300,000. If occupancy costs are budgeted at 8 percent, then Anne, the head of real estate, needs to keep the total leasehold costs to $80,000 or less. If marketing is 5 percent, then John, the head of marketing, has to be effective with store advertising and promotions while spending no more than $50,000. It is usually easy to get senior people to sign up to accomplish their tasks; what is more important is to get them to achieve their results while staying within budget. Being over budget in each area by just a couple of percent can wipe out a store's profitability. Conversely, being under budget in several areas adds profit directly to the bottom line.

Everything matters when it comes to making the numbers.

CHAPTER 11

Wellsprings to Expansion

I HAVE A FRIEND named Danny Piecora. He and his family operate two Italian pizza restaurants in the Seattle, Washington, area. I said to him one time, "This is such a great concept. We could grow the heck out of this thing."

He said, "What do I need it for?"

Danny is making a good living. He has no desire to become a "major player." He does not want to deal with the headache and heartache of becoming involved in tremendous corporate growth. He enjoys his life, his family. He just bought the real estate under his store. He does not need or want a third or fourth store, never mind a thirtieth or fortieth store. Danny is a smart guy. He knows himself and what he wants. "To thine own self be true."

Another guy might realize that he could never manage a huge company-owned concept with tens of thousands of employees, but he could take a simple concept—perhaps a variation on the "take and bake" pizza idea—and package it into a $50 million franchise. Other people understand themselves well enough to know that they would be happiest running a single sandwich shop in Texas or at most a handful of sandwich franchises. "To thine own self be true." That's the first step.

Precisely because revenues tend to be lower for new retailers and gross margins tend to be, well, *marginal*, retailers should first look to expand in "safe" ways, without the cost and risk of additional retail outlets. Having a "hidden wellspring," a source of revenue separate from normal retail operations, is one secret. One of Starbucks' strategic advantages was having the Costco wholesale account for coffee beans. Top Pot Doughnuts, which has two stores in Seattle, uses its excess manufacturing capability to provide doughnuts to other restaurants and food service stores in the area. Other approaches are less obvious. Danny sells pizza at Bumbershoot, a major Seattle street fair, and at the Puyallup Fair, the largest county fair in the state of Washington. Such sales can create a substantial increment to retail in-store business. There are people who sell $10,000 in Kettle Korn in a single week at a county fair. Danny could also market his special pizza sauce at his store. Some restaurants have a small shelf of items for sale; others es-tablish a small retail store next door. Danny could sell his sauce or pre-made frozen pizzas through one of the high-quality grocery stores in the area, becoming the preferred local alternative to Tony's Pizza.

Also, think "education." Everyone from the local potter to a famous chef can parlay educational courses into extra business and brand loyalty. Such activities can range from demonstrations that draw customers into the store to full-blown classes that would bring in addi-tional income. One glassblower has coordinated with the state univer-sity so students receive college credit for his classes. Women's shops can offer fashion shows, makeover clinics, and fittings for intimate apparel. Outdoor stores can do lessons or safety workshops on different sports, from rock climbing to snowmobiling. Remember, Elephant Pharmacy built a large part of its concept around the education of consumers.

Parlaying the Internet into additional sales is another way to make incremental dollars. Very few "pure" retailers exist anymore. Catalog companies have moved to the Internet, and many are opening retail outlets, including the venerable Lands' End, now a part of Sears. Retail companies use the Web as just another sales and marketing channel. There are bicycle shops that began with brick and mortar and moved online, and there is at least one bike store that began online and later opened a retail store. The Internet does not favor large, established concepts over the entrepreneur. The medium belongs to the company that can show the most imagination. Integration of every marketing channel is the name of the game.

Sticky Fingers Ribhouse, a small chain of barbeque restaurants in the South, began augmenting its restaurants with a catering business and with a wholesale business involving its barbeque sauces. Now the sauces are available in more than two thousand groceries, and the company's Internet business offers priority delivery of everything from a rack of frozen barbeque ribs to pecan pie and T-shirts. While the wholesale and mail order business today represent only a small part of the chain's overall sales, the wholesale business is growing at 40 percent annually and mail order has doubled every year since it began in 2002. In addition to expanding the revenue base, the two side businesses are excellent vehicles for brand awareness and brand exposure in markets where Sticky Fingers does not have restaurants. As Starbucks learned, the mail order business helps pinpoint possible areas for new physical stores.

A little imagination goes a long way in the real world as well as in the digital world. Around the Northwest, many of the local farms are going bankrupt. One of them, Remlinger's Farm, decided to turn agriculture on its head. The owners built picnic shelters and designated meeting areas that people can rent for company meetings and gatherings. They built a little amusement park, a petting zoo, a climbing structure, and a miniature train. They grew a "pumpkin patch" for Halloween and held other child-oriented events. They provided food service. They converted a house into something like a Trader Joe's supermarket. They sold fresh produce, fruit, frozen pies, cheeses, wine—you name it. All branded, of course. The lesson? Retail works in a lot of dimensions. Even the smallest operation can think in terms of vertical integration. Just because I am a farmer doesn't mean I am limited to growing corn. Just because I am a pizza maker doesn't mean I am limited to tossing pizza dough into the air.

Such approaches to expansion are not free of concerns. You might face channel conflict between different companies reselling your products, or you might see poor sales without ever knowing that competitors are paying incentives to obtain better placement in the aisles of a store. The handling of returns can be an issue logistically. A related problem is that a lack of inventory depth may make it difficult for customers to find exactly the right product, especially if your product comes in different sizes or colors. Ensuring that resellers are properly trained can be difficult, as well as ensuring that the brand is properly presented and positioned. In fact, many of the issues with using other retailers to sell your products are exactly those faced by franchise operations and licensing, approaches that are described in detail in the following sections. Serious thought and proper planning are requirements to enable this manner of expansion to succeed.

Expanding the Good Old Retail Way

If you have the personality, the desire, and the concept, though, one day you will want to expand the good old-fashioned way—by opening more stores. Before you do, think hard about the particulars. Some concepts have limited expansion potential. A fine restaurant with a great chef, a small interior design firm, a bookstore with an erudite proprietor—any retail operation that depends primarily on the skills of the owner/operator is limited to the two or three stores that this individual can personally manage. Surf shops, ski shops, kite shops, T-shirt shops, guide outfits, equipment rentals, charter excursions—there is an entire class of "tourist" or outdoor concepts that flourish close to scenic areas or recreational centers. Their viability diminishes as a square of the distance from the attraction. If the locality is the hero, or the person preparing the product, then the concept has limited capability to expand. (A beach shop or restaurant or charter service or similar business could expand, of course, up and down the coast to become a local or regional chain, as could a ski-related concept in the same mountain region.) The good thing about retail, though, is normally the *product* is the hero. If the product is the hero, the concept has a tremendous potential for expansion.

Expansion is something that most retailers look forward to, but too many people expand for the sake of expansion. They have one successful store and they figure they can manage another one, so they expand. However, you need to be very careful about making assumptions about how successful you can be in a new city—or a new neighborhood. It is much harder to develop clientele, control costs, and maximize efficiency in unfamiliar territory. Understanding each trade area is a prerequisite for success. So is understanding your operational strengths and limitations relative to where you plan to expand.

Several early steps will smooth the way for expansion. One is to establish a broker network to ensure the rapid acquisition of new sites (or relocations for an established chain). Early on, local brokers fill this need. As you expand, regional and national brokers need to be involved. Another thing to do early is to develop relationships with major mall property managers, those who own multiple malls, many of them in the most desirable locations. The largest ones in the U.S. are the Simon Property Group, the Taubman Company, the Westfield Group, and the Rouse Company/General Growth Properties. Other fast-growing retailers may provide access to excess property, unique terms through sub-leasing, or property that can be co-developed. Big Box stores and other mass merchandisers also seek complementary brands as subtenants to augment their offerings. Even if these relationships do not result in formal strategic alliances, the informal partnerships might unlock some attractive locations. Finally, identify and hire an external design firm, site surveyors, engineers, and others to speed planning and the permit process for potential new locations. As your organization grows, you will need to begin establishing relationships with service technicians and with companies that provide facilities management.

To put expansion in context, two or three stores provide a very good living for someone not planning to expand. If you plan to expand, you and your partner(s) will live somewhat less well as store income is plowed into growth. Typically, three successful stores set the stage for serious expansion. Three stores give you solid operating experience, and the net income should be sufficient to pay for the next store. At 12 to 15 percent, the net annual income of three stores is roughly the cost of the build-out of one new store of the same size. You will move somewhat less quickly if you fund all of your expansion out of cash flow and somewhat faster if you borrow or seek additional investment capital. At this point, you are still learning to walk so there is no rush.

From both a financial and management standpoint, a mom-and-pop-sized operation can open one new store a year. At six stores or so, you take another step on the ladder as you begin to hire senior managers and leverage marketing and operations, especially if the stores are clustered. This is also the time that you have to begin taking infrastructure seriously. Oakley, which makes fashion eyewear, outdoor performance wear, and accessories, was a wholesaler for the first 20-odd years of its existence. The company opened outlet stores to relieve inventory and to test a retail concept. At six stores, Oakley found it had a winning proposition. It had also reached the limit of being able to beg, borrow, and steal employees and corporate managers from the wholesale operation to run the retail operation. The company put together the team and systems needed to go further with its company-owned stores.

At ten stores, you begin to feel that you have a real company. You can probably open two or more stores a year. At 25 stores, you take another big step. You now have a lot of purchasing clout, you can hire more specialists, and you can open stores faster and faster. At this point, the speed of deployment is proportional to the teams and systems you put in place and the real estate strategy you developed, particularly if you expand out of your region. Potbelly, as one example, has gone from 25 to 50 stores and should exceed 80 stores in about three years. Oakley expanded from 15 to 30-plus stores in one year and should continue to open about 15 stores a year for some time, a fairly expansive rate. Chico's, with more than 550 stores, has been adding another 90 or so stores annually.

Store numbers also relate to potential investors. If you have fewer than 20 stores, venture capitalists may be interested in your concept. At more than 30, investment bankers are interested. At greater than 50 stores, Wall Street will definitely be knocking on your door to analyze the opportunity for an initial public offering (IPO). At 75 to 100 stores, you will have proven that you have the personnel and systems to become a major national chain. Many entrepreneurs go public as early as possible, often with the "encouragement" of their venture capitalists, in order to obtain additional capital to continue growth and to enable the initial players to get their money out, usually as part of a planned "exit strategy." Going public, however, has its own pressures, the biggest being quarterly reporting that can promote short-term thinking. An IPO is not a step to be taken lightly.

Once you begin to roll, you can use the economic model to tell your real estate development team how many stores they need to open each year to keep up with the chain's sales projections. Similarly, the physical constraints of finding the right locations and of spending six months to locate, execute a lease, and build out each store puts an upper limit on projected growth. On $1 million in sales, each store nets $150,000 a year, and weekly store net income is $2,885. It is a simple calculation of the number of new stores open for so many weeks of each year to determine the projected new income, minus of course the cost of construction and inventory. Such numbers become the basis for a 3-year planning cycle.

Preparing to Expand: Count the Ways

Expansion can take many forms. This section describes the variety of ways and their corresponding strengths and weaknesses.

Franchising

This is the most rapid way to expand and the least risky financially. It provides the most revenue for the least capital investment, but also returns less overall revenue and true value than company-owned stores. With rapid expansion comes the difficulty of creating a national management structure and managing the complexity of national distribution early in the organization's life. The key to success is a simple concept with excellent operational systems supported by excellent operating manuals and training. Franchises require fairly good investment in field personnel who can identify the right people as franchisees and find the right locations to support the concept. Quality control is the biggest problem, and protection of the brand is the biggest concern. Remember the poor ice cream restaurant in Chapter 1, "It's About Your Values." Other headaches range from failed franchises to franchisee lawsuits.

For franchisees, the value comes in the ability to buy into an established brand for a fraction of the cost of creating a new concept. Also, mom-and-pop retailers who feel that they cannot compete with national brands may take the strategy of joining them. It is hard for a local ice cream shop to compete with a high-quality national brand such as Cold Stone Creamery, as one example. Typical franchise fees run $10,000 to $50,000 per location. Because design and construction standards are already established, the total startup cost, including build-out, could easily be half of that for a new concept—under

$250,000 for some quick-serve restaurants. The "turn-key" setup usually includes everything, all the way down to the cash registers and computer systems. The franchisee benefits from the chain's national advertising, its buying power, and its distribution system. In exchange, the franchisee pays royalties ranging from 4 to 8 percent and a marketing fee that runs another 3 to 5 percent so that the franchisee's annual cost can total from 8 to 15 percent of revenue.

For franchisees, the biggest risk is that the national chain franchisor may locate another franchise too close to your store so that it cannibalizes sales. (Some franchisees avoid the problem by buying a franchise territory, usually a much larger market in a particular area.) Franchisees are also limited to products provided by the franchise itself. A quick-serve franchise restaurant cannot add nachos to the menu on its own or make up a special kind of sandwich that locals would like. Other rules designed to enforce consistency often get in the franchisee's way. One franchisee complained that he could not put up team schedules or other local school announcements because the only allowable signs were those with the franchise logo. Other problems can be more serious. The national franchise may not develop new product lines, or it may do a poor job of marketing, or it may respond to financial difficulties by increasing product or equipment costs, squeezing the franchisee's income. An individual store may do very well, whereas the national franchise itself could go out of business.

That said, many of the most successful chains, particularly in food service, are built on the franchise model. Speed of market expansion and quality control and consistency are the heart of success.

Licensing

Licensing is a variation of franchising. Licensing gives the licensee the specific use of something—a company or product name, the formula, the product itself, or some combination. A licensor typically does not have the responsibility to support the licensee, nor does the licensor have control of the licensee's operations, as is true of a franchise. Consequently, the costs to the licensee are usually lower than to a franchisee, but the licensee also receives no operational support and no direct marketing support. From a practical standpoint, licensing for most retailers will apply only in very specific applications. When Starbucks wants access to space controlled by another company—at an airport terminal, a grocery store, or a bookstore, for instance—it licenses its name and product line to the other vendors and operators. Starbucks consults on the design, provides the product, and trains the trainers, but it has no formal power over the operations other than making sure that the licensees execute to standards (for instance, make lattes properly). Under U.S. law, a loosely written "license" can turn out to meet the definition of a "franchise." A legal specialist is needed for any potential licensing opportunity.

Preparing to Expand: Company-Owned Stores

Company-owned stores are the most capital-intensive route for expansion, which means they usually expand the slowest. They are, however, my preferred manner of expansion. My overwhelming concern is to protect the brand. Company-owned stores provide the greatest capability for a retailer to control quality of the product, the presentation, the staff, and the brand. For a brand seeking to differentiate itself, the company-owned approach is best. Company-owned stores also provide the greatest overall return on investment. Consider a concept that has a franchise fee of $25,000 and store units that generate $1 million in revenue, of which the franchisor receives 5 percent. After 10 years, each store will return to the franchisor approximately $525,000 ($50,000 a year plus the initial fee). A company-owned store netting 15 percent on $1 million in sales will return $1.5 million over 10 years. The retailer will have spent $400,000 on the build-out (annual revenue divided by 2.5) and will have the cost of depreciation. Even so, a company-owned store with $1 million in annual revenue will easily return $200,000 to $250,000 more than a franchise over a 10-year period. If you have ten stores, that represents $2.5 million. Further, a standard Wall Street valuation of retail stores is 24 times earnings. (By comparison, Starbucks' P/E ratio is 50 as of this writing.) If each store nets 15 percent and the chain as a whole nets 10 percent, then a ten-store, company-owned chain has earnings of $10 million and a valuation of $240 million, far higher than a comparably sized franchise.

Another way of looking at expansion is to use the net income of the concept from the very beginning as a signal as to whether to franchise or to own each store. Maybe your concept will not generate as high a rate of return as I prefer, but the concept is still financially sound.

Franchising might be the best approach for concepts on the lower end of the scale in ROI. However, the very best concepts are the most successful financially. They take longer, but company-owned and run concepts ultimately deliver more revenue and assets to the company itself. If you are going to do all this work, reap the rewards yourself. Even if you do not want to go national, a nice regional company-owned concept can be personally rewarding and financially successful. You can pay Midas $25,000 and 5 percent of your revenue, or you can build a great muffler chain yourself—assuming you know how to compete.

Expanding by Other Means

Chains can increase the rate of expansion by using other approaches besides pure company-owned expansion and pure franchising. P.F. Chang's China Bistro, the upscale-casual Chinese restaurant chain, has a double-barreled approach to expansion. For every P.F. Chang restaurant in an area, the chain plans to develop several smaller, fast-casual Asian restaurants called Pei Wei, which diners can enjoy closer to their homes or businesses. Sales from the two related concepts reinforce each other. Brilliant! It is worth noting the benefits that P.F. Chang's has from its relationship with the venture capital firm Trinity Ventures. Trinity has been involved in rolling out Jamba Juice and Starbucks. This experience has been as valuable to P.F. Chang as the funds Trinity has invested to support expansion.

What follows is a summary of other approaches to expansion.

Area-Owned Management

Two approaches, one from a franchise standpoint and the other from a company-owned standpoint, try to blend the best of both. One is the concept of a master franchise licensee who owns the franchises for an entire area and sublicenses them to others. Quiznos uses this approach. The other takes a proven operator from a company-owned store in one region and assigns the operator a new territory. The individual oversees all of the stores in the new region. In return, the operator receives, for example, 10 percent of the business. As a part owner, the operator has a vested interest in the success of all the stores. Outback has used this approach successfully. Both approaches attempt to get the equivalent of a regional supervisor to function in more of an entrepreneurial role. Usually the exit strategy for an area licensee is to sell his region back to the parent company at a defined multiple of earnings once he has built out his territory. The sale assumes, of course, that years later, the concept has endured and the parent company is solid and desires to buy back the region.

Acquisition

Sometimes an entrepreneur buys a brand and retains the name with the idea of growing it, as Bryant Keil did with Potbelly. Or entrepreneurs may buy a substantial existing chain with the goal of reinvigorating it, as the new owners of Eckerd Drugs seek to do. Sometimes a large chain will buy a smaller chain in a related category to diversify its own business, maximize operational expertise, and drive revenues of the new business. Too often the larger chain does a poor job of running the smaller chain and often both companies suffer. A few years ago, McDonald's bought Mexican, pizza, and chicken concepts, but the acquisitions caused the company to lose focus on its core business. Seeking to revitalize its core hamburger business, McDonald's has begun selling off most of those other businesses.

More typically, an acquisition occurs with rebranding in mind. Acquisition can give a retailer instant presence and credibility in a market. Acquisition can be costly or it can be a relatively inexpensive way to obtain good real estate as well as brand presence. Such purchases also bring potential management and financial headaches. A major part of the due diligence in an acquisition is to determine why the other chain can be acquired. In many cases, the acquired company is struggling. You need to avoid thinking that your concept is so good that it can succeed where the other did not. It may be that the chain's economic model is weak or that it has a large portfolio of poor locations or expensive leases.

Of course, there are also legal and administrative expenses, but the biggest potential costs may be in the minds and spirits of the employees you inherit. An exodus of employees can drive up training costs. Unhappy employees can result in poor service and lost business, particularly for a brand with loyal customers, who might be looking for subtle clues in employee behavior as a signal as to whether they

should continue to frequent the establishment. One of the most difficult tasks in acquisition is conversion of one store to another. The best
guideline is to make the conversion as quickly as possible. The longer
you wait, the more uncertain employees become, the more second-
guessing there is of new management by old staff.

Quick, positive support of the staff can ease the transition. When
Starbucks bought The Coffee Connection in Boston, some employees
bolted, unwilling to work for an out-of-town chain. Others took a
wait-and-see attitude. We immediately put a team in each store to help
with the transition and to explain our plans. When employees realized
that they would receive better training, higher pay, medical coverage,
and stock options, they changed their mind about what some of them
thought was conquest by a competitor.

An acquisition should include "hidden" benefits. The Coffee Connection had learned that Northeasterners preferred a lighter coffee
roast than what Starbucks sold, and meeting this immediate market
demand sped up our decision to provide a wider variety of coffee
blends. The lighter roasts later proved to be successful on the East
Coast and in the Midwest. The Coffee Connection also had an iced
coffee beverage. The recipe was not very good—servers made it by
pouring the blend into a machine from 5-gallon buckets—but the
drink sold well. This is a fact we noticed in our due diligence prior to
completing the purchase. Buying The Coffee Connection accelerated
our research and development of ice-blend coffee drinks. The formula-
tion we developed was considerably different, but The Coffee Connection provided the perfect name: the *Frappuccino*™ drink. Today the
Frappuccino™ category represents a tidy percentage of Starbucks'
overall sales. Acquisitions should be about more than adding stores or
increasing your company's revenue base. Acquisitions should also
make you smarter and put more tools in your brand marketing toolkit.

Joint Ventures

As a complement to company-owned stores, joint ventures represent
interesting ways to extend the brand. Joint ventures enable expansion
for half the cost and half the risk, although potential problems exist in
a concept that attempts to serve two masters. A joint venture needs to

have a compelling business or social reason, an opportunity to launch your brand far beyond where you might be able to reach otherwise.

I have believed for many years that the greatest sales opportunity in retail lies in inner-city America. Such areas have tremendous population density, and everyone has heard of the major brands. Few retailers venture there, though such areas have proven successful to those companies that do invest. Earvin (Magic) Johnson, the former L.A. Lakers' basketball star, has been a catalyst in bringing new retail ventures into inner-city neighborhoods. After meeting with Ken Lombard, who was the president of Johnson Development at that time, I wrote a one-page proposal to Starbucks' senior management outlining a joint venture to open Starbucks stores in various inner cities. There was some skepticism about whether a 50-50 joint venture made financial sense, but Magic was an icon to the African-American community and I knew the stores would do well enough to justify the effort. Howard and the rest of management were willing to try the experiment for the "soft" reasons of being a small part of revitalizing communities. Magic was excited about the Starbucks proposal. He crystallized the underserved nature of the neighborhoods where he went to church in central L.A. There, he said, the only coffee he and other people could get was at convenience stores. "I want the folks in these neighborhoods to get the same good products you can find in every other neighborhood," he said.

When we opened the first store in Ladera Heights, more than 250 people showed up, including basketball player Shaquille O'Neal and other celebrities. Once again, we learned operational lessons from doing something different. Magic recommended that we provide sweeter products, more flavored syrups, and baked goods with the coffee drinks for this market. We took his advice, and the stores have done well financially—enough to justify the "hard" reasons for the venture. If you do partnerships such as this, do not settle for a one-off project. Look for relationships that are symbiotic and will lead to multiple stores. These have more impact on the communities and provide a sounder basis for operations. Before I left Starbucks, we had opened 30 stores with Magic; there are more than 60 now. Since we went into inner-city neighborhoods, 24-Hour Fitness and Washington Mutual have also done cooperative deals with Magic's development firm in Los Angeles.

Wholesale/Retail Expansion

Whether supplementing its retail business by adding wholesale channels, as Starbucks and Top Pot Doughnuts have done, or supplementing its wholesale business by adding retail channels as Oakley and Nike have done, a business can draw from the added economic wellspring of a second channel by minimizing conflict between the two. For a wholesaler-becoming-retailer, the biggest challenge is to convince existing wholesale customers that a retail outlet will help create additional brand awareness and therefore bring additional benefit to their own stores. A scuba diving shop might sell a collection of Oakley glasses and an Oakley dry bag, but the customer might not know that Oakley also sells ski gear, bicycling gear, or watches. For Oakley, which remains best known for its sunglasses, having a store that showcases all of its products together provides the customer with a total view of what Oakley is about. By broadening awareness of the entire product line, the retail stores help drive everyone's business, including the retailers that are wholesaling parts of the line. Oakley's advertising also generally promotes the Oakley brand rather than a particular Oakley store, so that it drives business to every retailer that carries Oakley products and not just its own stores. The company's marketing goal is not to take business from the local bike shop or other Oakley partner, but to increase the overall number of Oakley fans.

Tuning up the Engine of Success

If the economic model is the engine of success, the retailer has to do everything possible to tune it up. The numbers have to be solid and the financials need to be substantial enough to drive expansion. My preferred method of expansion is company-owned, but then I am interested in higher quality concepts that tend to have higher margins. Other concepts might prosper through franchising. Most financial analysis focuses on cutting costs, but increasing revenue is equally profitable and a good deal more fun. Chapter 6, "Merchandising: Maximizing Your Profits," showed ways to increase gross margins and return more profit.

If the most difficult question a retailer faces is when and how to open the first store, the next most difficult question is when to embark on the road to major expansion. Assuming this is your desire, there is a pragmatic way to know whether you are expanding too soon or not soon enough. You are expanding too soon when you have not obtained all the efficiency and profitability from your initial store or two, when there is more money to be made by running them better. You might extend your business by finding new sales channels, by introducing new product lines, or by expanding to new day parts. Here is another reason to know the industry average for gross and net margins for your category and to know how your competitors have extended their businesses.

Another way to tell that you are expanding too fast is if your service model collapses. This is the surest indicator of problems with the qualitative aspects of expansion. Rapid expansion is not the same as reckless expansion, and every step of the way must be taken in the context of protecting the presentation of the brand and preserving the authenticity of the concept. Expand only when you can maintain quality control. All it takes for the wheels to come off a food concept is to have a food-borne illness as the result of poor quality control. All it takes for the wheels to come off other concepts is to have two or three dirty stores or low sales that result from poor hiring practices or slipshod inventory management. Because of the Internet, bad experiences by even a few customers can lead to widespread negativity and to your concept becoming irrelevant. Other symptoms of qualitative problems are the same as those of other stressed businesses: high personnel turnover, a drop in sales, and headhunters recruiting your staff. Pay attention to these warning signs, and put a brake on expansion for as long as needed to make the necessary changes.

Although the desire to be the first in a market forces the issue of speed, it is more important that you move intelligently through the expansion process. Make sure that your concept has really taken root in current markets. Make sure you have fully fleshed out the concept. Make sure every new store enhances the brand positioning and does not detract from it because of a loss of quality. Make sure your organization does not implode from the stress of overly rapid growth. Do not let the business reason *for* expansion push you into taking actions you are not prepared for, which are the operational challenges *of* expansion. What I mean is this. You have a great new concept—food, clothing, consumer electronics, whatever it might be—and others begin to copy it. For business reasons, you want to expand quickly to cut off competitors. But if you have no infrastructure, no people, no processes or systems in place, you are moving too soon and your expansion is likely to falter. You also know you are expanding too soon—or at least, too fast—when you choose the wrong location, or settle on a secondary location, just to get open, or lower your hiring standards to fill your staffing needs. Conversely, you know that you are not expanding soon enough or fast enough when the economic model is working, the operational systems are functioning well, and you are paying overhead for highly trained managers who are underutilized. At this point, it's time to *move*.

PART THREE

Own Main & Main

If you don't know where you are going,
any road will take you there.

—*Lewis Carroll*

CHAPTER 12

How to Grow Rapidly without Stumbling

A FRIEND OF MINE met Sam Walton in the early 1970s, when Sam's company Wal-Mart was still a small regional chain. My friend asked Sam why he had stores in Bentonville and Berryville, two Arkansas towns with just a few thousand people, but none in Little Rock, the state's capital and by far its largest city.

"How many state capitals does Arkansas have?" Sam asked.

"One," my friend said.

"How many county seats does Arkansas have?" Sam asked.

"Seventy-five."

"If your choice was to put one store in Little Rock and compete with Sears, JCPenney's, and Montgomery Ward, or to put 75 stores in the county seats without any competition, which would you do?"

"Do you really think that will work?" my friend said. At the time, Wal-Mart had a few dozen stores in the rural towns of Arkansas and Oklahoma.

Sam said Wal-Mart planned to open 18 more stores in the next quarter.

Not certain that he had heard correctly, my friend said, "You mean 18 *next year?*"

"No, sir. 18 next *quarter*. And 18 the quarter after that. And 18 the quarter after that. And then ..." Sam leaned back in his chair, waved at a map of the United States, and smiled.

Twenty years later, Wal-Mart had redefined the retailing of general merchandise and Sam had become one of the richest men in the world. His story proves that a concept does not have to appeal to the wealthy or be located in the largest cities to succeed. The target demographic of the music store Sam Goody is middle class and lower middle class children and teenagers. Its stores prosper in non-major markets as well as in major markets, providing the area has a strong concentration of its target group. The primary market of Omaha Steaks, the largest direct response marketer of premium meat, poultry, and seafood in the U.S., is suburban households, and its stores generally perform better when they are located in regional shopping centers near major supermarkets. Everything depends on the concept. Before any concept can succeed, however, you have to know the location of the customers who support your *particular* retail idea.

For every success story, there is also a cautionary tale. Pep Boys, the automotive service chain, became established in Los Angeles in the 1930s. The chain grew up in a car-crazy town, one that has a peanut butter spread of demographics—customers stretching throughout the L.A. basin. Pretty much anywhere they opened a store, they succeeded. In the mid-1990s, Pep Boys embarked on a rapid expansion on the West Coast, only to back off and retrench nearly as fast, closing dozens of stores. Pep Boys' target market is the middle class. The wealthy take their new cars to dealers for service, usually on new car warranties, whereas the poor can't afford to have their cars serviced very often. But Pep Boys' segment is a particular slice of the middle class: people who have late-model, used vehicles, and people who like to work on their own vehicles. When Pep Boys expanded into other metropolitan areas on the West Coast, they didn't know where to find the same deep vein of customers they had mined in Los Angeles. They picked the same kind of generic locations along busy arterials and streets that had worked so well for them in L.A., but in other cities and states, the customer base was more isolated and concentrated. They seemed to open many stores in major trade areas because other retailers were there, following the herd instinct instead of doing the right demographic analysis to find out where *their customers* actually lived. It seems to me that Pep Boys expanded without doing an adequate job of researching the locations close to the population segments that defined their customer base, where their stores would have maximized revenue. Their lack of discipline caught up with them.

Starbucks' target market is urban professionals, high-income individuals from the age of 18 to 45. Stores need to be located where these professionals live, work, or play. Starbucks established a beachhead in a number of large American cities by targeting major urban core areas and the bedroom communities for these areas. In the many 100s of other prospective cities, and of the prospective trade areas within those cities, we need to know: Where do we go next? How can we more effectively find our customers?

We created a database report of potential markets, using high income and large population size as the primary criteria. The result was a list of the country's major Metropolitan Statistical Areas (MSAs), more or less in order of population size. An MSA is an area with a large urban center surrounded by other communities that are similar economically and socially. There are about 140 MSAs in the U.S. Each MSA has at least one and usually several trade areas, where retail activity is concentrated.

I wasn't satisfied with the initial results and the somewhat generic ranking of MSAs. There is more to demographics—or to finding coffee lovers or car lovers—than starting with the largest city and working your way down. We were looking for any kind of unique demographic profile or insight to help us plan our market development more strategically. After mulling over the data, I asked my team to generate a report sorted according to an additional statistic: people who have 13 or more years of education. People with college educations are more likely to experiment and try something new, and they are more likely to tell their friends about it. They want to impress their friends with how knowledgeable and worldly they are by taking them to a new restaurant or coffee shop or to involve them in some other new experience.

College-educated people tend to have higher incomes, as do their friends, but the anchor is education. When we further narrowed the query by doing an additional sort on level of education, the rankings shifted substantially. The San Francisco MSA ranked number 29 for income and population; however, it ranked number 1 after education was included as part of the query. The potential new market rankings also showed a strong correlation with areas where we were already established and doing extremely well.

We defined the top two market tiers, those major population centers with the right combination of high personal income and high education. Experience at that time had taught us that an established market would support one store for every 25,000 people. (Since then, senior Starbucks executives have discussed a penetration of one store for every 10,000 people.) An MSA with one million people could support 40 stores over time, an MSA with half a million people could support 20 stores, and so on. We defined each MSA according to the number of potential stores. A *grande* market such as Detroit had the potential for 25 or more stores total. A *tall* market, such as Calgary or Salt Lake City, had the potential for ten to 25 total stores. Both of these also had the density of stores to drive mass media advertising and other large promotions. A *short* market, such as Ottawa or Reno/Tahoe, had the potential for less than ten stores. As we entered a new market, the goal was to open at least ten stores a year in a *grande* market, at least five stores a year in the *tall* markets, and at least two stores a year in the *short* markets. To achieve a marketing bang and brand visibility, five stores would open in the first 12 weeks in each new *grande* market and three stores would open in 12 weeks in each new *tall* market. A flagship store, the highly visible store in an influential location in an important residential or major commercial core, would be among the first to open. Whenever possible, we tried to synchronize openings. One year, we opened five stores in Toronto on the same day in June and another five stores on the same day in July.

This strategy gave us a process that we could follow logically. We would concentrate on tier one and infill with the best locations in tier two. We would leave tier three for the future. You might ask why we bothered with the *short* market at all. The answer is that we could not find enough of the right locations to open all the planned stores in the bigger markets alone. Sometimes a smaller meaningful market is located in between two large markets or near a large market, so placement of a store in the small market served to reinforce our presence. We had the money and operational capacity to expand and the *short* markets were the right demographics. We did our research and executed a disciplined growth plan.

Because it is seldom possible to find all the real estate quickly in one market, planning needs to remain flexible. If your plan says to open ten stores in Chicago, you would probably proceed even if you found enough good locations to open only six. If you could find only two or three suitable sites in Chicago, though, you would be advised to evaluate a nearby market with similar attributes and more potential available locations—Detroit, perhaps, a city smaller than Chicago in the same region. One strategy would be to open a substantial number of stores in Detroit the first year and use that time to find sufficient properties so that you could make a splash in Chicago the second year, rather than opening early but weakly in Chicago.

Other strategic factors may cause a shift in priority. In the early 1990s, we planned to enter Philadelphia, Baltimore, Cincinnati, and Pittsburgh. However, the South-central region of the U.S. was the last to come out of the late 1980s real estate recession. On a reconnaissance visit there, we were stunned to see the number of vacancies in prime locations. To take advantage of available real estate and terrific rents, we delayed expansion in the Northeast for a year to leap into Dallas, Fort Worth, and Houston. Adaptability does not mean the scattershot opening of stores all over the country, but rather a sensible variance in defined strategy. By swapping regions, we still entered big markets in force with high-quality locations that we could support operationally.

Proceeding in Rapid but Orderly Fashion

When we completed our initial round of strategic planning for 1997, we were ready to take on the opening of 22 new markets and 325 stores. We had the targeted demographics that defined our customer base. But there was still work to do to refine the order in which we prioritized the 22 new target markets. The premise for an expansion methodology is simple, though execution can become complex. "Own your home" first—wherever you are headquartered. Your "home" market could be a city or MSA or a state. The next market, chosen according to sound demographic principles, should be close to your current base of operations to leverage your brand recognition, administrative and human resource functions, operations, marketing strength, and budget. "Own" each new market in turn before going on to the next. (*See Figure 12-1.*) "Own" means to take prominent positions in the key trade areas and become the dominant brand in that area. Never go in tentatively or try to "test" a market. A retailer will have 20 stores in Minnesota, for example, and will open two in Atlanta. One store does well, one doesn't. Given ambiguous results, the retailer searches for all kinds of reasons—poor real estate, a lack of operational focus, and so on. Usually, the retailer closes up and leaves the market. The test is a failure not because of the particular reason that one store struggled, but because the chain never committed to the market in the first place. Its actions showed that it did not *intend* to succeed. Often times, retailers say that they are testing a market when they are really being *drawn* into a market, as opposed to marching into a market. What do I mean? Sometimes a retailer gets into a "gotta grow! gotta grow!" mentality, as one of our clients described it. Word gets out. A mall or shopping center needs your concept or demographic *now*. Real estate brokers and landlords start calling, offering locations in cities that should be good markets. Individually, each location looks great. The property is a nice structure. It has national brand co-tenants that support your concept. Lease terms are favorable. Eager to expand, you react by thinking, "Oh, this one's for me!" You forget that there are more than 3,000 very nice—and very similar—shopping centers all over the country. Before you know it, you have 60 stores in 60 markets. Unless your concept supports only one store per major market, this is not the correct approach. Never base your expansion "strategy" on who cold-calls first.

For retail concepts that can support multiple stores in each market, optimizing store locations does not mean opening one store each in the top 60 markets or two stores each in the top 30 markets. Optimization means opening ten to 15 stores in three to four markets. Conspicuous presence is the way to win each market strategically. Concentrating stores in a market develops sales momentum, maximizes the chain's

HUB AND SPOKE EXPANSION MODEL

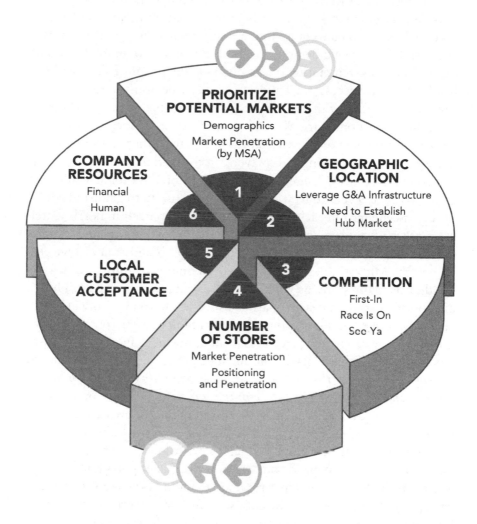

www.airvision.net

FIGURE 12-1

Retail concepts need to follow the hub-and-spoke model of expansion, conquering their own locale first, expanding into nearby locales and regions, and finally expanding nationally. Formal expansion methodology takes into account demographics, operational strengths, competition, store market penetration, the degree of local product acceptance (in terms of willingness to try the brand), and company capabilities.

infrastructure, and deters competitors. Remember our mention of the "herd" mentality? Know for sure that your competition within and outside your core market is studying your expansion. Normally a retailer will be tempted to jump into a market where its competition is successful. However, a demonstration that you are committed to rapid expansion in a given market might dissuade them from going head to head with you. Success is often determined by demonstrated *intent*. You are competing with hard-nosed businesspeople, many of whom are defending their home turf. Whether your "test" is deliberate or inadvertent, putting just one or two stores in a market that can support more stores is like putting two players on the field to test whether you can compete against 11-man teams in professional football. You're not giving yourself a chance to win, just an opportunity to get drubbed.

Use ascendancy in each market to establish yourself in nearby satellite markets. Establishing your presence in a major market and leveraging regional growth from that market is the "hub-and-spoke" concept. To win the Midwest, in general you would establish a hub in Chicago, building as many stores as your concept can support before establishing your first store in nearby markets, such as Detroit or Milwaukee. Similarly, in the Southeast, you carry Atlanta first; after you are established there, you spread to South Carolina, northern Florida, and eastern Tennessee. Achieve market dominance in the hub before moving to the spoke, and *open the first store in the spoke only when it can do more business than the next store in the hub.* The presence or absence of competitors and other factors, discussed in the following section, determine the order of attack in new markets, but the hub-and-spoke model is the overall strategy by which to proceed. The definition of "hub" and "spoke" depends on the concept. The original hub for Wal-Mart was the largest town in a rural area, and market saturation was one store. The spokes were the closest county seats to the initial store, for operational efficiency. But the principle was the same: dominate your primary market before moving on.

The number of stores to establish in each hub depends on the concept and the availability of real estate. For Starbucks, this approach could mean opening 20 stores in Chicago before opening the first one in Detroit. For a mainstream clothing or computer store, the hub-and-spoke strategy might mean six stores in the hub before the first one in a spoke. For a white-tablecloth restaurant, the strategy might mean three or four stores in a hub to balance market visibility and the maintenance of high-quality brand positioning. For outdoor or other specialty wear, this could be one or two stores in the hub. For an exclusive specialty retailer or a large format retailer, this could be a single store.

Most concepts, however, support multiple stores. In this context, establishing a flagship store and "infilling" with other stores in the trade area is not only about visibility and brand presence but also market power. Consider a tale of two coffees: Two high-quality chains were established in the mid-1980s. One, Gloria Jean's, rapidly franchised its coffee concept in a 100 cities, locating mostly in malls, but it did not develop a critical mass of stores in any one market. The other, Starbucks, expanded rapidly but systematically city by city, reaching critical mass before continuing on to the next. Twenty years later, Gloria Jean's remains a specialty provider known locally in only a few markets, whereas Starbucks is the most recognized coffee brand in the world.

Starbucks' lesson with its hub-and-spoke approach applies to almost every retailer. In addition to the marketing bang, the rapid opening of numerous stores in one locality maximizes your investment in construction, labor, training, and general and administrative costs. There was no sitting around by our management hired to operate a new market. Multiple stores not only made the brand more visibly present, but it also maximized advertising and other promotional dollars. Hiring becomes easier because friends tell friends about new job opportunities. Human Resources also benefits because of the ability to cover absences in one store with employees from others, or to fill store management positions from a larger employee pool. Finally, this approach maximizes efficiency for real estate. You become more credible with landlords, who recognize your seriousness in the market and begin to offer better locations. The benefits of the hub-and-spoke model are endless.

Evaluating the Competition

Another consideration in choosing the order in which to tackle hub markets is the competitive situation. The best hubs in terms of raw demographic numbers will also usually have the greatest number of competitors. National chains will have done at least some homework and will be in these markets, while some number of local competitors will have sprung up over time because of the population base and opportunity. The analysis, then, should determine those hubs with the best fit and the fewest competitors. As of this writing, there were 95 competitors in the category of office supplies in the Los Angeles-Long Beach area, but there were only 23 in the New Haven-Bridgeport-Stamford area of Connecticut, and only 18 in the Bergen-Passaic area of New Jersey. The East Coast areas have demographics similar to the area in California. Assuming operational support in the New York area, an office supply company would be better able to penetrate that market, establishing the brand and generating the revenue to later tackle tougher hubs.

The competitive landscape offers three strategies. In the order of preference there is *First In*, *See Ya*, and *Race Is On*. The best position is to be the "First In" competitor in the market and to be recognized as the market leader. You will have the best choice of real estate and the strongest opportunity to set the standard, work out any operational problems, and establish your brand. The next favorable position is *See Ya*, in which there is an existing but vulnerable competitor. Let's say you want to open a muffler shop in Allentown, Pennsylvania, and there is an existing operator, but his facility is old, he hasn't repainted the building in years, his parking lot is in a state of disrepair, and he never advertises. If you come in strong with several modern muffler shops in good locations, and properly market the business, you will own the market. It is like the Roadrunner who says, "beep beep" to the Coyote and leaving him in the dust. The most difficult situation is the *Race Is On*, in which a competitor is already entrenched in the market, perhaps a local company with a well-run business or a national chain that has been there for a long time. They have tremendous brand loyalty and they may be expanding rapidly. You would seek to enter *First In* and *See Ya* markets first. Both help establish your brand. When you're ready for the *Race*, you would remain as quiet as possible prior to opening to benefit as much as possible from the element of surprise. Normally, upon opening you would come up with tremendous promotions and attempt to grab market share quickly. In some cities, however, a national brand that comes in with heavy promotion can generate a backlash in favor of a well-loved local business, so the marketing may need to be quieter—for example, direct mail to individuals rather than large ads in the local newspaper, or the selection of a specific popular charity to support.

As the name implies, *Race Is On* is the most difficult competitive situation. You must act as if the other company will speed up with you. In Boston, The Coffee Connection in 1994 had ten stores and a fanatically loyal customer base. Knowing that Starbucks would be coming to town, The Coffee Connection raced to obtain capital for expansion. They opened an additional 15 stores and had plans for 60 more before we had our first store. I knew Boston would be extremely difficult to crack. Grade "A" real estate rarely is available in Boston and the surrounding towns. There is almost no turnover in the quality community shopping districts. There is also tremendous loyalty to local operators, and Boston was home not only to The Coffee Connection but also to Dunkin' Donuts, which had a 40-year head start on us. So we made the Connection an offer they couldn't refuse—$23 million in Starbucks stock. Their leadership decided that getting more than a million dollars a store was a better deal than trying to raise the huge amount of capital that they would need to fund the expansion to keep us out. There was no question that a fight for market share would have been costly to both parties and the outcome uncertain. The deal was good for all concerned, including The Coffee Connection employees, who ended up with higher pay and better benefits when they became Starbucks partners.

In New York, there was no one major competitor, but the total cost of rent and labor was exceedingly high, and we knew that the minute we entered the market, other competitors would take the corner opposite us on every street. Because coffee was a hot concept, every entrepreneurial immigrant would also open a coffee store. This was one of the few times we made a considered decision *not* to be the first in. Sure enough, when we said we were planning to enter New York, other companies rushed to expand in Manhattan. But we had never actually said we would move into the city. We opened our first stores in Fairfield and Westchester counties, north of Manhattan, where many of the Wall Street crowd lived and where many influential types summered. We flipped our usual strategy of establishing ourselves in the urban core and then moving outward to the suburbs. In smaller towns, such as Rye, New York and Greenwich, Connecticut, we were more relevant than we would have been among the teeming masses of the nation's largest city. People discovered the Starbucks experience as a place to visit on the weekends. We became locally relevant.

Meanwhile, I was able to evaluate the competition "down below" in the city. They all tried to clone "standard Starbucks." They opened stores similar in size to the 1,500-square-foot stores that we were typically opening in Chicago and Los Angeles. They copied our old design, unaware that we were about to unveil a new one. They put up a store on any corner they could find. Our point of differentiation became clear, and Howard was convinced that we had to go into Manhattan *big*. We opened in some of the most expensive neighborhoods in New York City. The stores were 2,000 to 4,000 square feet, double the usual size. Because the competition was opening smaller stores they had fewer than 20 seats. We provided twice the seating capacity. Knowing that New Yorkers were impatient and wanted fast service, we increased the number of points of sale (cash registers) and doubled the number of baristas to handle the larger crowds at peak periods. We rolled out our new designs, making each store *unique* in its look and appeal. Our store on Broadway near West 86th Street catered to the upper west side Central Park crowd. Our store on Second Avenue at East 81st Street (the one with the open second-floor loft) had a bohemian feel. The third store, at Astor Place in the village near East 8th Street, was the most bodacious of all, 4,000 square feet. It is still one of the top producing stores in the entire Starbucks chain.

We also had to tread lightly to enter the Berkeley market, the bastion of specialty coffee in northern California. Berkeley is the home territory of Peet's Coffee and Tea. Alfred Peet, the legendary Dutchman who started the company in Berkeley in 1966, was the original purveyor of fine coffees on the West Coast. Jerry Baldwin, who grew up in the Bay Area, fell in love with Peet's coffee, which was his inspiration when he and two others founded Starbucks Coffee in Seattle, Washington, in 1971. Later, the relationship between the companies and principals became quite tangled. In 1979, Alfred sold Peet's, and in 1984 the new owner sold Peet's to Starbucks. In 1987, Jerry Baldwin and his partners sold Starbucks to Howard Schultz and other investors. Jerry retained Peet's for himself to operate. In the 1990s, few of Peet's customers would have known that the original Peet was gone—that, in fact, he served from time to time as an advisor to Starbucks—and that

Starbucks' entry into Berkeley would have been "new Starbucks" versus "old Starbucks." The locals would have known only that their sacrosanct Peet's was being threatened by an outsider. Rather than move to Piedmont Avenue in Berkeley close to Peet's and create a backlash, we moved into a great location nearby in Oakland. In the minds of Peet's loyalists, we had not technically "invaded" Berkeley because we did not open on the neighborhood walking street that Peet's was on. We opened less than one mile away in a supermarket-anchored shopping center with great visibility and a lot of parking in the Rockridge neighborhood. There was no local outcry. Peet's did not open its first stand-alone store in Seattle, Starbucks' home, until 2003—in the Fremont neighborhood next door to Blue C Sushi! Peet's is now a publicly traded company that is expanding nationally.

Starbucks was not so lucky with every location where we might encounter a local competitor in northern California. A landlord in Mill Valley asked us for a confidential letter of interest outlining the terms that we would want to lease a small corner location in the heart of the downtown community. This landlord was already our landlord in another location. We submitted an offer based on our projected sale revenues. She went back to the existing tenant, a local coffee retailer whose lease was up for renewal, and used our offer to leverage an increase in their rental rate. Instead of quietly making the deal with the landlord, the tenant shrewdly took the story to the press and spun it to show how a large corporate chain from Seattle was increasing the rents and forcing the poor little guy out of business. As the person in charge of Starbucks' retail expansion for ten years, I have to say that we respected good local operators that provided high-quality coffee and unique environments. Invariably when Starbucks opens a location, nearby coffee houses continue to do well *if they are good operators*. The area becomes known for coffee houses, and many operators actually do better because of the corridor's increased customer traffic. As for rents, we were often accused of paying above-market rents. In fact, we paid top market rates for top quality real estate because our economic model could support such locations. Local residents often carp about the "big company" coming in and driving out locals. They seem to forget that national chains would love lower rents as much as the little guy. Landlords could just as easily rent to Joe's Local Juice as to

Jamba Juice, but they raise the rents, leaving only the national brands able to afford the property. The *local* retailer suffers and the *local* landlord benefits. The ironic part of the Mill Valley story is that this coffee house operator was a chain store in the region. No one knew it because he named each of his stores differently.

Of course, the story did not play out in all its complexity. Taking the inevitable David versus Goliath aspect of the story, the press did not bother to ask how this whole saga began or to investigate current rental rates. In fact, no one contacted us. When the story came out, all hell broke loose among potential local customers. If we had gone in, we would have faced a boycott. The landlord received her rent increase from the local operator, who remained in business and was quite profitable despite the rent increase. In fact, Peet's Coffee is located diagonally across the street from the operator and is also doing well. But Starbucks has never opened in downtown Mill Valley.

Sometimes in "going long," you have to know when not to go at all.

Assessing Other Factors

Another consideration for a target market is the availability of strategic partners. Barnes & Noble and the Albertson's grocery chain are two important partners for Starbucks. A potential hub in which Barnes & Noble has a number of stores or Albertson's has a strong presence would take precedence over a hub that has few or no potential partners. Barnes & Noble was an important partner because their brand was positioned by their chairman, Len Riggio, to offer the finest customer service, store environment, and depth of selection in their category. They pioneered the book superstore concept, and successfully grew to over 840 units, covering over 16 million square feet of retail space throughout the country. Ensuring that you align your concept with a company that will be successful over the long term is critical.

It's also important to evaluate the potential customer base and its knowledge and its willingness to accept new positioning within a concept, or a new concept entirely. At Starbucks, this meant the level of local coffee knowledge. Was the overall level of coffee sales in supermarkets in the area high or low? This could be measured by the number and variety of specialty coffee blends presented in the aisle. Before going into Cincinnati, or any city, we would find out whether lattes and cappuccinos were being sold in fine restaurants to determine the level of knowledge about high-quality coffee. We would evaluate other concepts related to community: the number of movie theaters or performance theaters, the presence of bookstores or music stores that were large enough to be gathering spots, the number of shopping streets and high-end clothiers—and, yes, the number of coffee shops.

Indicators differ for other categories, but most potential markets vary enough that you should be able to make reasonable evaluations of priority. Eugene, Oregon, and Little Rock, Arkansas, are two metropolitan areas of comparable population, but Eugene dresses down and favors the funky lifestyle of a college town whereas Little Rock dresses up and aspires to be as worldly as its neighbors, Dallas and Memphis. Running, biking, hiking, and snow skiing dominate Eugene's outdoor activities. Camping, water skiing, hunting, and fishing dominate Little Rock's. Clothing retailers, as just one example, would have to understand the fundamentally different mindsets and activities of the respective populations and do the right research to determine which market would be most receptive to their concepts. Many ways exist to assess the openness of a market to an idea. A running shoe store could look at the general level of outdoor activity, the number of running-related events, and the subscription levels for *Fitness*, *Runner's World*, and similar magazines. A store selling hip clothing for the young could examine the number of colleges, the relative number of young singles in the population, and the vitality of the night life of an area. At Starbucks, we looked for evidence that an area was willing to try cutting-edge concepts. We would look for gourmet food markets, such as Eatzi's in Dallas, which has fresh pasta and salads, fine oils, and specialty meats. We would look for the quality of poultry, fish, and meat sold in high-end supermarkets. We would look to see whether ethnic offerings—kosher, Hispanic, Asian—were broader than usual. Anything that showed people were willing to experiment with new foods created a target demographic.

For companies that have direct sales, the mail-order business provides precise data on where demand for product is demonstrably strong. Before expanding from its first few stores, Williams-Sonoma created a catalog business and "followed the ZIP codes" of catalog customers to establish its next set of stores. Starbucks' first East Coast venture was into Washington, D.C., because it had the highest concentration of mail-order customers in that region. Mail order is a way to create "brand soldiers," who prepare the way for expansion by clamoring for your product. Another way is to initiate specialty sales locally ahead of the opening of a store. Starbucks not only asked how much specialty coffee was being sold in restaurants, but would also create strategic alliances with the highest quality restaurants and hotels. By serving our coffee, lattes, and cappuccinos, the restaurants would introduce our brand to the decision makers and idea leaders in each locale. When customers asked about the coffee, restaurateurs would say, "Yes, this is Starbucks. You can get it by mail order, and next year they're opening a store in town." This kind of top-spin can enable you to blast past your competition again and again.

Brand soldiers can appear and do battle on your behalf at unexpected times. When Howard and I approached Steve Wynn, one of the major hoteliers in Las Vegas, about partnering with Starbucks, Steve invited the individual presidents of the Mirage, Treasure Island, New York New York, and the Golden Nugget hotels to our presentation. After I outlined the advantages of having Starbucks branded kiosks in the casinos on the way to the retail shops, and the increase in sales they might expect from serving Starbucks in their banquet facilities, Steve asked the hotel heads for their opinions. One by one they said no. They didn't see the value of switching to our brand, they had existing relationships with other vendors, and so on. When they were done, Steve started talking about our brand. He was familiar with Starbucks, but his wife *loved* Starbucks. "If she talks this way about something, it must be special," he said. He proposed a test. They would put a Starbucks kiosk in Treasure Island and a generic hotel-managed coffee shop in the Mirage to see which unit generated the greater revenues. Four months later, Starbucks had done much higher volume, and our relationship with Mirage Resorts took off.

Strategically, the process is to target the MSAs in which you have the potential to maintain the leadership position and possibly dominate, then develop a portfolio of superior real estate locations in concentrated trade areas. Select the order in which you will go after MSAs by any number of factors including the competitive situation and operational capabilities. Try to be the *First In*. Be sure to look for areas of economic growth—Las Vegas, Orlando, Scottsdale, among many others—because growing regions offer most concepts the best chance of success. At all costs, avoid scattering your stores across a number of markets. The analysis should not so much produce a list of favorable locations as it should create a sustainable, connect-the-dots real estate process by which to guide a disciplined expansion.

Many good demographic tools are available by which to make your initial analysis, though you need highly skilled analysts to make the data meaningful. If you don't have the data (I'm surprised at the many retail chains that don't seek out the level of detail they need) or you don't have the staff in-house, you can find consultants to help. An investment of $150,000 to $250,000 for a comprehensive national plan is a small price to pay for strategic market analysis for national chains. Costs could be lower depending on the scope of work. You could consider the cost to be the entry fee for succeeding at the regional or national level, but in actuality, the data will more than pay for itself in two to three years. If you have in-house staff, you could obtain much of the research for considerably less and do the analysis yourself—as long as it is the right analysis. A small retailer wanting to be smart about local or nearby expansion can get a thumbnail demographic sketch of a similar concept for perhaps $5,000 to $10,000. One 15-chain store recently obtained an analysis for approximately $20,000 that provided good guidelines on locations without precise metrics or recommendations on specific sites. A one-store or two-store operation can pick a major company similar to its business and evaluate the competitor's approach to locationing in a particular market. In fact, there's an urban legend that one of the major fast-food operators spends relatively little money on demographic analysis. Knowing that McDonald's has done its homework, the company simply locates near this major competitor.

Developing a Method to Expansion Madness

Real estate expansion begins with a rigorous demographic analysis to precisely identify your customers within the larger population. This process enables you to prioritize the MSAs within the country that map to your customers. (This process becomes more intense as you evaluate particular trade areas within each MSA, which is the theme of the next chapter.) After you have a preliminary listing of MSAs in priority order, the next step is to evaluate each MSA for competitive openings. Try to be the *First In*, and be aware of the costs and effort that will be required if you are not. Identify opportunities for strategic alliances, acquisitions, underserved markets, and niche opportunities in non-traditional locations to improve your competitive chances.

Avoid the temptation to step out until you "own" your own market first—saturating the market with enough stores to become the dominant brand. Then own each successive market before going on to the one after that. Use the "hub-and-spoke" approach by dominating the major city in a market and using that city as a base for expansion into each region. Scrutinize existing stores afresh, relocating stores in good MSAs but poor locations, and closing stores that show poor performance and are located in poor MSAs. Cluster markets and regions for maximum operational efficiency. Whatever else the demographics may tell you, for most concepts, one of the best ways to ensure success is to target an established market that is also growing. Finally, never go into a market half-heartedly. Either stay out, or go in with enough stores and enough marketing to create a brand presence that is powerful enough to win.

CHAPTER 13

Hot Spots, Oil Stains, and the Perfect Location

L ET'S SAY THAT your strategic planning has identified the
Houston, Texas Metropolitan Statistical Area (MSA) as
your next target market. How then do you find the best specific
locations in Houston? The answer requires a three-step process.
The first is market planning, in which you use demographic
data and detailed analysis to identify the best trade areas or
retail trade zones within the Houston MSA. The second step is
site selection, which requires identifying potential individual
locations in each trade area and evaluating them in person. The
final step is to build sales estimates for the proposed location(s)
to ensure that the economic model is profitable.

Every major metropolitan area has a number of generally
recognized trade areas. In Houston, these are the central business district, Galleria, the Woodlands, Sugarland, Champions
Village, and others. In retail, the trade area has a more specific
meaning, which is that locale from which your particular concept draws the vast majority of its customers. Usually this is a
subset of the general trade area, but not always. The downtown trade area might be a mile long and half a mile wide,

whereas the trade area for a downtown store might be only a few blocks in size. In a suburban area, the trade zone for a particular concept might extend beyond the general trade area into part of another general trade area or even into a nearby town. The Gap's trade area contains at least 200,000 people, so it could encompass an entire small city. Drive time is also an important factor in determining the size of the trade area, as discussed in Chapter 14, "A Walk Through the Locationing Process."

Virtually everyone involved in retail real estate selection at the regional or national level does some kind of demographic analysis to determine trade zones, but capability varies considerably. At the simplest level are the reports provided by landlords to prospective tenants that show the population at a radius of one, three, and five miles from the shopping center. Concentric circles from a spot on a map bear little relation to where people actually live and work, so this data is nothing more than a starting point. One step up from this is "thematic" mapping based on population density, household income, and age. Most commonly these maps are based on postal code. Using Geographic Information Systems (GIS) to tie the data to particular geographic locations, these maps can look impressive, but they are basic in many ways. Postal codes were designed to systemize mail delivery, not to provide demographic data to marketing people. Although they have some relevance in areas with homogeneous populations, postal codes do not segment populations by age, wealth, or occupation. Alone, they seldom lead to meaningful demographic data. For example, the 97701 postal code for Bend, Oregon, which is the fastest-growing resort and retirement area in the Northwest, contains large numbers of both the city's white-collar and blue-collar populations, the "student" demographics around the local community college, and sparsely populated ranchland stretching nearly ten miles west of town. Nor do postal codes take into account the physical landscape. Demographics can change radically at a city boundary or in the crossover to the proverbial "wrong side of the railroad tracks," even if these are both in the same postal code. In addition, a river or a line of foothills effectively cuts off a geographic area, and any trade area. In Bend, a haven for sun-seeking Seattleites, the Deschutes River winds through the middle of town, creating a zigzag of mini-population groups on its north and south banks, whereas Awbrey Butte, the town's most visible geographic feature, is an upper-class residential demographic unto itself. A major state or interstate highway or a rail line generally extends the trade area along its route but cuts off everything on the other side of it, as occurs with both a major railroad and a highway that run north and south through the middle of Bend. These factors are why simplistic "ring" maps or maps based on postal codes—common as they are—rarely provide meaningful information. In fact, in areas with relatively small populations, a postal code map might not provide any distinguishing characteristics. (*See Figure 13-1.*)

Another issue is the underlying data itself, which comes from the U.S. census. Census reports are created two years before each decade. Census data delivered in 2001–2002 was being prepared in 1997–99. Because populations shift over time, often rapidly, "current" census data will be approaching "vintage" state by the time you read this— old enough that reliability is in question. Even major chains do not often have recent, reliable customer data, so the basic census data must be freshened in some way. Data-gathering companies, such as Claritas and ESRI BIS (formerly CACI), enhance census data and provide their own data from market research. Specialized data might include detailed demographic information of a particular population segment, or information on the locations and sales volumes of competitors, or segmentation/lifestyle data, such as Claritas's PRIZM® and Experian's Mosaic. Claritas uses entertaining names to define its lifestyle segments. You know instantly from the name that the group called "Kids & Cul de Sacs" represents suburban professional families, whereas "Shotguns & Pickups" represents rural blue-collar families. With each segment, Claritas includes several identifying traits. For example, the top five demographic segments in Bend are, in order of size and with just one trait listed: "Greenbelt Sports," who drive Ford pickup trucks; "Big Fish, Small Pond," who go cross-country skiing; "Boomtown Singles," who watch MTV; "White Picket Fences," who eat at fast-food restaurants selected by kids; and "Traditional Times," who drive a Buick Park Avenue. (Claritas provides a summary of demographic segments by postal code on its Web site as a free sample of its work.)

Few retailers or GIS analysts have the capability to do more than the simplest "thematic" maps, but to be useful, a demographic map has to: 1.) identify the unique attributes of your potential customer base; 2.) generate the actual shape of the customer population mass;

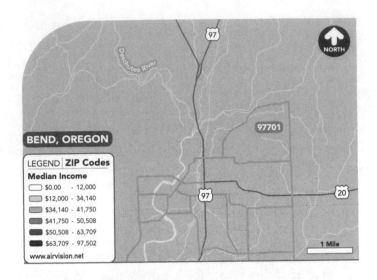

FIGURE 13-1

Even using six income brackets, a postal code-based map (top) provides no meaningful information on where potential customers actually live in the 97701 zip code: The result is a uniformly gray map. Further, the map's census-based data is too old to apply to a rapidly growing region such as Bend, Oregon. A suitability map (bottom), based on current data, specific customer demographics, vehicle traffic, and other demand generators, creates "hot spots" (darkest regions) showing locations likely to draw the right customers. Awbrey Butte, a high-income area in the left center, is clearly visible, as are a number of intersections that would make potentially good store locations.

and 3.) reflect the true travel patterns of the trade area—the way in which people actually circulate to shop and work. In fact, a sophisticated methodology exists to combine demographics, traffic, and other factors to identify concept-derived trade areas, and sometimes even specific locations within the trade areas in a particular MSA. This approach enables a model to be built based on a number of factors that tie suitable customer characteristics to location. Customer characteristics vary according to concept and to your brand positioning, so the factors chosen to build the "suitability model" can vary considerably. Unlike a simple thematic map, the suitability model pinpoints the *number* of likely customers for a concept as well as the *actual distribution* of those customers in a trade area. Like radar maps of weather, the resulting map uses color to indicate different levels of intensity for well-defined customers and other positive attributes ("demand generators") in the area. The densest areas show up in red, creating what we call a "hot spot"—an intensity of customers and other positives that reflect the likelihood of success in a particular trade area. In addition to determining the size and shape of the trade zones, the map might also determine, to use our example, that Houston has only 15 trade areas strong enough to support your stores even though the city population should theoretically support 20. The use of suitability factors creates meaningful results that aid in locating a store.

Because the sophistication of market analysts varies considerably, you should ask about the methodologies used before you commission any demographic analysis, and you should look carefully at any data that an analyst presents. Anything based strictly on postal codes, as we've shown, requires another level of analysis. Specific criteria vary according to the concept, but the demographic analysis should include at least the following data to produce any kind of meaningful results:

- The income levels and the household size and makeup of the population living and working within the trade area, according to where they actually live.
- The day- and night-time population that fits with your concept.
- The number of businesses within the area.
- The number and sales volume of competitors and where they are versus your possible locations.

- The major retail establishments, how they relate to your concept, and whether they are bad or good for you. You want to know if a Wal-Mart or Best Buy is the anchor store in a neighborhood, or if the anchor store is a Target store. In reviewing malls, Nordstrom's or Saks Fifth Avenue anchors indicate a higher-income mall position versus JCPenney or Sears.
- Traffic patterns according to residents, workers, shoppers, and passers-by and how they relate to your category and concept.

Determining Traffic and Traffic Flow

After identifying the hot spots for your concept, you need to understand traffic flow and how it affects your concept. Good flow can make a hot spot even more attractive, whereas poor flow can offset the positive features of an area. For example, a breakfast café must be properly located to take advantage of the "going-to-work" side of the road to capture the commuter trips in the morning day-part, whereas a quick-serve restaurant benefits from morning, noon, and evening traffic and the number of shopping trips. Dry cleaners should be located on the going-to-work side of the street; video stores should be on the going-home side. You should be located on the side of the road that has more traffic at the time of day when people are most likely to stop in your store. Because weekend traffic flow can be radically different than work-day traffic flow, make sure you know what the weekend traffic flow is and how that will affect you. Some soft-goods or clothing retail shops cater to non-working women. Others cater to working women. Which clientele is present in this area? Do workers in this area leave at the end of day or stay to visit restaurants and shops in the evening? Do returning workers stop at the restaurants and shops on their way to their nearby homes? Do businesses cater to transients—travelers who pull off the highway to eat or spend the night? A few years ago, a Bread & Circus store that opened in Wellesley, Massachusetts seemed perfectly positioned for traffic from Newton, an adjacent town whose demographics fit the company's ideal customer profile. However, traffic patterns did not bring those shoppers past the site. Residents traveled in the other direction instead, to Chestnut Hill and Boston. People rarely change their traffic patterns. You have to account for *where they go* more than *where they are*. Do not try to go against the flow. The odds of changing behavior patterns are against you. Why take the risk? Access also shapes traffic flow. Two streets may have the same vehicle count but see dramatically different effective levels of *customer* traffic because of access. The same may be true of two parts of the same shopping center regarding vehicle access, or two streets regarding pedestrian traffic. Vehicle traffic patterns affect some concepts more than others, and site analysis should take into account the interplay of roads and traffic flow according to the concept category.

Related to *where they go* is how long it takes customers to get there. Success of a concept will depend on the driving distance—or, more precisely, the driving time—from various points to the potential location. Customer visits decline directly with the customer's drive distance/time from the store. In lightly congested areas, distance works as a measure. In highly congested areas, drive time is the necessary measure because a mile in one direction might take two minutes whereas a mile in the opposite direction might take five minutes. If an area is lightly congested today, evaluate growth and probable traffic trends. If one stretch of a major highway has good vehicle flow but nearby stretches are beginning to go bumper-to-bumper, the odds are that congestion will soon create delays on this stretch too.

Varying by concept and traffic congestion, customer "decay"—the loss of customers over distance or travel time—can be determined from customer surveys or from customer databases that provide addresses. Generally, the less expensive or less specialized the product, the shorter the distance (time) customers are willing to drive to get there. The more specialized or expensive the product, the longer the distance (time) customers will drive. How surprised should we be at Starbucks' capability to locate stores close together in major cities? After all, how far are you willing to walk for a cup of coffee? Quick-serve restaurants, the epitome of convenient restaurants, define the main trade area in terms of a three-minute drive time. The outermost size of a trade area for any one store location is a seven-minute drive. Recreational vehicle dealers, on the other hand, can expect customers to drive from one to several hours. These characteristics define "convenience" and "destination" concepts, respectively, and dictate factors such as store proximity and cannibalization for a multi-unit retailer, competitive impact, and network optimization. Network optimization is the number of stores in a given trade area. Alhough there is a continuum between convenience and destination concepts, most retailers can be classified in one category or the other.

Thus, a combination of demographics, natural or manmade barriers, and drive times or distances together define the shape of the trade area, or retail trade zone, for a particular concept. This shape is usually referred to as a trade area "polygon," although an accurate rendition more closely resembles an amoeba. Hot-spot analysis and traffic flow identify the particular areas within this trade area that are most likely to lead to a successful store location. The more specific the data, the better the results, as the next section illustrates.

Seeking Proxies and Other Nuggets

Bringing all the demographic factors together in a meaningful way depends greatly upon the intuition and experience of the analyst. Disposable income is an important measure for any luxury item, whether small or large, but there is no one direct measure of disposable income, for example. Even high overall income can be misleading because $100,000 a year does not go nearly as far in San Francisco, California, or New York as it does in Peoria, Illinois, or Peoria, Arizona. Context means a lot in demographics. One way to find meaningful factors is to search for a proxy, in which sales of one item stand for sales in another. For grocery stores, bread is a proxy for milk and other staples. For certain kinds of apparel, the money spent on eyewear might apply. For every concept, sales of related consumer products might indicate a buying preference. Sales of Starbucks coffee in an urban area might indicate a good market for other small luxury items, an affinity for gourmet foods, or a busy morning trade area. For drugstores, the amount of money spent on hair spray might strongly correlate to a basket of other products, so hairspray is a proxy or an "indicator species" for the many similar sundries that drugstores sell. Tracking one critical item is less costly and less complicated than identifying or tracking multiple variables. (It is for this reason that biologists focus on a single species to gauge the overall health of a forest ecosystem. If a particular

owl population is healthy, then the forest and all its wildlife populations are healthy.)

Real estate people tend to have a "windshield view of the world"—
they have confidence in what they can observe directly. They may focus
too much on one physical factor and ignore other intermediating issues. Sometimes it's hard to convince them that a specific but seemingly
unrelated attribute may be the defining characteristic for real estate
selection. Sometimes the factor is a solid demographic trait, such as
household income. Sometimes the factor is a proxy. Sometimes the
factor is an artifact of population density, such as an occupational category that relates to store sales for certain concepts. For example, pro-
tective service is a rare occupation that appears only when population
density reaches a certain point. Its presence signals a population of
middle income, blue-collar households in dense suburban trade areas,
and the occupation serves as a positive indicator for concepts that appeal to this demographic.

You never know what the one factor may be, and sometimes you
can't explain it even when you know what it is. In the Midwest markets for Starbucks several years ago, a high correlation existed between
coffee sales and Hispanic households within three miles of a store.
When we told the real estate group to focus on areas with concentra-
tions of Hispanics, their reaction was, "Huh?" We told them, "Trust
us." Our team had evaluated more than 400 demographic characteristics around stores, slicing the data in every conceivable way. No matter
how we cut the data, one pattern emerged: We had higher sales near
Hispanic households. The conclusion was not that Hispanics drank
more coffee than everyone else. We couldn't even prove that Hispanics
represented a strong consumer base for us then. We concluded that the
presence of Hispanic families related to areas that were becoming more
cosmopolitan and the Hispanics happened to be the one population
among several that was large enough to demonstrate a correlation.
This factor correlated strongly with the sales of current stores, so we
had high confidence that it would predict the sales of future stores. It
didn't matter what was actually behind the factor—today, the presence
of Asian-Americans might serve as the bellwether, or a rise in median
income—it only mattered that at this moment in time this one variable
was a *defining* characteristic. An experienced market analyst constantly

pours over data to find such indicators, however oblique they might seem at first glance. The two lessons here are: 1.) don't look only for the obvious and exclude real learning; 2.) update your demographic models relative to the speed with which you grow your portfolio or to the speed of demographic change around stores.

From the five or six most important factors that define success, including any non-obvious ones, the analyst builds the suitability model for a particular concept. The hot spots generated by the analysis show the trade areas in which these factors are concentrated together. In preparing a site selection model for one client, for example, we had a variety of metrics, only two of which might be considered "standard": the number of households in certain income brackets and the distance of a site from a major highway. The other elements included locations relative to certain kinds of shopping districts or centers, locations relative to certain other retailers, and some intangibles that our experience has taught us, including a certain kind of traffic flow and the need for a store to be in an area with a growing economy. In another situation, we identified six variables to evaluate in our database: income, population density, casual dining dollars spent, amount of education, property values (a proxy for disposable income), and the number of potential competitors in the market and their locations relative to major roads. For another, the variables were traffic density, the "Pools & Patio" households and a similar demographic segment, the consumer spending for a certain product, and the density of favorable co-tenants. Among the other benefits, the use of multiple variables reinforces the rule that you should never locate a store based on only one source of customers.

Different demographics lead to different "hot spots" for every concept. Potbelly's demographics take it to high-traffic locations in fashionable neighborhoods, preferably close to high-end grocery stores or retailers, such as Pottery Barn or J. Crew. This ensures a steady stream of its core customer of young professionals with disposable income. Oakley, which benefits from high pedestrian traffic and the presence of other major brands, may locate on the highest traffic areas in upper-tier malls, such as Bellevue Square in Bellevue, Washington, or on the busiest high-end retail shopping streets, such as Rush Street in Chicago.

For most retailers, hot-spot mapping at the trade area level is sufficient before you begin to search for specific locations for a store. At this point, you have a good idea of the neighborhoods in which you can succeed, and it really doesn't matter which one. Your strategy will be to find the one best location of all the neighborhoods. For a mature retailer that seeks to in-fill submarkets within an MSA or trade areas, the hot spots need to zoom in more tightly, possibly down to particular intersections. In this case, you're looking for *where else* in the neighborhood you can succeed without cannibalizing sales of existing stores.

Eyeballing Oil Stains: A Street-Level Look at Locations

At Starbucks, I would send the hot-spot maps to my field people and say, "I'm coming out in two weeks. Drive me around the areas indicated in red on these maps." Today, before driving through the different red zones to seek out available targets for clients, I often take an extra step. Several vendors now provide inexpensive aerial photo-mapping software. You can view on your PC areas of town, intersections, or individual street addresses in most major cities. You can rotate the view to look up or down a street or tilt the perspective to observe a property from different angles. An aerial view enables you to see the physical density and height of surrounding buildings, the layout of streets and arterials, and the proximity of the site to highways, rivers, parks, and other physical boundaries. Such a preliminary view will help to eliminate properties that have obvious drawbacks and to prioritize the ones you actually want to see. But nothing—neither terrific demographic analysis nor the equivalent of spy-satellite surveillance—substitutes for inspecting each location in person.

Before setting out, you should write down your criteria for site selection. You'll be more definitive about your needs and you'll be less likely to waver if you see something appealing but off strategy. Remember: Establish your criteria and do not be swayed from them. Stay disciplined! For Omaha Steaks, our real estate strategy was to obtain highly visible, brand-building stores that would reinforce product positioning with consumers. This strategy meant that we would not settle for something set back from the street or in line in a typical shopping center, where we might be lost among other storefronts. We would strategically locate a *network* of stores to achieve the market penetration we needed in the right demographic areas, usually higher density corridors.

The criteria must be centered on the hot spots. The red zone represents a Grade A trade area, the densest concentration of potential customers. The next-densest layer, yellow, is a Grade B trade area. Green is average. The thinnest layer, blue, would be ignored by most retailers. Particular locations are also rated A or B or worse according to your real estate selection criteria. A mature retailer can have a Grade A location in a Grade B trade area, or a Grade B location in a Grade A trade area, but never a Grade B location in a Grade B trade area. A new retailer—one without an established brand—should take only Grade A locations in Grade A trade areas. When a real estate broker wants to take me outside a red zone, I generally decline, but I also apply common sense. If there is a great intersection on the edge of a red zone, but not actually in it, will I take it? Assuming that the site is on an arterial used by the target demographic as they come to and from the red zone, and assuming that the site is appealing in other ways (visibility, access, and so on), then sure, I will take it. Also, remember that even the freshest data cannot take into account new, fast-growing areas, so the great intersection might actually be in a newly emerging red zone.

In visiting each trade area and each potential site, observe your surroundings from two points of view. The first is the view of the businessperson: What evidence is there that the area and location will generate the sales you need? The second is the view of the customer: Would you come here to this location to shop? Both of these perspectives take a certain amount of street sense.

Recently I was evaluating real estate for a person on the East Coast. He was reasonably satisfied with the sales volume of a particular store in the shopping center and didn't necessarily believe me when I told him a better site in the trade area would improve sales. I took him to the far reaches of the parking lot and asked him to describe the asphalt pavement of the parking stalls. It took him a few moments to understand what I wanted. Finally, he said, "The pavement's pretty clean." Then I took him a few blocks away to the shopping center housing his main competitor. I felt that location was much better because of the co-tenancy. We inspected the parking stalls on the outer edges of the competitor's parking lot. The asphalt had oil stains. "They're dirty," he said. I asked him, "And so my dear Watson, what may we deduce from the evidence?"

"More cars park out here in this lot," he said. He pondered this fact a bit more and said, "Damn." The presence of oil stains in the *outer* parking area meant that his competitor's lot was full of cars far more often than his own. The competitor had far more business. More people were coming and going to this center than to his center because of the draw of other stores.

When you're looking for a location in your own town, you can stake out an area for intense examination. You can measure the traffic during the morning, afternoon, evening, and weekend day parts. You can count the number of people entering stores or the number of cars in the parking lot. In a perfect world, you would always do your due diligence for all the day-parts: weekdays and nights, weekend days and nights. However, outside your local area, perfection is seldom possible. Having to do a site evaluation on a Wednesday morning instead of a Saturday evening or another potentially busy time, you must take advantage of various "unobtrusive measures" to determine whether one particular physical site meets your needs or whether the surrounding area matches the demographic profile the analysts claim is there. (Some areas turn over rapidly. In Los Angeles, it's not unusual for a neighborhood to shift from Caucasian to African-American, then to Asian or Latino in a matter of a few years.)

One way to check out a neighborhood is to see the mix of clothes that are hanging on the racks of the local dry cleaner. If shirts predominate, you can deduce that this probably is not a high-volume cleaners and it does not draw a high-income customer. A variety of jackets, suits, coats, and women's clothes, on the other hand, indicate a high-income neighborhood because people wear more elaborate clothing professionally or socially. People need to have their clothes cleaned more often and they have the money to pay for it.

I learned this and other street-wise rules from Michael Epsteen, a long-time friend who has spent a lifetime in the real estate business in California. Michael was my partner in the late 1980s and to me remains the guru of real estate locationing. It was Michael who taught me to check the specialty sections of supermarkets for the extensiveness of ethnic foods, as both a reality check to what the data says about local demographics and as a way to determine whether the area has an investigational palate—one willing to try new foods. He's not the only one to use such observations. In its early days, before the rise of modern demographics, McDonald's had no direct way to measure the number of children in an area. To help determine new locations, the fast-food chain measured the length of the milk aisles in supermarkets, milk being their proxy for the number of kids around.

Michael has other rules too. *Don't fall in love with a piece of real estate.* Instead, use objective measures to determine whether a particular piece of land suits your needs. *Never use the word never.* People judge real estate based on their own experience in other markets. Someone who comes to Los Angeles from the Midwest might see a property and say, "I'd never take that." In reality, because of the peculiarity of the trade area, the property might work fine. After a while, they'll come back to it. Or after their brand takes hold, it might make for a great second or third location. *Don't listen to anyone else (including yourself).* By that Michael means to be open-minded about every location. Learn the trade area. Don't prejudge a property or the neighborhood. The location might be perfect for your specific opportunity. Let the property speak for itself, again according to its objective merits

You don't want to listen to anyone else in another way, too. That is, don't become enamored with a site because someone else has found the location to be successful. This herd-induced form of falling in love with real estate happens so often that I call it the "fools-rush-in" phenomenon. I continually see a drugstore locate on a corner and then another one move in and another one after that. Then they all wonder why they are struggling. It's true that sometimes the presence of multiple competitors helps everyone's business by drawing more total customers. It happens with coffee houses and consumer electronics stores, among others. The Home Depot and Lowe's tend to end up close together, at least partly because both require at least ten acres of land and city zoning tends to put such parcels near one another. In addition, each has a somewhat different target customer. Lowe's caters to a do-it-yourselfer and its customer service draws more women. The Home Depot has a larger following among contractors, although it is trying to catch up to Lowe's among weekender types. Automobile dealers discovered that congregating in the same corridor causes sales to go up.

Cars are differentiated by size, design, and price. Starbucks and the local coffee vendor draw different crowds. Consumer electronics stores differentiate themselves by product selection, brand, and price. There is always a *reason* for this kind of synergy to occur, usually based on differentiation. Don't just go *there* because everyone else has. Understand the dynamics of your particular market and competition. Watch for the phenomenon of a trade area being over-retailed or overfed. Look for the underserved markets.

Let me give you an example. In the small town of Bellingham, Washington, I did a site analysis of a small piece of real estate located near Western Washington University. This site was close to the usual array of quick-serve restaurants that surround a college: McDonald's, International House of Pancakes, Denny's, two Vietnamese restaurants, a Chinese restaurant, plus a higher-priced Kobe Japanese restaurant. The site in question was a former Burger King, which had recently relocated nearby. A fool would have rushed into this area to put in another fast-food restaurant, and I knew that several people were interested in the property for just that. But in carefully observing all of the restaurants at the dinner hour, I found that the Kobe restaurant had a full parking lot and people standing in line to be seated. The next-most crowded restaurant was a mid-price steak house across the street. None of the quick-serve restaurants was that busy; the trade area had too many of them. The right concept was not another fast-feeder but a nice sit-down restaurant featuring Asian cuisine or steaks. The higher quality, medium-price restaurant concept was the one concept in this trade area that was underserved.

It doesn't pay to be the fool that rushes in where you see people in your category or your direct competitor do well. Locate close to a competitor only if you can differentiate yourself. Rather than be just another drugstore, offer mailing or copying services. Find a way to draw from a different target audience (seniors, college kids, urban professionals). And, of course, if you're *First In*, the first store of that type, provide a variety of services to preclude a competitor from coming in with value-added services that you are not offering, and make sure that your store's location cannot be outpositioned by a competitor coming in after you.

Approaching Your Location Like a First Date

After you have done your homework, the best demographic report to use is your own knowledge of the street. Every piece of real estate, every storefront, and every shopping center and mall has its own personality. Some factors cannot be measured other than by a personal visit. No demographic models, for instance, measure the amount or convenience of parking near a location. Criteria in hand, you head out to every potential location. Approach each site as you would a first date. Be interested but skeptical. No matter how much you prepare, no matter how much you've heard, you can't know whether things will work out until you come face to face with a new person—or a new location. You want it to be really good, but you also want to be ready to walk away if it's not a good fit.

Always check first for traffic, vehicular and pedestrian. Does the location take advantage of the vehicular traffic on the street? Every city in the U.S. measures Average Daily Traffic (ADT) on its arterial streets. Never get even one block off from the road on which you are basing the site's traffic count. You want to put your sign and your storefront in the face of as many potential customers as possible. If the rent seems too expensive, consider some portion of the cost to be marketing dollars rather than space dollars. A store doesn't just sell things; it builds name and brand recognition. Within each and every shopping center, different locations provide different levels of visibility. A position on the end of the center (an "end cap") with excellent street visibility is usually desirable, but an end cap set back from the road may not be. A good site serves as a marketing billboard. A storefront set back away from the main street, or angled in a way that customers on the road cannot see it, is a lost marketing opportunity. A sign that customers see regularly becomes part of the "pattern recognition language" in their brain. Because they see your shop every day driving by, they will recall your service when they need it. Most of the time a corner site is best. A corner doubles the visual opportunity for registering your brand in the customer's mind. It also provides additional light and views of your patrons. Corners are very good for restaurant concepts.

Customers also must have easy access to your store. Does a left-turn lane or an intersection with a signal enable people to turn into your location quickly and safely? Is there so much congestion that customers have trouble *leaving* your store? You don't want to give anyone a reason not to stop. Consider tradeoffs carefully. One location might be on the correct side of the street for your concept, but another might have superior visibility and co-tenancy. Choosing the latter might be the best bet, especially if the presence of other major tenants has already "trained" customers into making a left turn into the center. Is there sufficient parking for customers close to your location? Seniors do not like to carry bundles farther than necessary. Other considerations include the overall quality of the area, in terms of both the age and conditions of the buildings, the cleanliness and attractiveness of the streets, the amount and quality of business traffic (vehicle and pedestrian), and the crime rate.

Visibility is the number one consideration for most concepts. First from a distance, then from up close, imagine your concept in that space. Are there great sight lines? Once your name is on the fascia, will it stand out? Will drivers be able to see your sign from the street? Will pedestrians, from the sidewalk or from other parts of the center see it? Does the building design provide a clean sign bank on which to install your sign? Understand the local signage codes and the landlord's signage code and your ability to obtain a sign variance. If the center has uniform signage, it is unlikely that you will be able to get your sign in your colors or even possibly in your logo typeface. If the façade is dark colored, such as brick construction, you want to be allowed to install a lighter color sign so the contrast makes the sign readable from farther away. If possible, negotiate placement of your name on a "monument" sign located on the street, or a free-standing pylon sign that has only your store name on it.

Now, compare all of these factors against other locations in the same area. Could a competitor locate on the opposite corner or on the opposite side of the shopping center or farther down the street and siphon off customers before they reach your store? At Starbucks, we talked about using strategic locations to "control the customer opportunity." Other experts talk of intercepting the flow of customers or "capturing the wind." In a race, a sailboat can position itself to block the wind from its competitor. Without the wind, the other boat loses speed. The same thing can happen with one store versus another. A competitor can pick a site so that the prevailing customer flow passes by that store first instead of yours. The ability to siphon off sales is why corner locations in central business districts are so highly coveted, though one corner can be substantially better or worse than another because of the direction of traffic. If you can cut off customers from an existing or potential competitor, then you have the strategic location. If the competitor can cut you off, then the competitor has the strategic location and you should look elsewhere—to a better site in this neighborhood or to another trade area entirely. Always look at a potential location with an eye toward competitor positioning. You want to be reasonably sure that you cannot be out-flanked.

After you are certain that the site will enable you to stay "upwind" of any competitor, then observe the kind of care that has been taken with the architecture and design. Does the location seem to "read" retail use? Is it appealing to you? Even strip malls, which tend to be similar in layout and design, have major differences in quality. Is the quality of the building at least as good as the quality of your product? Always consider the architecture from a brand-building standpoint. When Starbucks first moved into Boston, I wanted a particular location in an old building in the historic Beacon Hill neighborhood, so much so that I had to talk the landlord into it. He had never heard of Starbucks and was not aware of our product quality or financial strength.

Previously this site had been a convenience store, which made it underutilized in terms of the quality of the physical environment it offered and the building's personality. This location had two strong disadvantages. The first was the neighborhood association's restriction on signage. Starbucks couldn't use its trademark green; the store name had to be non-illuminated letters in gold on a black background. I was fine with that; the gold and black would be elegant against the limestone facade of the building. The more serious concern was that customers had to walk up a few steps to enter the store. The entrance to your store should be welcoming. Unlike an apartment building, where you want to convey an element of privacy, a retail store should never have steps up or down. Also be considerate of the ease of access. A double-door entry generally works much better for customers than a single-door entry. Why make it difficult for pedestrians to enter your store, especially when they're often carrying packages? Why make it difficult for pedestrians to leave, when you hope they're carrying even more packages—or a hot cup of coffee? There should be a seamless connection between the sidewalk and the store. Never, ever take a space down any stairs. Except for a speak-easy, any location below grade is always associated with a "bargain basement."

Only one time in a 100 should you take a space that requires shoppers to go up stairs. This was that one time. The location was a Beacon Hill corner across from the city's Public Gardens and close to the State House. The site presented the brand to a huge audience of local residents, workers, and tourists. The quality of the location, the quality of the building, the quality of the surrounding tenants: Everything about the location created the kind of brand statement that Starbucks wanted to make, in a neighborhood representing the crème de la crème of our demographic profile. Real estate should never take away from a brand's positioning. Real estate should always support the brand. This location dramatically reinforced our brand in this new market. It remains our flagship store in Boston.

Knowing Who You're Next To

In retailing, you are judged by the company you keep. Customers assume that stores located next to one another carry similar quality of goods. The company you keep also determines your sales. If you are selling the same kind of goods that Sears carries, the best location for you is in the Sears parking lot! You should find a subset of what they do, do it better than they can, and leverage their sales and marketing to pick off customers on their way to Sears. Co-locating with similar brands is so important that some location strategies become parasitical. For many years the Fashion Bug, a women's soft-goods retailer, had as its expansion strategy nothing more than "find the K" in every city. If Kmart had a successful store somewhere, Fashion Bug knew that it needed to be in the same area, preferably the same shopping center, to sell to the same blue-collar demographic.

It is fairly easy to determine what demographic a shopping center draws, and therefore the message that it sends to the marketplace. A center that has as the anchor tenant a high-end grocery store such as Whole Foods Market in the eastern U.S. sends a different message about quality and price than a center with a thrift shop or hardware store as the anchor tenant. I have seen high-end dress shops in malls that cater to blue-collar customers such as those that frequent the

Fashion Bug or Dress Barn. The owners opted for the less expensive rent, assuming incorrectly that customers would come to them despite the lack of other shops that appealed to their tastes. Co-tenancy is as important as location and building presentation. Never locate near tenants who target a less affluent customer than you do. Always seek to locate near tenants who target a "better" customer than you do and attract more of them.

At Starbucks, we were careful to select sites alongside established high-quality retailers in highly visible corridors convenient to the everyday shopping experience. Seeking "the corner of Main and Main"—the best corner of the best intersection of a particular shopping area, whether it was the central business district, an urban shopping street, or a suburban mall—we avoided locations with proximity to fast-food restaurants that might devalue our name and our brand positioning. When we started, coffee was associated with cheap food. Landlords did not believe we could pay the monthly rent selling single cups of coffee. Nor did they believe we would have the kind of customers they would want next to their existing upper-end tenants. When we showed them the quality of our store designs, the demographics of our customers, and most important our financials, they quickly changed their minds. After a few years, landlords were coming to us. They wanted us to anchor a corner of their street or shopping center. The quality of our brand created a cachet that not only drew customers but other high-quality tenants as well. In fact, during my tenure at Starbucks, I ran across an article saying that people were buying homes in up-and-coming neighborhoods in Portland, Oregon, using Starbucks' location strategy as an "indicator species." If we opened in neighborhoods, people figured it must be a good place to live. Our investment convinced them that the area was a safe investment for them too. I had sensed that this phenomenon was happening, and the article confirmed it. We weren't just bringing in customers or co-tenants but new *residents* to the area!

Another consideration of co-tenancy is *draw*. Starbucks preferred to locate stores near video stores and dry cleaners because each of these has a two-stop store visit: one to drop off, one to pick up. Both also tie in to the morning day-part, the peak time for coffee sales. A post office or UPS Store is another wonderful traffic generator. Regional stores, such as The Home Depot and Target, can bring a lot of traffic your way, but you must be physically close to their front door to benefit. If you are on the far end of the shopping center or around the corner, the location may not do you much good. You may be better off in a nearby center with great visibility, where customers see you on their way to and from the regional store.

To make the evaluation as objective as possible, consider using a simple rating system for the major attributes of a store location. On a scale of 1 to 5, with 5 being the highest, you can grade a site on all the things we've discussed: the general quality of the neighborhood, the quality of the shopping center or storefront, vehicle traffic volume, visibility, ease of access by vehicles, ease of access by pedestrians, availability of parking, number and quality of co-tenants, and other customer generators such as a nearby major office building or other shopping center, and any other factors you deem relevant. If a location scores poorly across the board, forget it. If the location scores generally well but has one or two poor ratings, think carefully before proceeding. Perhaps the area is not the greatest, but traffic volumes and flow more than compensate. That may be fine, but you would want to do more research to determine whether the area is rising or declining. Objectively evaluate each shortcoming to ensure that other criteria (including the fact that the area may improve in the future) more than make up for any shortcomings.

Using Analogue Stores to Confirm New Store Financials

After you have made your preliminary site selection, based on all the issues we have covered, you still need to ensure that the store will succeed economically. Fortunately, you can combine the demographic techniques described here with the financial history of existing stores to predict the probable results of stores in new areas. Building the sales estimate is the final necessary step to ensure that the new store location will provide the proper return on investment. The analogue store report, as it is known, compares and contrasts the proposed new location with stores in similar trade areas according to demographics, co-tenants, other nearby shopping centers, office buildings, military bases, and similar traffic generators. Based on the sales of the analogue stores, and adjusted for any differences, you can predict the sales of the new store. (A small retailer expanding locally can pick a major retailer that has a similar concept to provide the "analogue" or comparison stores, deducing the big company's siting strategy and approximate sales figures from published data and direct observation. See also Chapter 10, "Kicking the Economic Model Into Gear," on the topic of the economic model.)

Typically we create three categories of analogues from existing company stores. The first is a store that best matches the demographics of the proposed store location. The second is a store in an area that has, within a one-mile radius, a population closest to that around the planned store. The third is the retailer's nearest store, if there is a store in the same trade area. For the analogue stores, we pull all the data related to the factors that drive success. Usually these are the same factors we put together to initially select the new site. For one client, the one-mile and ten-mile customer draws were important factors, so we looked at the total population within the one-mile and ten-mile radius as well as the daytime population. We also broke down the number of the demographic segments that supported the concept and the total populations that these segments comprised. We also took into account the major co-tenants at each store, including the proposed one, the respective traffic counts on each road, and the number of nearby shopping centers for each.

We then looked at respective sales. The store with the best demographic fit to the proposed store also happened to be the lowest performing store. The reasons were clear when all the data were lined up. The lowest performing store had only one-third of the nearby population, one-fourth of the number of households, and one-tenth of the daytime population. For our comparison purposes, we chose to disregard it. Two other analogue stores were doing close to $900,000 in business, and the existing store in the same trade area was doing close to $940,000 in sales. The new location was superior to the other locations according to several of the criteria described in this chapter. In particular, the site was in a new shopping center located at a major intersection that benefited from the presence of a regional mall, and co-tenants included a major grocery chain, a bed and bath store, a movie theater, and a music store. No one analogue store had all of these traffic generators. Given the sales of the existing stores, we could confidently predict that the new store would do $1 million in annual sales. In fact, we believe that the store has tremendous growth potential compared to the others, although for planning purposes, we kept our financial projections conservative.

With enough units, data on existing store sales will enable you to tune your financial projections for new stores according to the quality of location. Among your next five stores, you may end up with two stores in average locations by your criteria; two stores in above average locations; and one store in an excellent location. By analyzing existing sales, you discover that an above-average store does 10 percent more business than an average store, and an excellent store does 20 percent more. Assuming $1 million in average store sales, you can estimate with reasonable certainty that the total actual revenue from the five stores ($1.0 million, $1.0 million, $1.1 million, $1.1 million, and $1.2 million) will be $5.4 million total rather than $5 million. To once again emphasize the importance of location, the additional revenue generated from above-average and excellent locations for similar-sized stores represents *pure profit*—all the stores will have approximately the same operating costs. If a store in an excellent location underperforms, you know to look carefully at how well it is being operated.

Similarly, this kind of financial analysis by location and demographics provides valuable data if your concept should ever stumble or an economic recession causes you to retrench. One multibillion-dollar retailer had never seen a need for extensive location-oriented analysis until circumstances forced it to close more than 50 stores. At that point, the company realized that it did not have the systems in place to peel back its expansion. It did not have a precise definition of its customer base or where the customers came from. It could not say what was driving profitability in various locations. If it closed a store in location "X," it could not determine whether the customers would probably shift to nearby location "Y," or whether the customers would be lost entirely. Nor could it predict which locations had the greatest growth potential. In the analogue stores example, if the question were which store to close, the answer would be readily apparent. The lowest performing store would be closed, not because of low sales but because poor demographics (one-third of the nearby population, one-fourth of the number of households, one-tenth of the daytime population) made growth unlikely. As you might have surmised, this store had opened without the benefit of careful demographic analysis. Even barring a rollback, the store would be a candidate for relocation or closing as part of a regular review of the company's real estate portfolio.

Investing in Knowledge to Drive Growth

Finding the best location in a particular town, especially one with which you are not familiar, is never easy. Doing it right takes time and money, but it will make you money and save you grief further down the road. One of several books on the topic will help you get started by showing you how professionals evaluate real estate for retail stores. *Location, Location, Location,* by Luigi Salvaneschi, who was president of Blockbuster Video and before that the head of real estate development for McDonald's Corporation and KFC, provides a good insight into how major chains approach new market locations from both a strategic and a tactical perspective. Salvaneschi works through the process as if he were choosing the next few locations for his own company stores, covering everything from general trade areas to traffic flows to why the "far corner" of an intersection is usually better than the "near corner." *The Site Book: A Field Guide to Commercial Real Estate Evaluation*, by Richard M. Fenker, treats practical, on-the-ground site issues and how to use field surveys to ascertain every positive and negative aspect of any site. A third, *Site Selection: New Advancements in Methods and Technology*, by Robert W. Buckner, is relatively technical. The book discusses various models, consumer surveys, and other sophisticated analyses by which a retailer can assess trade areas and store siting.

Taking different approaches to the topic, the authors of these books all agree on three important points: 1.) analysis should begin at the national level and work down through the MSA and local trade areas before specific sites are evaluated; 2.) a well-thought-out methodology should be used to create specific site selection criteria; and 3.) any real estate plan should incorporate the idea of strategic positioning vis-á-vis competitors. Just as you used demographic analysis to initially select and prioritize MSAs, you use the same type of analysis to identify the best trade areas in each MSA. On-site inspections determine which location is the best among the many possible locations in each trade area. Carefully considered financial comparisons ensure that the proposed location(s) will generate the necessary return on investment. Chapter 14 provides detailed examples of how such combined effort improves site selection and increases the likelihood of success for any concept. It also shows how location affected one particular company in an unexpected way. Knowledge is power, and the more you know about the makeup of your customers and potential store locations, the more likely the sites will turn a powerful profit.

CHAPTER 14

A Walk Through the Locationing Process

THE PREVIOUS TWO CHAPTERS delved deeply into the methodology a retailer should follow to expand into new markets. This chapter provides specific examples of work that we have done with businesses to find the best metropolitan areas for expansion and the best locations within those areas. The actual data is disguised for reasons of confidentiality and has been consolidated to portray a single fictitious company, but the problems are typical of many retailers and the analysis tracks exactly the process we have followed many, many times. The numbers used to describe Metropolitan Statistical Areas (MSAs), the number of stores in various trade areas, the number of competitors, and similar data are purposely chosen to represent ranges that apply to many companies. The same is true for the dollar amounts used in store sales. Obviously, numbers for your concept could vary considerably, but any demographic analysis you commission should achieve the same depth of analysis, obtain a similar level of detail, and enable a well-informed set of decisions about expansion and relocation.

Our featured company is Opportunity, Inc., which sells high-end consumer soft goods. It has a number of stores in both small and large markets, and the performance of those stores has been spotty. Like many other retailers, its expansion had been somewhat helter-skelter. Before embarking on a major expansion, the company sought a complete reexamination of its real estate selection process. "Save us from ourselves" is how one company executive explained the task.

It is not sufficient to rank potential expansion areas in order by population size or income levels, although both elements play a role and income is often a deciding factor. The goal is to create identifiable tiers according to your selection criteria so that you end up with a reasonable number of top MSAs on which you can initially concentrate. Some analysts create two tiers. Our own methodology is to use four. We find that a model with four tiers does a good job of predicting store performance, particularly in tiers 1 and 2. The specific cut point for income to create a tier depends on the concept. A concept appealing to a lower income demographic would use a lower income number to sort the tiers; a concept appealing to a higher income demographic would use a higher income number.

Because the demographic is defined by other factors before tiers are created by income, sometimes the cut point varies considerably even for concepts that appeal to customers with similar income levels. Choosing the cut point therefore requires great care. Tiers defined by the number of customers with $100,000 in annual income, for example, would yield many fewer tier 1 markets than tiers defined in terms of $50,000 in annual income. The smaller yield might be positive if you needed to create focus, or if the product itself was expensive, such as with luxury vehicles or yachts. The smaller yield would be negative if the goal was rapid expansion because the model would generate too few target markets to fuel high growth. A high cut point might also create too many lower quality markets in tier 2; that is, you could end up with a tier 1 of ten markets and a tier 2 of 50 markets, which is too many to effectively prioritize. The same thing can happen if the cut point is too low—so many markets appear in tier 1 as to make the division meaningless. It can take time and effort by a skilled analyst to find the right balance; for example, the right balance might be a model that yields ten tier 1 markets and 20 tier 2 markets.

Our analysis for Opportunity, Inc., quickly identified four discrete market types. Tier 1 was an MSA with greater than 400,000 people who had high income, which equates to a propensity to spend. (Remember, the 400,000 figure is not an arbitrarily large number, but a cut point that comes directly from the demographics for this one concept and the need to create manageable tiers.) Tier 2 was an MSA with greater than 400,000 people and lower average income. Though tier 2 had fewer propensities to spend, the sheer size of the population provided enough concentration of high-income earners to make the areas attractive. Tier 3 was an MSA with high income and low population. Tier 4 was low population and lower income. The top two tiers provided 80 percent of Opportunity's revenue, and this was not because the top two tiers had more stores. In fact, Opportunity had only 67 stores in the top 75 MSAs.

Further analysis showed no regional differences in sales, but a wide variation according to tier. Nearly two-thirds of the weakest stores (which accounted for nearly half the total number of stores) were located in tier 3 and 4 MSAs. The weakest stores earned barely half the chain average. The per-store revenue for tier 1 and 2 stores was 20 percent higher than the overall chain average and was nearly three times that of the weakest stores. Further, we found a strong correlation between store revenue and the number of high-income households within eight miles of the store. More than one-third of Opportunity's stores, however, were located in areas with low income. The implication was that new locations could dramatically improve sales for a number of stores.

Our analysis showed how competitive their particular category is. Of the top 25 markets, five had 100 or more competitors. Another ten MSAs had 50 or more. Most others had between 25 and 50 competitors. Only a few MSAs had a small number of competitors, and these were not close to where Opportunity was well established and could support operationally. These latter MSAs would provide Opportunity a chance to capture untapped markets in future years, but they would not enable the company to improve its market position quickly. Overall, competitors left few openings to be exploited. Falling back on the fundamental idea of "fishing where the fish are," we recommended that Opportunity's short-term emphasis be to own a particular state—

in this case, Texas. Despite the presence of strong competitors, Opportunity's most profitable stores were there and it had the operational capability to support more. Four of its tier 1 MSAs and five of its tier 2 MSAs were located in that state. Its strategic drawback (here and elsewhere) was not the strength of its competition but an insufficient concentration of its own stores.

"Owning Texas" and bolstering its presence in the other top MSAs in the country would maximize sales as well as operational efficiency by putting a number of stores in close proximity. By siting 50 new stores in three years in MSAs with the greatest potential, we estimated, Opportunity could improve its sales by 13 percent per year, even if the new stores did no better than the current average store sales. If Opportunity could double the number of stores in three years in the correct MSAs—a stretch, but it was possible—and saw modest revenue increases in the new stores as the result of better locations, the company could increase its overall sales by at least 24 percent annually.

Prioritizing MSAs according to customer profiles and operational strength gave Opportunity an orderly way to proceed over the next several years as well as the greatest opportunity to turn around its retail business. Opening new stores provided the twin opportunities of expanding the core business while upgrading the brand through new store designs. Using the evaluation criteria developed for new stores, Opportunity was also able to create a systematic method to determine the future of existing stores. Opportunity agreed to close poor performing stores in areas that had poor demographics and therefore little likelihood of future growth. If a store was in a poor location but in an area with good demographics, we recommended relocation at the time of lease renewal—unless relocation would generate more revenue than the cost of terminating a lease, in which case an immediate move would occur.

Because Opportunity already had a number of stores in smaller markets, you might wonder why we did not recommend that Opportunity target the small-town market as Wal-Mart did with general retail merchandise. (Wal-Mart followed the *See Ya* strategy in overwhelming existing small merchants.) The answer is that Opportunity sold to a broad range of customers. Its stores were operating in a representative sample of cities of all sizes. When we analyzed the customer base, we found that the customers who chose Opportunity over its competitors

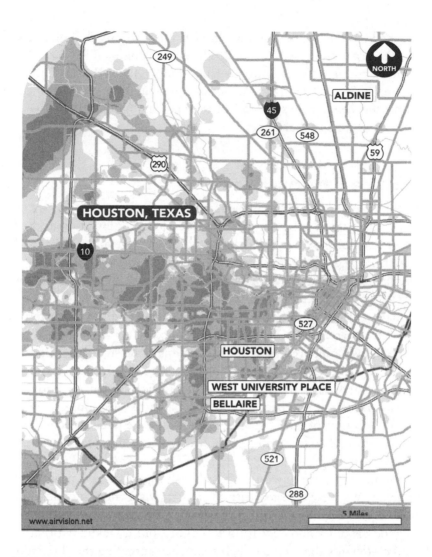

FIGURE 14-1

Based on the customer profile and competitive considerations for the company Opportunity, Inc., the city of Houston, Texas turned out to be a prime candidate for expansion. Demographic analysis identified a number of "hot spots" (darkest regions), indicating potentially good locations in the metropolitan area. Additional analysis would identify the best two or three trade areas for Opportunity's concept; Opportunity would select the best locations available within those areas. If this were the first store for the company in Houston, the specific trade area might not matter. However, if Opportunity already had stores in the city, then "hot spot" analysis would drill down perhaps as far as individual street intersections to determine the best places for the company to in-fill with stores without reducing sales at existing stores.

happened to be in major markets. In fact, Opportunity did relatively better in larger cities than in small. Thus, we recommended that Opportunity put new stores in top metropolitan areas. If the customers had been in Small Town, U.S.A.—or if Opportunity had determined to become *the destination* store in its category for small markets—we would have gone in that direction.

Picking a Particular Site

After we had chosen Texas as the targeted expansion territory, we examined each of the MSAs in the state. We identified Houston as the top market to enter based on the company's competitive and operational strengths. Using the methodology and demographics detailed in the preceding chapter, we developed a "hot spot" map of trade areas specific to that concept. The maps guided us to specific trade areas and sub-markets that contained good prospect sites based on the criteria we knew were correlated with store performance. After we identified these prospects, we compared them to existing analogue stores that had similar characteristics to validate our "on-the-ground" evaluation and to develop comparables-based sales forecasts. Finally, we were ready to examine the actual prospect sites to make a store selection. Chapter 3, "The Importance of the First Store," discusses site issues specific to a street location. The following example discusses site issues specific to a shopping center.

Our analysis pinpointed two possible shopping centers as worthy of pursuit. We were charged with the on-site inspection and recommendation as to which location was preferable. The first shopping center had good visibility and decent traffic counts, but it lacked national brand co-tenants that created high-frequency shopping that best supported Opportunity's concept. In addition, the shopping center was in the middle of a block, so it had limited turn access into it. The second shopping center had higher traffic counts and several national co-tenants that were attractive for the concept. In addition, the second center was located at an intersection with a signal, making access easy. These factors enabled us to quickly eliminate the first shopping center from consideration.

Another advantage of the second shopping center is that it offered three separate possible locations for the Opportunity store, so we visited the site to see which of the three potential areas of the shopping center would be best. All of the issues with the three sites and with the shopping center itself are representative of the issues that any retailer is likely to find in a typical shopping center, so we'll examine the possibilities in detail.

Figure 14-2 shows the three retail spaces available to rent at the center in the locations marked A, B, and C. The question for the client was which of the three would be best for a general retailer. In order, we looked at traffic, access, and co-tenancy. From our traffic database, we found that Rocket Road, running north to south on the left side, is a major artery carrying 50,000 vehicles a day. Yao Parkway, running east to west across the top, carries about 30,000 vehicles a day. The map of the shopping center had already showed us several things. Site A was in a corner location on the main building, close to Lum's Restaurant and Walgreens Drugs, which drew high-frequency customers, but there was no entrance close by. Site B had good access and visibility and had high-traffic stores on either side, but the store shape was long and skinny. Site C was located on Rocket Road, by far the busiest street, and had great visibility, but access was limited from Rocket Road. Touting its features, the shopping center landlord was eager to rent Opportunity one of the spaces at Site C. This space rented for $30 per square foot versus $24 for B and C, and usually rent is proportional to the quality of the space.

Many things jumped out at us during a personal inspection of the site that were not evident from the map. For Site A, we saw that Lum's and Walgreens took up all of the limited parking on the east side of the shopping center. Also, the Walgreens building would block Site A's store signage from Yao Parkway. For Site C, we saw that a lot of the traffic on Rocket Road came from people traveling east on Yao Parkway and turning north onto Rocket *before* they reached the center. The 50,000 vehicle count dropped dramatically on Rocket Road south of the intersection by the shopping center. The on-site inspection also showed why there was no access to the site from Rocket. The retail building was ten feet below the grade level of the road. Not only would customers not have access from the road, but a store also would not be nearly as visible from Rocket as we expected. (When a map shows the lack of an entrance on a street, there's always a physical reason, such as grade, or a practical reason, such as traffic congestion.)

TYPICAL SHOPPING CENTER SITE PLAN

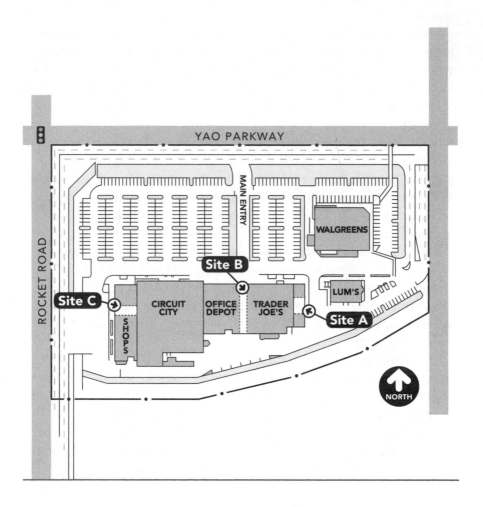

FIGURE 14-2

After a potential location is identified, a physical inspection is required. The map indicates that Site C would be the best location for Opportunity, Inc., because of the proximity of the two major cross streets. However, an on-site visit made it clear that Site B was superior to both Sites C and A. Among other factors, the visit revealed that Site C was ten feet below the grade of Rocket Road and hard to see.

For Site B, the only drawback was the shape. Office Depot and Trader Joe's, two high-frequency co-tenants, were on either side. The site was only a 100 feet from Circuit City, which draws customers from the overall region. From the map we were leaning toward Site C—and the landlords were guiding us that way—but an onsite inspection made it clear that Site B was really the best for Opportunity's needs. You can work around most space problems, but you can't get around the visibility and access problems. Best of all, Site B was $6 a square foot less!

This example shows why a personal inspection of the site is mandatory. Every location has some kind of physical issue, good or bad, that cannot be discerned from maps, schematics, or aerial photos.

One final issue. What if Site B were not available? Would we recommend that Opportunity take Site A or C? What if no sites were available at all in this shopping center—would we recommend the less desirable site at the first shopping center? There's no perfect answer. Because we have already done the analysis, we know that all the sites should be "good enough," capable of yielding a profit, so the expectation is that the better site will yield more profit, not that the lesser sites will result in a loss. This assumes, of course, that our site inspection did not determine that the physical shortcomings of one of the other sites did not render our projections meaningless. Let's say the location you want could generate a 15 percent return but will not be available for three years. Let's say your on-site inspection causes you to drop the estimate of the return on the secondary location to ten percent, but the revenue begins this year. There is value in having less money today rather than more money in the future. Too, you have no way of knowing whether you will be able to obtain the better space in three years anyway, or at a price that will make it more profitable than the second choice. (If the prime location becomes available, then your problem is whether you need to take the space for strategic reasons, to prevent a competitor from obtaining it.)

If, after seeing the sites first hand, you still have confidence in the financial projections for each location, then the next consideration is whether you absolutely, positively have to be in this trade area. In most cities, two or three trade areas provide the most brand visibility. They are so strong and have so much trade activity that you simply have to be there to get brand exposure and to succeed financially. This is the one exception in which a small retailer might take a B location in an A trade area. Another issue is the strength of the particular shopping center or mall. In Seattle, Washington, University Village is so powerful that you would think long and hard before saying no to a space, even if it were not the one you wanted. In San Ramon, Calif., one shopping center is heads and shoulders above all the others in the trade area. You would take a small space at the preferred center, even at less than favorable terms, over any other spaces, on any other terms, at the other shopping centers. It's that, or find another trade area.

Objective guidelines such as these make it easier to balance the ever-present trade-offs and provide you a greater comfort factor in making difficult site selections.

Mapping Concept to Destination

Because Site B was the preferred choice for a high-concept consumer brand, would other concepts do as well in Sites A and C and at the other center on Rocket and Yao? The answer is yes—a retailer with an appointment-oriented business. Site C has a nail salon and a company that makes window blinds. An optometrist would be a logical addition, or an insurance agent. Any of the shopping center sites would work for a business in which a customer would most likely search it out rather than drop in on a convenience trip. Site C also has a nutrition center, the kind of business that customers are normally willing to seek out.

Similarly, any of these sites will work for a *local destination*, such as a sandwich shop, where customers will come back regularly once they discover you. (Site C has a pizza shop.) The sites will also work for a *regional destination*, where people will drive some distance for your products. All of western Washington State has only one IKEA furniture outlet, and people will find it. Wal-Mart draws people from an entire county. Nebraska Furniture Warehouse in Omaha draws people from the entire state. Outlet malls are probably the best example of a regional destination that can be situated almost anywhere. They locate along freeways between towns or on main highways in out-of-the-way towns to avoid competing directly with mainline stores selling the same national brands, but customers will drive from Portland or Seattle to, say, the Oregon coast or the Washington interior to seek out bargains.

As the previous examples show, you can get away with a secondary site at a good location—*if you meet a need that the customers already know they have.* Most retailers, however, are *convenience*-oriented lo-cations. People will drive ten miles to go to The Home Depot, but they will drive only one mile to go to a dry cleaner. People won't drive out of the way to buy milk or gas or most other commodities. If you sell specialty items and you're off the beaten path, how will customers even know you're there?

A few retail categories may fall in between *convenience* and *destina-tion*. Starbucks began as a convenience location—it had to be "on the way"—but as the company became ingrained in American culture many Starbucks stores turned into local destinations, places that people seek out in their neighborhood for a break in the day. Radio Shack is a cross between convenience and destination. Some traffic consists of convenience drop-ins who want to check out the latest electronic toys and other gifts, whereas other traffic consists of destination customers who come with a specific mission—to get a connector or battery or similar part.

Knowing exactly who your concept appeals to and where it fits into the destination or convenience category can be difficult for some new enterprises. The problem is compounded by what we've seen with every location having some kind of "gotcha" or some kind of "aha!" Stuart Skorman, the founder of Elephant Pharmacy, the high-service, high-touch drugstore in Berkeley, California, found out within a few months of opening that he needed more local drawing power. Although the target market was perfect demographically—a well-educated and upscale Berkeley neighborhood—and the store site was physically per-fect within that demographic base, the community simply wasn't large enough. There were just not enough people in the one- to three-mile range to provide the business that Elephant needed, based on the draw of a traditional pharmacy. Stuart had selected the site because it con-formed to the Walgreens model of "local" site selection. Like Star-bucks, Walgreens saturates a market with a number of local stores. As it turned out, his great local base of customers protected his downside but did not maximize his upside. A supermarket offers many reasons for customers to come once or twice a week, but the core of a phar-macy's business, prescriptions, is a monthly draw. Because it can take as long as five years to change a customer's prescription-buying habits, a new pharmacy brand will not necessarily see a rush of business upon opening. Elephant therefore had to work hard to draw in customers more often. Although the company needed more consumables to drive more visits, the pharmacy also had to stay true to its core demographics. Where a Walgreens' food mart offers frozen foods, the town of Berkeley doesn't "do" TV dinners and beer. It does fresh fruit and organic vegetables. Elephant had to choose consumables to match the location—the neighborhood—in order to entice people to come daily. In addition, Stuart lowered his margins to increase traffic and started a direct-mail catalog touting all of the free classes, which sparked a surge in interest. The first four or five months were hard, but the store has slowly generated higher traffic. That Elephant Pharmacy did not map to a strict definition of "local," "convenience," or "destination" proves that every entrepreneur needs to carefully study the initial reaction to a concept. Retailers should be prepared to rapidly adapt the store's offering to the actual needs of the customers in a particular location.

A sophisticated demographic model can drive intelligent decisions regarding expansion, and on-site inspections of potential locations help uncover any street-level issues with a site. The final piece, then, is to be sure that the site maps to the kind of destination that your concept actually is. A location problem, as Stuart says, is an expensive lesson to learn. Once again, we see that location will make you or break you. For all the possibilities of being local or regional destinations, though, most retailers are strictly convenience retailers. There's no real issue about distance or the need to become a destination. For 90 percent of retailers, customers have to see your store—before they see your competitor's store—and be able to get to your store easily. Visibility, strategic location, and access are everything. You have to make it easy for customers to find you and stop because *most retailers meet a need that customers don't know they have until they see your store.*

Practicing the Art of Real Estate Expansion

As these last three chapters have shown, consistently locating and securing good real estate for a retail concept is exhaustive and time-consuming work. But there is more to it than segmenting the market, analyzing the demographics and finances, and pounding the pavement. Real estate acquisition is a process, but real estate strategy is an art form. Whenever I prepare to talk to someone about real estate expansion, I show them the Jasper Johns painting "The Map," which I have as a reproduction on the wall in my office entry. The painting consists of a large, irregularly shaped object worked through with thickly daubed primary colors. The colors are so brilliant and the texture is so interesting that you see the object as a whole, as an abstract painting that seems strangely familiar. It requires a careful look to recognize that the painting is actually a map of the United States, with each state boldly colored and clearly labeled. A typical U.S. map for a retail chain, which shows stores as dots in different cities, is informative but not beautiful. Johns' painting is art, and it has become an icon for a thoughtful real estate strategy. You don't look at real estate as separate pieces. Rather, you visualize the end result that you seek, in completed form and in terms of the pieces that must fit together to roll out a retail concept. People can identify with the beauty of the painting and begin to understand that what we're doing is more than just a job or the drudgery of process. Real estate strategy requires that you always keep in your head the totality of what you are trying to create and that you think of the process as a series of interlocking events. The steps lead to particular locations, so it is easy to think about them separately. The painting is a visual reminder that the mission of real estate is to pick all the right pieces so that they can be quilted together to create a single, distinguishable—and distinguished—brand.

CHAPTER 15

Real Estate: Who Needs Who More, When

AFTER FINDING THE RIGHT PROPERTY, you have to be able to lease it for a reasonable sum. Real estate deal-making is about "who needs who more, when." If the landlord wants you because of a vacancy, or because you fill a particular category of merchandise sales that his shopping center lacks, or because of the co-tenancy you provide, then you will receive relatively better lease terms. If you need the space more than the landlord needs you, then you will receive relatively worse terms, a landlord-sided deal. For this reason, always look for real estate when you don't need it. Great locations do not become available often. Even if you do not expect to expand soon, stay in the game with a real estate broker. Let the broker know that you are an active tenant looking to expand. You want to be the one who hears about a great location first (and possibly says no to if you're not quite ready to take it) rather than the one who finds out last, after somebody else has already said yes.

Leasing Versus Buying

A discussion of landlords and leaseholds assumes that you will lease rather than buy your space. Leasing is the usual procedure, but buying makes sense in some instances, such as when you plan to have only one or two stores. Real estate itself may offer a higher long-term return than the retail operation or other investments and you won't need additional funds for expansion. Buying also makes sense for *destination* locations, small or large. It's common for companies, such as carpet retailers and other big discounters, to buy their property and heavily promote the location, and customers will drive the extra distance for the price savings. The same approach applies to Costco, Target, The Home Depot, and other big-box destination stores, which buy their real estate. They are large enough to have core expertise in acquisition and development, and buying enables them to control the development process better. ShurGard and other storage companies often buy the land. They have an inexpensive, one-story concept. As the area around a storage facility develops, the land becomes more valuable. In five to ten years, the owner can replace the storage facility with, say, a three-story office building and dramatically increase the worth of the holdings for the company's portfolio.

For sophisticated operators, periodic buying and selling of property is a good way to manage cash and improve profits. Here's how the process works. An operator with large cash reserves buys property and develops its own stores. The balance sheet is largely unaffected by the transfer of cash to physical assets, and the stores are more profitable because they are not paying rent. Periodically, the chain bundles up some number of stores, leases them to itself on favorable terms, and sells the stores as a whole to other investors, usually a Real Estate Investment Trust. REITs are always looking to buy properties that have long-term leases in place with credit-worthy tenants. In this manner, over some number of years, the retailer saves development fees that a landlord would have charged, pays no rent for some number of years, has good long-term lease rates, makes money on the actual real estate sale, and frees up cash at the end to fund the development of another round of stores.

A small but expanding retailer might also buy, but here the reason would be to find a better location than might be available through leasing. However, be careful not to fall in love with the idea of owning real estate and end up buying a secondary location. If you are serious about locating your concept in the best sites, do not be swayed by any other consideration, including whether or not the property is available for purchase. If you do buy in order to obtain a great location, you can also think of doing a sale-leaseback, probably to a local investor. This strategy will work only after you have established the profitability of your concept, and thus there is an additional risk in purchasing as opposed to leasing.

Interestingly enough, immigrants to the U.S. tend to buy property for their stores far more often than existing residents do. It is a cultural phenomenon. I'm not sure whether they are better at thinking for the long term, or they consider real estate safer than other investments, or they feel the need to literally "own a piece" of their new country in order to establish a legacy for their family.

In all of these instances, the retailers are land-banking. They not only bet that their business will succeed but also that the underlying real estate will increase in value and add to their assets.

For most small, entrepreneurial retailers, buying usually is not the best approach financially. The primary consideration is retaining cash for expansion, but the retail concept could also be more profitable than the potential return on the real estate investment. This is a point that Starbucks CEO Orin Smith (then chief financial officer) made to me early on. Starbucks historically made more money by reinvesting in new store development than it ever could have made in owning its real estate. Buying real estate also increases the risk for a new company. If the business fails, you have a double whammy. You not only lose the business and whatever you've put into it, but you also risk having the property repossessed if you can't lease or sell it to someone else quickly. Starbucks has begun to acquire real estate for free-standing drive-through store development because the lease price of well-positioned real estate has increased dramatically. Purchase enables the company to control its occupancy costs.

Except for the rare case of buying to obtain a one-in-a-million piece of property, generally you would consider whether to buy the real estate and make it part of your growing assets once you have a proven, profitable economic model for your concept, and only then. But consider the tradeoff carefully between the quality of the location for your business and your desire to own an illiquid asset.

Finding the Right Broker

Finding the right real estate broker is essential. This doesn't mean someone who is a friend of a friend of a friend and who is involved with residential or commercial real estate rather than with retail real estate. This means someone who specializes in retail real estate in your trade area. If you have a large-box store, find the real estate broker who works for someone such as Toys R Us. If you have a furniture store, find the real estate broker for Ethan Allen or Levitz. If you have a drugstore, find the broker for Walgreens, and so on. If your concept takes less than 3,000 square feet, find the broker who handles fast-food, fast-casual chains, or Starbucks. The issue is not just familiarity with the good locations and appropriately sized spaces, but also the particular needs of each category. A furniture retailer, for example, has different requirements for location, visibility, access, parking, and delivery than a shoe retailer who relies heavily on foot traffic; and these two have substantially different practical requirements than a grocery or restaurant.

Sometimes you can glean the name of good brokers from the lease signs on available spaces, but usually these will be the names of the brokers who specialize in representing the landlord side. Just as when you are buying residential property you want a broker representing you and not the seller, you need to be sure that you find a broker who serves as the tenant representative rather than the landlord representative.

A good broker will provide a "market plan," which shows the trade areas in town and the simple demographic profiles for the one-, three-, and five-mile rings around a particular site. As we have discussed, major shopping complexes often have similar packages for their market areas indicating where the users or customers are coming from. These plans are useful starting points and good points of reference, but they show only *where everybody else is* rather than *where you should be*. In-depth analysis will determine who your true customer is and where that customer lives, enabling you to build a more accurate profit-and-loss pro forma for the store as well as determine the number of stores you should have within a market. One of our clients believed that its stores were regional, drawing customers from as far as 15 miles away. Our detailed analysis of "customer decay" for the stores showed that the customer draw was actually more concentrated, about five miles.

This information meant that, once a store was established, additional stores could be added in neighboring trade areas without cannibalizing the sales of the first. Such facts may have a bearing on the lease terms, such as the "radius clause" discussed later in this chapter.

Probably the most useful research that brokers can obtain is financial information about targeted shopping centers. If you have a food concept, you would want to find out the sales of other existing food concepts in the center and how those sales compare to the national chain-wide average. If a Mexican restaurant is doing $1 million in business against a chain-wide average of $1.2 million, you know that the center is under-performing for that food concept and more due diligence is necessary. If other concepts, such as clothing, are performing at above chain-wide averages, then you know the center is good for general retailing. The information could have several implications. First, the center has good co-tenancy for general retail, which indicates that food service should also do well. However, the center may be so good for general retail that it does not have enough parking spaces turning over during busy times, so that food concepts under-perform. Next, the success of clothing retailers implies that most customers are shopping somewhat later in the day, or the majority of sales are occurring on the weekend. The key to success for a food concept in the hypothetical mall might be to focus on evening dining periods, to provide more seats, and to remain open later. As one example, the Stanford Shopping Mall in Palo Alto, California, has some of the highest mall sales in the U.S., approximately $760 per square foot. During the week, sales are about the average U.S. mall number of $300 to $400 per square foot, but on weekends the mall is *packed* and sales zoom. The key to success at Palo Alto would be to gear the design, staffing, and financial model toward peak volumes for the weekend. Food service opportunity also might revolve around evening entertainment—a large bookstore that serves as a gathering place, a movie theater, or some other form of entertainment.

Experienced brokers can also be of practical value as you proceed with building and opening a store. They have real estate people, store operators, and contractors from many different companies in their cars all week long. They can provide referrals for everything from surveyors to architects and engineers to sign manufacturers.

Contending with Commissions

A good real estate broker who specializes in retail leasing begins "dialing for dollars"—calling the target list of desirable tenants— before the space is vacated and a "For Lease" sign is put in the window. If a center needs a clothing retailer, perhaps targeted to youth, the listing broker immediately begins to call companies such as Oakley, Pacific Sunwear, or Quiksilver. Having an experienced tenant broker who knows the decision makers at major shopping centers increases the odds that, regardless of your concept, you will find out about an opening well before the space becomes available to the general market.

Commission structures are paid by the landlord and vary, but U.S. retail real estate brokers typically receive 5 to 6 percent of the lease value for the first five years, then about 3 percent for years six through ten or a declining percentage over the six- to 10-year portion of the lease term. Sometimes, the fee may be a flat fee such as $4 to $5 a square foot. The commission is normally split equally between the broker and the tenant brokers. (So as not to split the fee, a few aggressive listing agents work with tenant brokers only as a last resort.)

Don't be penny-wise, pound-foolish and attempt to negotiate down your broker's fee. You will accomplish nothing but to ensure that the broker will not pay much attention to your needs. The same will be true if you have a non-exclusive contract, though you could have different brokers in different trade areas in a region. No broker can perform in a professional manner if multiple brokers are calling a shopping center on your behalf all at once. At the same time, do not let the broker take advantage of you. I know of one national brokerage firm that demands a minimum flat fee of $50,000 to bring major tenants to shopping centers, regardless of the established landlord commission. The landlord might agree to pay an inflated commission because it can be amortized into the tenant's rent to make up the difference. So the tenant ultimately pays more.

Some major urban markets across the country are very difficult to locate in. It is a good idea to *incent* your broker by guaranteeing a minimum fee per lease deal. Paying any difference between the actual commission and your minimum is particularly important if your concept requires about 1,500 to 3,000 square feet, the most common size—the "sweet spot" for leasing. A small tenant might offer a guarantee of between $7,500 and $12,500. A big-box client might offer between $50,000 and $150,000 depending on the size and the quality of the location. A recent client with a small space requirement offered a minimum of between $5,500 and $12,500 depending on square footage and the market location. To prevent any side deals between the landlord and either his broker or yours, you should specify in the letter of intent that all fees be fully disclosed in the lease agreement. Brokerage agreements are separate written agreements, and such disclosure is not typical. However, you have a right to know.

Incenting your broker is a business decision designed to get you the best possible space in a Grade A location. If your concept works perfectly well in a Grade B or C location, then there is no reason to offer special incentives. Lower quality locations, being more plentiful, are far easier to obtain. If, however, you have a rapidly growing concept that seeks a strong brand positioning and you are fighting for space against national chains, it is worth the investment to give your broker a financial incentive. You need every advantage possible to ensure that you get the first call when prime space in a shopping center opens up (or is about to) or a major street corner becomes available.

Before committing to any broker—and absolutely before committing to any lease deal—you should familiarize yourself with market rents in a given area. Knowing the going rates will give you the ability to independently evaluate whether the broker is bringing you good lease proposals—working hard for you, in other words. Determining the rates can be as simple as an Internet search or a drive around the trade area to locate the "For Lease" signs. Find out what is available, how big the space is, what the rent is, and what allowance the tenant typically receives for improving the space. Use these numbers as a base for comparison.

(Pricing terminology varies, by the way. Most leases speak in terms of dollars per square foot *per year*, but some leases speak in terms of dollars per square foot *per month*. A quote of $4 a square foot sounds like a great deal to someone used to numbers in the $40 range, but not if the $4 is *per month* and the $40 is *per year*.)

Proceeding Toward a Lease

Leasing space will be the first or second largest commitment that an entrepreneur will ever make. The total obligation for the leasehold will be on the same scale as the initial investment cost in designing and building out the concept. The long-term commitment may be the biggest risk you take, even beyond the physical cost of the store, because you probably will be forced to secure the lease with a personal guarantee. For many entrepreneurs, a personal guarantee could mean using their life's savings or their house as collateral, if not both.

There are several ways to mitigate the risk. The most obvious thing, and the least likely to occur, is to negotiate an unsecured lease. It's very tough to do. The next thing is to go to the landlord and say, "I know I'm not as financially attractive as a national chain, but my spouse is not going to agree to use the house as security. I'll take the space in existing condition. You won't have to pay a cent for improvements." You could even offer to pay the landlord's brokerage commission. The landlord trades higher risk for lower costs. Another thing is to agree to use your house or other personal assets as security but only for the first two years, until you have proven the financial viability of the concept. There is no reason to expose your personal assets for the entire term of a five- or ten-year lease. When asked, banks also will usually agree to a cap on financial exposure and to divide the total guarantee among the partners so that no one person's exposure is excessive.

These concerns lead to the idea of various legal forms for ownership, including sole proprietorship, partnerships, limited partnerships, limited liability corporations, S-corporations, and corporations. Different kinds of legal entities provide different layers of insulation between your personal obligations and the obligations of the business. Each legal form has different strengths, weaknesses, methods of tax reporting, and associated costs. See an attorney to discuss the form of legal organization that is right for your business.

One business acquaintance had a practice of signing relatively short leases, five years, to reduce his risk if the site performed poorly. In my view, he was trying to solve the wrong problem. He would have been better served to improve the rigor of his site selection process and take longer leases. Short leases create practical and financial problems. For one, you have to amortize the cost of improvements over a shorter time, which hurts the profitability of the store. Perhaps as important, taking short leases *presupposes* a habit of choosing poor sites and might subtly reinforce that habit! For the small proprietor, short lease terms can also diminish the sales value of the business. One couple ran a small retail shop for nearly 20 years. When they were ready to retire, they found that their year-by-year lease rendered their business almost valueless. No one wanted to invest in the business or in improvements without the security of a long-term lease. (The couple would have been better off buying a property early in their career, even if it meant moving the store.)

Generally, the longer you can control property, the better off you are. I normally insist on a ten-year lease with two five-year options. However, I *do* tie that commitment to a kick-out clause (also known as an "early termination" clause), which is the ability to vacate the premises or "kick out" partway through the lease, usually after 36 months. Every retail concept will make it or not in three years. You know by then whether it is taking off. A kick-out clause does not mean that you are planning for failure; rather you are creating an exit strategy, a remedy if you need it. One 40-chain store with ten-year leases decided to change its concept, but the change did not take hold. If the chain had had a three-year kick-out clause, they would be nearing the end of that time as of this writing and could terminate the leases. Instead, they have another seven years of pain. In most states, by the way, landlords are required to mitigate lease losses by finding replacement tenants. Thus, if you walked away from a lease obligation, you would more likely owe something like a year on the lease rather than whatever remains on the full lease. Still, it is far better to have a contractual right to leave versus a protracted legal wrangle over the departure and over the actual harm done to the landlord.

Small retailers sometimes fall for the trick of landlords saying that banks won't finance the landlord's business with kick-out provisions in leases. Yet today major retailers readily obtain the 36-month kick-out option, and these tenants have much bigger impact on the landlord's financing than anything involving a small tenant. Sophisticated banks understand that such terms are common now.

In exchange for a kick-out provision, you agree to give the landlord three months' notice and three months' rent and to cover the unamortized portion of any improvements the landlord has made, including unamortized brokerage fees, tenant improvement allowances, and other out-of-pocket costs. By ensuring that you will reimburse the landlord for such expenses, you reduce the landlord's risk while retaining your flexibility. If I cannot get a kick-out clause, then I insist upon lenient subleasing (subletting) rights. If I cannot get that, I reduce the term of the lease to not more than five years, with two five-year options. But I begin with the idea of taking high-quality sites for the long term.

Having good leases involving Grade A property creates a practical asset for the company, though it's not an asset that shows up on any books. With ten-year leases and one or two five-year options, Starbucks controlled a property on the upside for as long as 20 years. But we also had kick-out and sublease provisions that protected our downside in the short term. These provisions were not standard when we began insisting upon them, and landlords resisted them, but they became much more common as the result of Starbucks' presence in the market and our discipline in insisting upon them. Once word got out on the street that a desirable, fast-growing retailer had walked away from locations because landlords refused to accept a kick-out clause, other landlords became much more receptive to the idea.

I should note that Starbucks closed only two stores of the thousands we built in the decade I was there—a testament to the care we took in site selection and the strength of the unit economic model—so kick-out provisions were not exactly abused. They are, however, worth having. One reason is the focus that the kick-out clause puts on retailers themselves. Knowing that you could close the store in three years, then the store has to be profitable within two and a half years, and you are going to have much more serious discussions at the start about projected revenues. People aren't just going to pull numbers out of the air. Another reason is that, even if the concept succeeds, it will evolve. Retailers need to reinvent themselves every seven years. The more flexibility you have to move, the better. You may need more space or less. You may want to close up and move across the street. But you do want to make the landlord whole if you leave. After all, the landlord backed you when perhaps no one else would.

Negotiating the Details

Everything I say here should be treated as a working guideline (and none of the following should be considered legal or tax advice). Reminder: Everything is negotiable. The ease or difficulty of the negotiations depends on "who needs who more, when," whether you have a strong financial position or a weak one, whether the landlord needs a tenant quickly or has other people in line to rent, and so forth.

Completing a lease agreement can take anywhere from a couple of months to more than nine months. The lease agreement is a large part of the retail store development process, which requires a number of well defined steps. (*See Figure 15-1.*) The first step is to draft a Letter of Intent (LOI). The LOI should contain all of the important terms of the agreement—location, square footage, terms, rent, and so on. The purpose of the LOI is to agree to business terms before going to the expense of involving lawyers. Whenever possible, avoid lawyers negotiating with lawyers. They will legal you to death. With proper disclaimers, the LOI is not a binding commitment by either side, but it will establish the major terms and the working relationship between the parties. To obtain a good lease, to save money, and to expedite agreement on terms, no other factor is as important as an LOI because all the thinking is done upfront, businessperson to businessperson. The lawyers are left to do their proper work, which is to provide legal language and safeguards once the basic terms are reached.

From the LOI, you proceed to the formal lease agreement. A major prospective tenant can often strong-arm the landlord into using the tenant's lease form, but most retailers will end up using the landlord's form. Because it will be biased toward the landlord, the landlord's form will cost you more for legal review. Many experienced real estate attorneys will accept a "not-to-exceed" price for a lease review. A good figure to use as a guideline is actual costs not to exceed $3,500. Legal experts who specialize in chain store rollout, who know landlords, and who offer more than just a legal review of the lease may charge as much as $4,000 per location for a rollout across the country. Other local attorneys may charge less per lease depending on the need and the overall business relationship with your company.

Rent for street-front spaces ranges from $15 to $60 per square foot across most of the U.S., though rent for the most exclusive pedestrian-oriented shopping streets can run more than $300 per square foot.

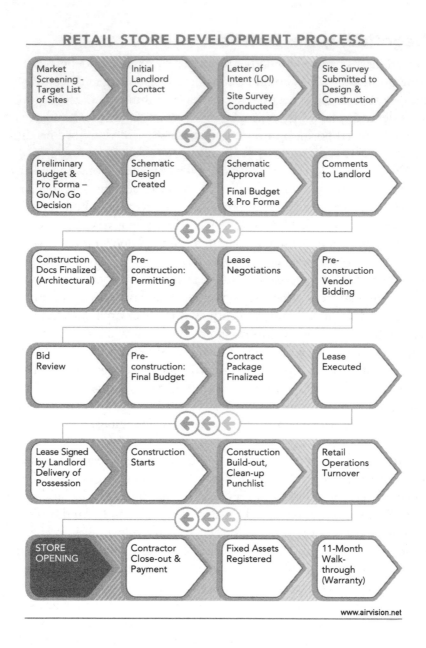

RETAIL STORE DEVELOPMENT PROCESS

Market Screening - Target List of Sites	Initial Landlord Contact	Letter of Intent (LOI) / Site Survey Conducted	Site Survey Submitted to Design & Construction
Preliminary Budget & Pro Forma – Go/No Go Decision	Schematic Design Created	Schematic Approval / Final Budget & Pro Forma	Comments to Landlord
Construction Docs Finalized (Architectural)	Pre-construction: Permitting	Lease Negotiations	Pre-construction Vendor Bidding
Bid Review	Pre-construction: Final Budget	Contract Package Finalized	Lease Executed
Lease Signed by Landlord Delivery of Possession	Construction Starts	Construction Build-out, Clean-up Punchlist	Retail Operations Turnover
STORE OPENING	Contractor Close-out & Payment	Fixed Assets Registered	11-Month Walk-through (Warranty)

www.airvision.net

FIGURE 15-1

The retail store development process requires a number of well-defined steps. Retailers need to track progress systematically throughout the entire cycle—from locating a potential site to store opening and beyond—as well as becoming educated about the many issues particular to store leases and to landlord relationships.

Mall rent for equivalent space ranges from $40 to more than $80 per square foot. Ancillary costs, called "triple nets" in landlord-speak, run annually from about $4 per square foot and up for street space and $15 to $30 or more for mall space. "Triple nets" originally meant the tenant's share of real estate insurance, real estate taxes, and "common area maintenance," or CAM. For a mall, CAMs also include the tenant's share of common area utilities, parking lot cleaning and maintenance, landscaping, security, other general and administrative (G&A) costs, and sometimes marketing. The cost of maintaining the building's structure normally is the landlord's responsibility, but a roof in a mall, the most expensive structure to maintain, conveniently falls into the "triple nets" or CAM. Some leases have wording making the tenant responsible for the entire structure—*never* sign such a lease.

Although the industry still talks in terms of CAMs or a variation such as "TICAM" (taxes, insurance, and common area maintenance), the actual wording in most lease agreements is now "operating expenses" precisely because landlords want to cover any cost they may incur, not just maintenance. However such expenses are described, make sure that all additional costs for which you will be responsible are defined and are appropriate in scope. The additional costs can easily add another 25 percent to the cost of the lease. For an upscale mall in the Seattle, Washington, area, for example, the base rent for a 2,192-square-foot space was $60 and the total lease cost was $76.53, including a CAM fee of $12.37, taxes of $2.31, and a merchant's fee (effectively, a marketing fee) of $1.85. Tenants that invest in marketing may negotiate no marketing allocations.

One approach with operating expenses or CAMs is to have a "not-to-exceed" number for the first year, with a cap on increases every year afterward. For example, the not-to-exceed number for CAMs might be $10 the first year, with a cap on increases of 5 percent each year afterward. Of course, with such provisions you will discover that the expenses always miraculously go up the full 5 percent annually, even if the rise in the cost of living is half that number. Another approach is to negotiate specific exclusions, for example for management fees or for legal compliance with various matters such as environmental costs. (See the section on hazardous materials following.) Another exclusion could be for new capital items, such as a new parking structure. You should pay only for replacement capital costs, which should be amortized over the life of the structure. The largest of these expenses will involve the roof and the parking areas.

Leases normally provide for tenant costs to be collected on the basis of estimates from the previous year. At the end of the year, the landlord collects the difference if actual expenses are higher and rebates any difference if the actual expenses are lower. You are more likely to hear if the landlord has under-collected than if the landlord has over-collected. It's worth the money for you to have an accountant audit the actual expenses every couple of years to ensure that you pay only your share of the costs itemized in the lease contract. Some accountants will take such work on a contingency fee. As just one example of the types of costs that might be passed on to you, a landlord in the process of expansion might include some of the preliminary costs under "G&A," but current tenants should not be paying this expense. Unless you audit, you have no idea of what you are being charged. Landlords generally have one formula for computing costs, even if every lease is different. A chain of 200 stores with a person dedicated to auditing occupancy costs could easily return $150,000 to $200,000 annually in overpayments. A few years ago, Starbucks did a major audit of its lease payments across the world. The audit recovered so much money in the form of overpayments for "triple nets" and CAMs that the company installed software to electronically monitor such payments going forward.

Some leases provide that the landlord collect "percentage rent," which is additional income based on annual sales over a certain sales number. Usually the percentage is 4 to 6 percent and the number at which it kicks in is usually fairly large. The idea is that terrific sales must be related to the property itself and the landlord should participate in your upside. If you project sales of $1 million in revenue, you should ensure that the landlord's sales percentage does not kick in until well above that number, say $1.5 million. Otherwise, the landlord will be taking a piece of the net profit that you need to make your financial projections.

Increases to rent are also usually built into the lease agreement, but do not agree to automatic increases based on an index. For a five-year lease, I recommend that the price be fixed for at least two years, then increased by 3 to 4 percent and fixed for the last three years of the base term. For a ten-year lease, I recommend a three-four-three approach: fixed rent for three years, then a 6 to 9 percent increase fixed for years four through seven, then a 8 to 12 percent increase (on top of the earlier increase) fixed for years eight through ten. One company took a ten-year lease with a 10 percent increase after five years. As mentioned, don't forget to cap any increase in the operating expenses as well, to no more than 5 percent a year. Otherwise, you could be the one to pay if the landlord decides to add earthquake insurance or decides to hire new people. Generally, you will not have any flexibility with your share of taxes and insurance, though you want to be sure that your portion is calculated correctly. However, real estate taxes normally jump substantially whenever a building is sold, reflecting the higher market value. Agree to pay additional taxes that result from a sale only once during the life of a lease. Otherwise, you're paying for the privilege of other people making money on the buying and selling of property. Landlords are reluctant to agree to such caps, but these terms represent a decent deal for both sides, giving the landlord reasonable increases while capping the long-term cost of your lease.

Because of all of these complexities, sophisticated landlords are shifting to gross leases with no extra charges tacked on and a fixed percentage increase in lease rates each year. For one thing, this approach gives landlords budget certainty. For another, they are tired of haggling with national chains—and knowledgeable small retailers—over all of the issues we've just discussed. They are tired of the complaints about the additional fees and the demands for documentation of the fees. For the Seattle-area mall space renting for $60 plus CAMs, taxes, and merchant's fee that brought the total to $76.53, the flat rate might well end up $77. In other words, the new approach may not offer a better deal on its face, but the simplicity of execution and predictability of costs is probably worth a small premium.

Online

For further reference, the book's website, **www.builtforgrowth. com**, contains a number of documents pertaining to this chapter: sample lease wording, letters of intent, site survey forms, and other supplementary materials.

Considering Other Leasehold Provisions

As every piece of real estate differs, so every lease differs too. It would require an actual lease agreement to cover every point. Suffice it to say that you should have an experienced real estate attorney walk you through the legal "gotchas" in your state and locality. In addition to the points already made, the following provisions or issues require special attention. They may show up in the standard lease (possibly to your detriment) or *they need to be included (to your benefit)*:

- **Use.** Define your business use in the broadest terms. You never know when or how your concept may evolve. When Starbucks opened, who would have imagined that a major part of its offerings a decade later would be "shaken summer drinks"? You might even have to close your existing concept and reopen with a new one. Remember that if you close, you are still responsible for paying the lease costs—even if the landlord won't let you reopen with a new use because it was not defined in the lease agreement!

- **Square footage.** Most of the time, the usable space will be smaller than the landlord claims. Always measure. Agree to a certain rental cost per square foot along with the right to measure the property within 60 days of lease execution. Also, don't pay for more space than you need. A fast-food concept would probably need more than 1,000 square feet, and 1,400 square feet would likely be enough, but 1,500 square feet might not lead to any more sales than 1,400. Consider "usable" space. Irregularly shaped spaces add to square footage but are virtually useless to most concepts. Sometimes the smaller actual size, or the smallest needed or functional size, will get you an effective rent reduction. At other times, the landlord will demand a certain monthly rent regardless.

- **As is.** Although you may take property in its current condition, without any improvements, do not accept the phrase "as is" in the lease contract language. "As is" has no precise meaning from state to state; even in a single state, "as is" may be applied differently according to circumstances. You could accept language that says you will take the property in "broom clean" condition.

- **Rent commencement.** The landlord will want rent to commence in 90 days or when the business opens, whichever is sooner. Because many variables can delay an opening, including actions or inactions by the landlord, commencement of rent should be contingent on several conditions. Typical phrasing would involve rent beginning when the business opens, or 90 days after *all* of the following: full execution of the lease, completion of all required permits, landlord's approval of all plans and signs, delivery of the premises in agreed-upon condition, and completion of all common areas and systems. Don't put yourself in the position of paying rent when the parking lot has not been completed or when the air conditioning system is not yet installed in the summer in Arizona—to name just two examples in which tenants have paid full rent for spaces that customers could not reach or did not want to reach.

- **Excess vacancy.** Your lease commitment should be tied to the presence of one or more anchor tenants, such as a large grocery store or a large department store. If they close or leave, you should be able to break your lease without penalty. If the center is new, you should not pay full rent until the major tenants are in and a majority of other tenants are in. (It won't do you much good if the anchor tenant is open, but no other stores are open on your side of the shopping center.) For example, you might pay a flat 6 percent of sales in rent, in lieu of all other costs, until the co-tenancy provisions are satisfied. If they are not satisfied within six to nine months, then you are free to leave.

- **Site plan.** The landlord should not be able to make, without written consent, any changes on the site plan that would affect your access, visibility, or parking. The landlord should not, for example, be able to put up a kiosk in front of your store that would block visibility or access, or expand the building in a way that blocks your signage or reduces your parking, or install a bank of handicapped-only parking stalls directly in front of your location. One retailer found a nice corner location that had off-street parking next to it in an area with limited parking. However, the lease did not specify that the parking spaces were dedicated to the tenant's use. A few years after the store opened, the landlord expanded the building to cover the parking lot and rented the new space to someone else. In addition to losing all that parking, the original retailer also ended up paying top "corner location" dollar for a location that was no longer on the corner!

- **Sidewalk seating.** Make sure you have the right from your landlord to provide sidewalk seating and sidewalk sales, even if local codes do not currently permit them. At the same time, understand the impact of parking lot sales or sidewalk sales by others that might negatively affect *your* business. Some shopping centers, for instance, stage motor home sales in their parking lots. These sales generate additional business for related concepts such as a sporting goods or auto parts store, but the parking congestion might hurt sales for a nutrition or greeting card store.

- **Radius.** This clause is the landlord's way of preventing you from putting in another store within a nearby radius that might cannibalize this store's sales. Such a clause does not make any sense at all unless the landlord gets a percentage of your sales, and even then it is questionable. A second store nearby might improve sales at the first store by increasing your market presence. Also, you might need to open a store nearby to take pressure off of your existing store. Your pizzeria might become so busy that you are turning away people at lunch, but you have no room to expand in this location. Or a good location might open nearby and you want to take that space to preempt a competitor from moving in. Most landlords won't insist on a radius clause with small retailer, but if the radius clause becomes a sticking point, you might negotiate instead a lower breakpoint at which the percentage rent kicks in. Another approach might be to treat a portion of the second store's revenue as part of the first store's revenue for purposes of the landlord's percentage share, or for you to make up any difference in the landlord's rent for some time if the sales of the first store do decline. Any radius clause should have three exclusions. The first, obviously, is for any existing stores. The second is for any stores you add through a merger or acquisition or as the result of your being bought out. The last would be to agree to add no more than one store within, say, a three-mile limit, or to exempt a location in one or two defined developments (for instance, an existing shopping center that currently has no vacancies, or a new retail center still in planning).

- **Exclusive use.** This is for the tenant. The landlord cannot rent other space in the shopping center to a tenant who sells the same products as you sell, as defined in the exclusivity clause, unless the products represent less than 10 percent of the company's annual sales volume at that store. Grocery stores and other big tenants are normally not included in the exclusion. The small retailer should pay particular attention to this provision, as it may be the only protection the retailer has against a bigger competitor that might otherwise move into the same shopping center.

● **Hazardous material.** The site survey should turn up any issues related to environmental hazards. For your own safety, as well as for your future liability, you need to know whether the property used to be a dry-cleaning plant or a gasoline service station or has lead-based paint, asbestos, or other environmental problems. The first step is to get a written representation from the landlord about the landlord's knowledge regarding any hazardous materials or environmental problems. Such a statement is normally required for the landlord's financing anyway. The second step is to include in the lease a provision that the landlord is responsible for remediating any such issues. The law already requires this of the landlord, so a "covenant to remediate" is not an additional burden. If remediation is necessary, you need protection from interference with your property or disruption to your business during the cleanup—a rent offset or, if the condition is serious enough, the right to terminate the lease. Although the agreement should specify that the landlord will pay for problems not caused by you, the landlord could turn around and pass back the cleanup costs to you as a part of the "operating expense"—with a 15 percent markup! This possibility is still another reason for a cap on your share of the landlord's operating expenses. The third step is a provision that the landlord will indemnify you for any hazardous or environmental issues that you did not cause and that you will indemnify the landlord for any hazardous or environmental issues that you do cause.

● **Tax issues.** Tax matters are not covered in the actual lease, but you should factor in tax treatment before settling the final structure of a lease. If you pay for leasehold improvements, depreciation on those improvements will affect your profitability, particularly for shorter term leases. Tax consequences vary according to how much of the improvements are equipment and how much are structural improvements, because equipment and structural improvements depreciate at different rates according to their useful life. If a lease is terminated before depreciation is completed, the remaining unde-preciated cost of the improvements may become an abandonment loss, unless the improvements are sold to the landlord or the new tenant. Tax consequences also exist for other equipment depending on whether it is bought or leased, and the rules get complicated in a hurry according to whether a transaction is a "true lease" or a "disguised purchase" as defined by the tax code. Small businesses usually strive to have lease terms meet the "true lease" requirements for ease of record keeping and potentially better tax deductions. However, occasionally a bonus depreciation for new equipment is passed into law to stimulate the economy; these depreciations may make purchase a better overall deal if your revenue is sufficiently high to absorb them. See a certified public accountant for an analy-sis of the best tax benefit for your situation.

- **Sublet issues.** The lease should give you the right to sublet the space. However, landlords have a legitimate interest in who you might sublet to. If you are in a high-quality location and sublet to a tenant that is undesirable or financially weak, the landlord could suffer appreciably. The landlord's wording normally states that per-mission to sublet will not be "unreasonably" withheld. Though common in many business contracts, such language with a landlord will invariably lead you to a legal conflict. Insist upon wording with specific provisions that answer the landlord's concerns: that you will sublet to someone whose financial strength is at least as good as yours; that the use will be proper for the tenant roster (for example, no adult video store in the shopping center); that the use will not conflict with any of the landlord's exclusivity clauses with other ten-ants; and so on. In addition, the landlord should receive a modest fee for legal review of the sublet and related costs. As the original tenant, you will probably have to remain responsible for the lease even if you sublet. The landlord should agree to remove that obliga-tion after two or three years with the new tenant in place without any problems.

- **Transfer/assignment issues.** Contract language that prevents leases from being assigned to other entities poses another set of problems, especially for the young, growing chain that might be bought out by a larger company. Here is a likely scenario: A major national chain wants to buy your 20-store regional chain for a multiple of eight times your revenues. During due diligence, the potential buyers discover that the leases for your top stores do not allow the leasehold interest to be transferred without the landlord's approval. When you ask to transfer your leasehold obligation to the purchaser, the landlord may realize that his shopping center has one of your high-volume stores. In this scenario, the landlord may be able to halt the sale of your business by insisting on hefty transfer fees, demanding higher rent, or making other changes to the lease that make the sale less attractive to the buyer of the business. The landlord's actions grossly change the economics, devaluing the offer to you or causing the sale to fall through entirely. Sometimes the landlord's reaction is personal. Perhaps the national chain went into Chapter 11 and left the landlord high and dry some years before. Perhaps the national chain sells liquor in some of its establishments and the landlord opposes drinking on moral grounds. *All of these things and more have killed deals.* Therefore, the lease should state that the landlord will approve the transfer of the lease to the new entity without triggering the transfer, assignment, or sublet clauses if 50 percent or more of your company is sold or transferred to another entity.

Scheduling a Site Survey

When you have greater than 50 percent confidence that the deal for the location will be completed—and prior to or during formal lease negotiations—it is time to commission a site survey. Performed by a licensed architect or engineer, a site survey includes an accurate layout of the leasable space and identifies every potential problem with the space from a mechanical or construction standpoint. The survey should cost no more than a few thousand dollars. If you use the same company for surveys of multiple stores, you should be able to reduce the price by half.

A site survey should begin with an executive summary highlighting the financials of the planned store, major design and construction issues, and basic assumptions about the site, including a description of the trade area and future market considerations. The financial summary not only includes estimated sales and return on investment, but also numbers of any analogue stores in the chain and of comparable operators. The executive summary is useful if a real-estate committee needs to review and approve the location; the document can also be taken directly to a lending institution to obtain financing. The ultimate purpose of the executive summary is to reinforce good mental habits, to remind you to judge this location on its objective merits. You may love the site, but if the cost of building it out distorts the financials, you will be less likely to ignore the information if all the data is directly in front of you.

A checklist for the site survey needs to be extremely detailed. You'd be surprised what lurks underneath the surface, and what work landlords defray or will not tell you needs to be done regarding the basic infrastructure of the property. Some hands-off landlords think "electrical service" means wire in a pipe somewhere near your space. One time, many years ago in my less wily days, we discovered that the nearest electrical service was a 200-foot run from my location, and we had to drill through concrete to reach it. (Drilling through concrete in some multi-level structures first requires an X-ray to make sure that you do not negatively affect the rebar structure. This step adds a few thousand dollars to the cost.) Wiring needs to be of sufficient size to meet your needs, delivered into your space, with all the necessary circuit breakers and panels installed. Heating, ventilation, and air conditioning (HVAC) are often inadequate. The facility needs to have enough rooftop space for any additional equipment and sufficient access to deliver required ventilation to your location. You also need to observe the lowest point of the ceiling level in the space. Distributing new HVAC air ducts may require a drop of more than two feet below the existing lowest level of ceiling height in the space. This change may result in the rest of the ceiling being lowered to that level.

Plumbing, including water and sewage service, fire sprinklers, and telephone service all need to be adequate to meet current and future needs. The amount of fire sprinklering, determined by an analysis based on local building and fire codes, can be very expensive to install. Also make sure you know the particular needs of your occupancy and use requirements before executing a lease. Food service has additional utility needs including the installation of a grease interceptor and exhaust systems. Restroom requirements are based on your use according to local codes, and must meet the standards of the American Disability Act (ADA) or similar laws in other countries. Meeting ADA requirements, primarily access to the premises (usually via ramps and wide doors), level floors, and accessible restrooms, is a particularly expensive task in older urban buildings. The survey should identify any environmental hazards such as those just mentioned. The most common are asbestos and lead-based paints. Inquire about refuse disposal and make sure that you are assigned a dumpster location that is close enough and large enough to handle your daily needs. The survey also should ascertain any limitation imposed by municipal, county, state, and federal building codes. It should note specific shopping center building requirements. Some localities have oddball codes, and some malls allow construction only at night, which means the cost of the build-out may include overtime pay for every shift.

In addition to all these things, a site survey should reveal "invisible things." One such item is access for your deliveries. Some spaces don't afford rear entry. Doorways or hallways may be too narrow. Another is backroom space, which should be ample enough to provide employees with a place to change clothes, an office for the manager, and a secure cash-counting area. Another is physical security. Is there a peephole in the rear door? Is employee parking close by and well lit?

Another invisible issue is the quality of work behind the scenes. One of my big pet peeves is the electrical panel. I want it to be properly enclosed, accessible and labeled, with no hazards. I also check the plumbing joints, to see if the welds are properly soldered. A solder joint should be neatly sanded and smooth; it should not appear to be covered with candle wax. Any sign of a lackadaisical attitude toward the underlying construction should be a warning flag about the overall quality of the facility's construction. In an existing space, construction short-cuts and shoddy workmanship will increase your maintenance costs over time. In a new space, you need to pay special attention that the work is completed to your satisfaction.

From the site survey comes a written exhibit that should be incorporated into the lease detailing the landlord's work needed to bring the space up to your requirements. In the U.S., the work to be done is called the landlord's "vanilla shell," a reference to the generic look and off-white color of finished, painted wallboard. Be warned that the phrase "vanilla shell" is a term of art that has no precise meaning. The landlord's definition may be different than yours. Be sure that the lease exhibit precisely defines the landlord's work in completing the vanilla shell. The expectation is that the landlord will pay for the vanilla shell work and also provide you with a Tenant Improvement Allowance (TA or TIA) to offset some of the tenant's costs for building out the store. In actuality, the amount of the TIA depends, as always, on every other aspect of the negotiation. In this building, the vanilla shell may be unusually costly. Or the location may be so valuable the landlord can pretty much dictate the terms. Or the landlord may be cheap.

If the landlord has a construction crew, the landlord usually does the actual work on the vanilla shell. On the other hand, the landlord may not have the expertise or the cash to do the work. Or you may have your own contractor and prefer to control the build-out—especially if you are building more than one location and can negotiate volume discounts from the contractor. Issues to consider are the increased liability that comes from doing the construction yourself versus the time and control that you gain. Any work on the roof, however, should be done by the landlord's roofing contractor; otherwise, your workers can void the landlord's roof warranty and you might be held responsible for leaks throughout the building, including those in other tenant spaces.

Lease negotiations should clearly define who does what work and who pays for what work. The Tenant Improvement Allowance (TIA) is expressed as dollars per square foot. If you ask for a TIA well above market rates, you can expect the rent to be increased. The landlord might request $25 a square foot in rent and offer $15 a square foot in TIA. You might ask $20 a square foot in rent and $50 a square foot in TIA. Ultimately, you both could compromise on $22 a square foot in rent and $25 in TIA. Payment for the TIA is usually made a set amount of time after you open, upon proof that the money was spent on the designated work.

Whatever the result of the negotiations, the most important matter is that you have a reasonable estimate of the cost to bring the space up to your requirements. Costly unknowns will wreak havoc with your financial projections, not to mention your mental state.

Leasing the Right "Coming Out" Location

From this lengthy inventory of issues, concerns, and checklist items, I close by calling out two of the most important points about leaseholds, landlords, and the property itself.

First, the liberal assignment of subleasing rights in a lease agreement ties closely to the idea of choosing only the best locations for your store. If you are going to take the large risk involved in starting a retail business, do it with Grade A real estate. Good locationing accounts for fully half of a business's success. *A good location will keep a so-so operation alive longer than it will take for a bad location to kill a good operation.* Should your business fail, Grade A real estate provides another equally important advantage. It's even harder to sublet Grade B real estate than it is to make a business a success in it. But with Grade A real estate, you have a much better chance that someone else will come along and take the location.

The second also relates to location. (Surprised?) Malls justify their higher lease rates on the basis of establishing a great destination location, doing a lot of marketing, and providing a high concentration of customers—all of which should result in greater sales volume for tenants. But many urban street locations offer the same kind of customer density and shopping appeal as a mall without the additional overhead. Many "high-rent districts" of urban areas are less expensive than equivalent malls, and I find the urban shops more appealing.

Where suburbia tends to have one strip center after another with little to differentiate them, each neighborhood of an urban area has its own special characteristics. Even urban shopping centers, usually integrated into older, refurbished buildings, seem more like a traditional department store than a modern mall. By and large, it is easier to establish yourself in a unique way in urban areas and expand into suburban areas than it is to establish yourself in suburbia and expand into the city. The caveat, of course, is "depending on use." A concept that appeals to adults with disposable income would favor an urban area. A concept that appeals to children or involves home décor might favor a rapidly growing suburban area. From this standpoint, the very first thought about a leasehold is whether your concept can be a strong urban "street concept" rather than, or in addition to, a "mall concept." If it can be a street concept, think carefully about starting in a

Grade A street location in an urban commercial or residential area. By and large, urban areas provide the most interesting "coming out" locations for a new store. Look for the up-and-coming districts and streets in your targeted trade areas.

In summary, lease negotiations come down to who needs whom the most at a particular moment in time. Oaklcy, the performance outfitter, has landlords eager to find a place for the company because Oakley appeals to such a wide demographic, everyone from the 19-year-old surfer to the 45-year-old golfer. Oakley will do better on lease terms than a generic clothing concept will, or one that appeals to a narrow demographic. To find the best properties and deals, hire an experienced tenant broker who specializes in retail real estate. Negotiate the business terms through a letter of intent before tackling specific terms in the lease. Use this chapter as a guideline and reference, but look for any other matters that might relate to a specific property, and get legal and tax advice appropriate to your locality. Don't be afraid to talk with other tenants (here or at another property of the landlord) to uncover other issues and to gauge the landlord's operating practices. Current tenants can tell you whether the landlord is a stickler for quality and neatness, eager to keep the property in top condition, or a penny pincher who is slow to do upkeep and repairs. Other tenants can tell you whether the landlord will work cooperatively to honor the spirit of the lease or try to use the fine print to squeeze you in some way. Due diligence requires diligence! A poor working relationship with the landlord can greatly complicate your business life. A national retail client called me once about a lease that had several of the onerous provisions mentioned here. The landlord had given the client only three days to review the lease, and said he could make only three changes, or the landlord would go on to the next retailer who had expressed an interest in leasing the property. "Don't sign," I said. The client, however, felt he had no choice. The location was just too good to pass up. The lease terms will come back to haunt him, I know that. "He's letting you know upfront what the relationship is going to be like for the entire term of the lease, the ten years that you're a tenant." I added, "Good luck." If the landlord insists on an unreasonable provision that benefits him or her, or the landlord balks over any reasonable protection for you, then your landlord is telling you what *your* relationship is going to be like for many years to come. Proceed accordingly.

Ensure that the lease unambiguously expresses what you and the landlord are responsible to do and that the language is clear and precise. You should need a lawyer to explain only occasional legal jargon (phrases that have precise legal meaning under the law), not the general provisions of the lease. Know your rights and insist upon them. Conversely, honor all of your obligations under the lease. Don't be the tenant who does shoddy build-out work and runs a sloppy store and then complains about the landlord and the condition of the shopping center. When you are done, the physical store will be the vessel for the success of your concept, and the underlying long-term lease agreement will be a major underpinning of your financial success. A sound lease with predictable costs is an integral part of the store's economic model.

PART FOUR

Push the Envelope

*There is one elementary truth the ignorance of which kills
countless ideas and splendid plans: that the moment one
definitely commits oneself, then Providence moves too.
All sorts of things occur to help one that would never
otherwise have occurred. A whole stream of events issues from
the decision, raising in one's favor all manner of unforeseen
incidents and meetings and material assistance which no man
could have dreamed would have come his way. Whatever you
can do or dream you can, begin it. Boldness has genius,
power, and magic in it. Begin it now.*

—Goethe

CHAPTER 16

Innovation as the Path to Growth

"PUSH THE ENVELOPE" is a common phrase today in business, meaning to take a concept or business practice to its outer limits, but few people know its original sense, which involved the testing of high-speed aircraft. Aircraft performance is often depicted in graph form on an X and Y axis. For example, power is measured against altitude or weight against balance. The predicted performance frequently takes the shape of a rectangular box—the shape of a letter envelope. In the early days of high-performance aircraft, engineers could not predict with any exactitude how new aircraft designs would handle, so "pushing the envelope" meant to fly at the edge of or beyond the known or theoretical capability of the aircraft and see what would happen. For example, the F-4 Phantom, workhorse of the U.S. military during the Vietnam War, was notorious for "bumpy" behavior during turns. Pilots feared that it might flip out of control, much as a car might flip off a road while cornering too fast. In "pushing the envelope," pilots learned that the Phantom would hold together during extreme maneuvers—knowledge that saved the lives of American pilots in combat.

The lesson is two-fold. First, risk is necessary for reward. However, second, the risk must come as part of an overall plan. Pilots didn't just take off in a new jet and start experimenting with barrel rolls and loops. The few that did, died. No one pushed the envelope except as the result of a disciplined methodology, and only after a great deal of experience handling the aircraft under constantly expanding conditions.

Sounds a lot like what we have talked about with retail expansion, doesn't it? Having a solid concept and plan, getting a great deal of operational experience under your belt, and then pushing forward in orderly but aggressive fashion. Constantly innovating within the brand context. Yet for all the talk about pushing forward, most retailers today want to stay safely inside the envelope, which contains little risk and less reward.

Several years ago, I met with senior executives at Jack in the Box. I learned in the middle of lunch that Jack in the Box actually owned and managed 80 percent of its 1,500 units. I was flabbergasted. I said, "Do you realize what you have?"

They looked at me like, "What?"

"To date you have been a me-too concept," I said. "You follow McDonald's and Burger King and Wendy's. But you own 1,200 of your 1,500 stores. You can win the burger wars."

"What do you mean?" they asked.

"Could you truthfully advertise that you are serving the highest-quality meat in the category and charge a nickel or a dime more for it?" I said. "If you sold a hamburger for $1.10 but it was the highest quality in the category, your business would sky-rocket. You're in a price war, and there is no end to a price war until everybody's dead."

At that time, the industry was in a bitter 99-cent burger war. The day that Taco Bell came out with the 49-cent taco was the day that the burger guys were forced into slashing the price of hamburgers. The price war drove down the average meal price. The 99-cent pricing diminished the whole positioning of the quintessential American casual meal: burgers, fries, and a shake. Below a certain price point, you cannot talk about quality, you can talk only about price. The downward cycle caught up every fast-feeder. Now, instead of going down below 99 cents, they are doing two for 99 cents. It's really a 49-cent hamburger, but no one wants to admit it.

McDonald's, the market leader, set off the burger price war. Usually the market leader resists price cuts because their brand is considered the industry premium. That was not the case in this category. Cutting prices was considered the best the company could do to face threats because it had not identified, or at least had not reacted to, true trends. The number one reason for McDonald's decline was its failure to act ahead of time or even to react quickly to changes in the fast-food category. McDonald's was too focused on unit growth and worldwide expansion.

We have talked a good deal about how to expand, but expansion must be accompanied by innovation. It's a truism to say that every business lives or dies according to whether it innovates or not, and for many businesses, the definition of innovation can be elusive. Not so in retailing—see the many specific examples to this point. Along the way, it is imperative that a company continue to innovate and be known as an innovator, especially the market leader. McDonald's diversification into other concepts was not a bad thing, but these acquisitions (pizza, Mexican food, sandwich shops, and chicken) were relied upon to be the company's growth vehicles, a tacit admission that McDonald's saw the need to have additional growth vehicles to complement its core brand growth. Within the core brand, McDonald's thought innovation was a new sandwich. At one level, it is. One new sandwich sale a day times 30,000 stores times 365 days is more than $50 million. But innovation, as we have seen, is an evolution of the company's mission and role. The brand needed a big idea—something more than a hit product, as welcome as that might be. McDonald's is approaching 55 in age. When it was created, it was an exciting idea—and it had the best fries of any fast-food restaurant. Yet until recently, it had not evolved with the times. It had not added anything as exciting as its original concept had been in the 1950s. Compare that static concept with Starbucks, a much younger company. In little more than a decade, Starbucks evolved from roasting and selling coffee beans to providing specialty coffee drinks to providing pastries to becoming a community gathering place (prior to 1992, the hard chairs encouraged turnover) to providing an extended beverage line ("everything in a cup") to becoming an evening hangout, to becoming a "hot spot" and therefore a place to work while away from the office. All while staying true to its mission.

McDonald's core demographic, of course, is children. So the company continued the Happy Meal and added play spaces to stores and came up with "Hollywood" promotions—action figures tied to children's movies and other disposable toys. McDonald's evolved into a *marketing* company. Good so far. However, it should not have become a marketing company at the expense of being a *food service* company. As a marketing company, it purchased a chain that had indoor playgrounds similar to those in Chuck E. Cheese restaurants, and yet as a food service company, McDonald's did not make comparable changes in menu to further appeal to the core audience. For example, it could have added peanut butter and jelly sandwiches or macaroni and cheese or other fare with more kid appeal, thus securing and enhancing the core brand. The indoor playground units were relatively large, so the overhead was high, and the interactive play area was nothing unique. Others could easily duplicate it (and did), and the experience was nowhere near as interesting as GameWorks, which developed soon after. The indoor playground move could have been exciting, but it was safe and became stagnant and predictably unsuccessful.

So, here was McDonald's, the industry leader, following other companies instead of staying in front. McDonald's did make a half-hearted effort to knock off Starbucks with their McCafe concept. They opened up a test store in downtown Chicago under the "El" that is still open. Seeing the rapid growth of Starbucks and the rise of innumerable other regional and local coffee shops, McDonald's read the emerging market as a breakfast concept that mapped to its high-volume brand and its values of consistent delivery of product. Both the McCafe name and the location—right next door to a McDonald's—show that the company intended the McCafe to benefit from the McDonald's brand position. The company picked up on the "quick-serve" aspect of coffee—this being McDonald's strength—rather than on the community aspect of a coffeehouse. McDonald's did not seem to notice that the successful coffee companies focused on quality as well as fast delivery; the brand values and their physical expression were anything but McDonald's-like. Unfortunately, the "Mc-" in front of a name now stands for "fast, generic, and cheap" as in "look at the McMansions on our old street." Operationally, quick-serve coffee is already available at McDonald's at all hours. There is no day part for the McCafe to capture. If the concept is intended to have an identical market position as a McDonald's, it makes no sense to put the McCafe next door and cannibalize the store's sales (or fail to gain any for itself). If the concept is intended to have a higher market positioning, it makes no sense to put it next door and have its positioning diminished by co-locating with a downscale concept. Nothing about the McCafe made any sense—not pricing, not location, not design. Realizing that the coffee concept is here to stay, McDonald's has announced a re-launch of the McCafe concept. It is not clear what direction this effort will take or whether the company will fundamentally alter its approach.

You could argue that McDonald's had to test McCafe this way because of the franchise system. Corporate headquarters has to sell their ideas to their franchisees and licensees, who have to put the money into the upgrading and into the growth concepts. Perhaps McDonald's felt that it had to locate the McCafe next to an existing store to get economies of scale, or perhaps to limit the investment cost because franchisees are sensitive to costs. That's no excuse. I say, "Imagine what the franchisees would have if they were given a growth concept that was on trend, with high margins and high profits."

Missing the Shift to Softness

As all this was going on, McDonald's remained focused on growing the number of its stores worldwide and on becoming ever more efficient. McDonald's stayed with very hard surfaces—Formica, iron, stainless steel, glaring lights, plastic-molded seats—anything to standardize, to make it easier to operate, to reduce maintenance. They missed, completely, the change to softness and texture, the high-touch trend, the move to comfort in the fast-food category. In the McCafe, they went as far as fake lace curtains and some kind of veneer wood on the front counter, as if that would vault them into the Starbucks' league of design. McDonald's could have differentiated its look and feel. Any one of the burger brands could have changed the whole paradigm, had they shown some leadership. Wendy's is now trying to warm up its look with stone in the front. McDonald's has built a couple of prototypes with wood, but the chain is using laminated wood, which is fake and shiny. Interestingly, McDonald's uses better and more appropriate designs when cities require it. In New Orleans, for example, McDonald's has a lovely A-frame building that blends in with older structures on the street-car line. The store, which is near several churches, is known by locals as St. Mac's. Why doesn't McDonald's move away from plastic everywhere? Every town should have a nice-looking McDonald's, not just special markets such as tourist towns and ski resorts. The reason they do not is perceived cost to franchisees. A fear of cost keeps the concept cheap. A cheap concept leads to price wars with other cheap concepts. Yet you have seen that design improvements need not be excessively expensive and that they can generate additional sales. Ultimately, good design, along with product improvements, can create differentiation that lifts a brand out of the price wars.

Now, you could say that the "hard" look *is* the McDonald's look, that it's their iconography, that they are supposed to feel streamlined, featuring Formica and plastic. How can McDonald's innovate without losing sight of its brand and losing its current market? Well, people will go to Dick's Drive-In in Seattle, Washington, and stand in line in the rain in a tuxedo at midnight to buy a Dick's Deluxe burger. The reason is that the value proposition to the customer is high. The food is good, consistent, and cheap, and Dick's is a local institution so the whole package is worth it. (Dick's also pays above-average wages, so the service is excellent.) At other fast-food joints, it is not. Customers are sick of neon-and-plastic stores with inexperienced kids giving them bad service in a dirty environment. It's okay to be what you are, in this case "factory produced," but then you have to differentiate yourself some other way, whether it's value or quality or experience. McDonald's fell asleep on all factors, all measures.

Contrast the cheap approach with In-N-Out Burger. A mom-and-pop operation founded in 1948 and still run by the mom, In-N-Out was the first drive-through restaurant in California. The simple mission statement is unchanged after 55 years: "Give customers the freshest, highest quality foods you can buy and provide them with friendly service in a sparkling clean environment." As of this writing, In-N-Out had 185 units across California, Nevada, and Arizona, all company-owned. In-N-Out has a limited menu, six items, almost unchanged from its beginning. But people will drive for miles to eat at an In-N-Out Burger. *The food is good.* The meat comes from choice cuts. All of the meat and vegetables are delivered daily. (Their restaurants must be within a day's drive of a meat-packing plant. Think about that as a site-selection requirement!) In-N-Out has no freezers or microwaves. The meat is cooked to order, where McDonald's meat is pre-cooked, shipped frozen, and "nuked" in the store microwave. In-N-Out's french fries are hand-cut from whole potatoes, as McDonald's fries used to be, many years ago, before the cost-cutters insisted on frozen fries. In-N-Out Burger's shakes are pure ice cream; McDonald's shakes are made from milk and various preservatives. Despite the simple red and white pallet and its ceramic tile, the In-N-Out brand has remained fresh in the literal sense. In-N-Out has advanced because it stayed true to the brand while the rest of the industry marched backward. In-N-Out's competitive advantage—quality—means that they do not have to fight on price. People are glad to pay twice as much for a hamburger at In-N-Out but ... they do not have to.

Of course, there are limits to what you can charge for quality in any category. You have to innovate and have competitive pricing. An acquaintance who won the sandwich concession in a local state office building planned to serve high-quality sandwiches in generous proportions and charge $7 a sandwich. I told her, consider the clientele. State office workers do not make a lot of money. You have to have something under $5. You're selling big sandwiches: Do half a sandwich for $4.50.

McDonald's Addressing Some Issues

Some final thoughts on McDonald's. Although it has been fashionable to criticize the company in the last couple of years, the main point of the example is to show what can happen to any chain, and often does happen, when management becomes caught up totally in the tremendous pressures of day-to-day operations and in the inevitable "gotta grow!" syndrome. It must be said that McDonald's has begun to address some of the problems at the heart of their brand. They are selling most of the secondary concepts they bought, concepts that proved distracting at best. They have closed or remodeled hundreds of stores. They are focusing hard on cleanliness. Addressing the negative attention focused on the health risks associated with eating McDonald's foods, the company is "right-positioning" the brand with foods such as healthier Happy Meals for kids and adult Go Active!™ Happy Meals that feature a premium salad (with Newman's Own® Dressing, no less), and bottled water. Along with other menu improvements, the company has ended the practice of super-sizing and has begun a number of exercise- and nutrition-oriented education programs geared to children. McDonald's is now aggressively responding to the high-protein, low-carb wave. The wonder is that these actions were so long in coming. The Atkins and other low-carb diets have been growing in popularity for a decade. Subway has been promoting healthy fast food for several years with their poster-boy, Jared. McDonald's barely dabbled in change until circumstances and fear of lawsuits forced the company to act. No one was willing to take bold steps, to push the envelope in an organized manner. To INNOVATE!

McDonald's was not alone. Although most of the fast-food chains missed a big opportunity and failure to innovate around the low-carb trend has hurt them in the short term, the trend has done them all a favor in the long term. "Atkins-friendly" and similar menus provide a way out of the price wars. National chains can talk about product again—about menu choices, about quality. They can give you less bread, less fat, and fewer chemicals—and charge you 50 cents more. We are beginning to see a reverse of the spiral taking place already. Jack in the Box did not take my concept-innovation advice back then, but they have been adding new menu choices every couple of months, from low-fat chicken pita sandwiches to deli sandwiches. The chain is also extending its concept by adding a convenience store and brand-name gasoline service to some of its locations. They have hired an outside design firm to try to develop a unique, stand-alone look—with the metal, strong colors, and wood, one could say an "adult" look—under the JBX name. Jack in the Box understands that reinforcing a company's commitment to innovation requires more than a menu change; it requires a change in product offering *and* an update to the design of the concept.

Most encouraging about McDonald's in recent years is a program to match costs of between $50,000 and $100,000 for franchisees who substantially renovate their restaurants. The goal is to make customers more comfortable so that they linger longer and spend more. Some of the new McDonald's have café tables and electrical and Internet hookups for computers. Some have TVs tuned to 24-hour news. Others now look more like traditional family restaurants, with the main seating area resembling a traditional dining room. Remodeled restaurants have increased business by at least 10 percent, and totally remodeled restaurants have done as much as 30 percent more. The minimum matching number ensures that the remodel is substantive, but the maximum figure also means that franchisees have to bear the bulk of the cost themselves. Operators are conservative, and many are cash strapped. Corporate headquarters seems to be encouraging as opposed to enforcing the updates. In addition, while McDonald's surely has some kind of corporate review of remodels before providing funds, the sheer number of different approaches could result in confusing or conflicting designs. One concern for the chain has to be achieving individuality while maintaining a consistent brand image, especially if the changes occur over a long period of time. (If the company remodels 500 stores a year, it will still take 60 years to complete the makeover!) These factors, which will slow any concerted effort at a new visual approach and an effective rebranding of the company, illustrate problems inherent with the franchise model, especially one that is global in size.

Ideating Ways to Innovate

Innovation is good, just often very late. It is a common tale in retailing. In fact, a stock analyst praised Gap Inc. for bringing Paul Pressler in as CEO from outside the retail industry *precisely* because retailers have so little imagination and so much fear of innovation. Before Pressler, critics felt Gap's brands (the Gap, Old Navy, and Banana Republic) had become indistinguishable from each other as well as from other brands. Today, the three concepts are clearly differentiated: the Gap as a specialty casual retailer, Old Navy as a value-oriented family store, and Banana Republic as a moderately priced designer retailer. Sales are increasing at all three. Pressler did not thrash around with wild experiments; instead, he went back to the core values of each brand and began to innovate within that framework. The core values became the basis for methodical—and continuous—improvement and expansion to products and displays. This is the answer to the retailer's question,

"How do I innovate while staying true to my brand?" "How do I know what is true innovation versus a departure from my brand?" In other words, "How far can I extend the brand without losing it?" Innovation requires three things:

- **License.** Your customer has to give you permission to extend the category or to enter a new category.
- **Timing.** You have to capture a trend.
- **Demographics.** The extension must fit with a demographic that is comparable to your current one.

Let's take each idea in order.

License

Recall the earlier comments that you have to extend your concept into the welcoming arms of your customer. Always ponder what your customer would want you to do next, and what the customer would see as a natural next step. A confectioner was wondering where he could go next. There were only so many different kinds of chocolates he could make, and he already sold them through a variety of outlets. What is chocolate? I asked him. Chocolate is a dessert. What do customers associate with chocolate? Chocolate ice cream, another dessert. What do customers associate with chocolate ice cream? The old-time soda fountain. The customer would give this vendor a license to be in ice cream more quickly and easily than a license to be in coffee or other beverages or some other tangential enterprise. The thought progression leads immediately to a range of possibilities, from an additional line of desserts sold through others to a chain of specialty dessert shops featuring his confections. Brainstorm for your concept the three to five things that people most relate to about your brand. These are the things that become the brand touchstones. Ask how each of these might be extended. This process is the heart of ideation.

For Starbucks, the natural extensions were coffee-based cold drinks, to make the brand an "all season" concept, and coffee ice cream. What could the company continue to do? The answers are fairly immediate: More and more products in the grocery aisles, and more growth globally. One is a natural extension of products, the other of markets. In Chapter 11, "Wellsprings to Expansion," we talked about the many ways to extend a brand. Product and brand extension should be an early question in any new or existing concept evaluation. Could Potbelly Sandwich Works have pickles in a grocery store aisle? Could Potbelly become a brand name for chips, pickles, condiments, and ketchup? For your brand, the extension could be accessories or new sales channels.

Another way of "getting a license" is to consider the customer's need state. For coffee, the need state depends on the time of day. In the morning, the customer wants a comfort hot drink, quick. At mid-day, the customer wants a place to "take five" during a busy work schedule. At night, the customer (in this case, a younger customer) wants a place to hang out with friends. The first need state was the basis for Starbucks' initial business. The next two were natural brand extensions. The initial need state for the Gap's customer was for casual weekend clothing. After a while, the brand stagnated. Now, the retailer is addressing the need states for the work week and evening as well, while staying true to its casual roots. The company has also introduced maternity wear, intimate wear, and of course its baby and kids' lines, some of which have their own stores. More recently the Gap began developing a clothing line for women over 35 years of age. All of these related concepts make sense because they are natural extensions that customers welcome.

By asking the questions about brand extension early and planning for extensions early, retailers can push the envelope without undue risk, yet feel reasonably confident that they can grow their income stream in a variety of ways. Existing retailers can use the approach to revitalize the brand, as the Gap has done.

Timing

This element has two aspects. The first is survival, the second is the ability to ride an important economic wave. To take advantage of timing, you have to stay in the game. Just as a surfer has to be able to stay afloat long enough to catch the big wave, you have to have a core concept that has a strong enough economic underpinning to keep you in business long enough to capture a demographic wave or trend. Subway Sandwiches, for instance, had a good brand and a solid franchise operation for a number of years before it jumped on the low-carb diet trend. Having served healthy sandwiches for a number of years, it could credibly present itself as a front-runner in the new fast food "health" wars.

Demographics

The extension must involve the same or similar demographic as your current customer set. A food concept that opens an evening day-part, for instance, must draw a customer crowd that is similar to its original customer crowd, or risk losing the first customer group. It is hard to imagine a restaurant that serves blue-collar families at breakfast, the high-powered business crowd at lunch, and the teenage crowd at night. It is easy to imagine a restaurant that serves blue-collar workers at breakfast and lunch, blue-collar families for dinner, and blue-collar teens in the evening. The Gap's extensions have involved the same customers dressing for different times during their week or lives, or the same customers dressing their children. Chico's focuses on professional women in their 30s but has discovered that its designs appeal to women both older and younger with similar tastes. In the same way, a concept that appeals to teens can expand to young adults when they have a similar demographic profile.

Maintaining the Premium Position

When extending the brand, retailers need to be careful not to dilute it. If you expand rapidly and become omnipresent in major shopping centers and malls, it is difficult to maintain an image of exclusivity. Your very ubiquity lessens the prestige of a premium vendor. The answer lies again with innovation. In today's world, the retailer wants to be either the quality leader, value leader, or the price leader. Being the quality leader, at the apex of the consumer pyramid, means "your product is worth top dollar." Being the value leader, in the middle of the pyramid, means "your product is the best value," representing the best combination of quality and price and a strong connection to the customer. Being the price leader, at the bottom of the pyramid, means "your product is the cheapest." Consumers know that at Giorgio Armani's they will get the finest up-to-date clothing, at Wal-Mart's they will get the best value for new products, and at Savers/Value Village stores, they will get great prices. The problem comes for the retailer caught somewhere in the undifferentiated middle, distinguished by neither quality nor value nor price, lost among the similarly afflicted. Good retailers constantly branch out, seeking ever more refined niches. The parent company of Urban Outfitters, geared to educated urban young adults, followed with Anthropologie, geared to sophisticated women from 30 to 45 years of age, and then Free People, geared to educated young women who prefer a "feminine, athletic, and preppy" look.

Particularly vulnerable are those brands that start at the top, but who think that unit expansion is all that is needed for sustained growth. The Nature Company, which offered a variety of unusual gifts based on a travel and nature theme, is one example of a company that was "first in," but lost its position because of a failure to innovate. They invented but never owned the category. New products failed to create an enduring bond with the customer. Over time, it became clear that the Nature Company was growing only through expansion. Meanwhile, other specialty gift stores emerged (Sharper Image, Brookstone, and others). One, Natural Wonders, directly challenged the Nature Company's position and did them one better in everything—store design and materials, product quality, interesting products, and product innovation. Landlords saw Natural Wonders as the committed professionals who were serious about the concept and as a result began giving them prime mall locations, which in turn raised the company profile and set up expectations of further success. The Nature Company went through the motions and fell behind, into the crowd.

A number of regional grocery stores that have been the premier brand in their local markets have suffered the same fate at the hands of Whole Foods Market, the chain that specializes in organic and natural foods. Unlike earlier natural food stores that reveled in their austerity, Whole Foods is a guilty pleasure, combining an array of organic products with an overwhelming assortment of natural foods. Whole Foods opened a 59,000-square-foot store in Manhattan, the largest supermarket on the island. The new store includes a sit-down sushi bar, self-service stations for ethnic foods, a giant pizza oven, homemade soups, free-range meats, and fresh fish. Not every Whole Foods store will be as large, but the chain is sending the resounding message that a "wholesome" competitor can become an 800-pound gorilla as easily as Wal-Mart or Costco. Some high-end regional groceries have lost 20 to 30 percent of their business to Whole Foods, whose visible market presence unavoidably drops all the others to a lower position. Washington Mutual on the West Coast is doing the same thing to other banks with its patented *Occasio* bank concept, which removes the teller counters, enables bank employees to interact more easily with customers, and provides more of a community feel to the banking experience.

Changes in brand positioning happen regularly; in a free market, retailers will always move up or down. Unfortunately, it is always easier to fall down than to climb up. But slippage is not inevitable. Eddie Bauer lost its market position as the design leader for outdoor wear, primarily because it chased fashion instead of function. Its loss of leadership is evident by chronic promotional sales. Yet Patagonia, another maker of outdoor wear, seldom has such sales and focuses instead on other distinctions. The company's use of organic cotton and recycled synthetic fabrics, a design philosophy based on rugged outdoor use, and strong environmental activism mark it as a company that knows what it stands for. That "committed-to-the-core" philosophy keeps its customers committed as well.

Discounting unsold wares, as Eddie Bauer and many others have to do, is a necessary evil for the retailer. Inventory management is hard, even in the days of sophisticated inventory control systems. But some mainline department stores have purchased clothing lines with the specific goal of discounting. These are the clothing lines that are routinely and successively advertised at 20 percent off, 30 percent off, and 50 percent off. Apparel vendors encourage these actions by paying "markdown money" if product does not move quickly, reimbursing merchants to help make up lost margins. But the more a store marks down, the more customers expect markdowns, and the cycle repeats. This strategy shows that the merchants themselves do not believe in their own concept's brand positioning. They are trying to maintain the pose of a high-end brand while engaging in the actions of a value brand. The result is that they do neither well. Their brand image becomes murkier and they disappear more into the unplumbed depths of mediocrity. Such a strategy is a terrible thing to do to a retail brand. It is the end of your company.

Compare this strategy with Tommy Bahamas. Ten years ago, the product brand did not exist. Today it is one of the most visible lifestyle brands. The company made a bold decision to create the highest quality products of silk, linen, cotton, and nylon, carving out a specific niche in the sophisticated island lifestyle, which was soon broadened to include golf. They run a "clean" department store business. They are one of the few product vendors who tell the stores, "you buy it, you own it—no returns." They do not offer markdown money, and they do not look kindly on retailers who mark their products down. If you mark down Tommy Bahamas products this year, you probably will not be selling them next year. The company position is that they will grow on merit. If that is 2 percent a year, good. If that is 5 percent a year, even better. Their rigorous adherence to brand standards has resulted in their growth being much higher than either number. And they have helped lift the brand image of the stores that carry them.

Thinking About Customers in Fresh Ways

While thinking about innovation, challenge the conventional wisdom for your category. Most grocery stores place the milk toward the back wall of the store, the bread on the far left or far right side, and other staples scattered throughout the rest of the store. The goal is to take the customer through the entire store in the hopes of encouraging a few more sales. Perhaps an opportunity exists for a grocery concept that places the most commonly purchased items close together along with a single express lane checkout so that the customers who need to dash in and out can do so. After all, the customers buying groceries for the week will still make the full circuit. Grocery stores give up customers to convenience stores despite the fact that convenience stores have older product for which they charge higher prices—*all because it is easier to get the most common grocery commodities at a gasoline station than at a grocery!* Who decided that grocery stores should be *in-convenience* stores? Sound far-fetched? Old Navy is trying to find ways to expedite customer trips through its stores rather than prolong them, recognizing that mothers shopping for their families, one of their prime demographics, are exceedingly busy. Make it easier, and they will come back more often. These approaches do not repudiate the idea of using design and layout to lead customers through the store. Rather, they recognize that different customers have different needs and may need to take different paths. You may be able to better serve sub-segments of your existing customer base by more carefully identifying who they are and how they shop (men versus women, adults versus teenagers, and so on) and catering to those differences.

Food service remains another occasion for innovation. The lunch day-part is crowded, but there is always room for a new entry, if the offering is more than plastic furnishings and processed food. No one realistically can own the dinner concept, which will always be a combination of convenience dining and more intimate white-cloth dining. An opening exists to reinvent the breakfast day-part. Customers are tired of IHOP, Village Pancakes, Shari's, Denny's and other fast-casual concepts. Since Starbucks began its rapid expansion more than a decade ago, no quality-differentiated breakfast concept has come forward on the national scene. One new breakfast concept would combine quality with simplicity. The approach could offer a maximum of five choices, including such things as organic eggs, a stack of pancakes or crepes on the side, bagels, and great coffee. The concept would be a two- to eight-minute "cup of luxury" stop for the on-the-go person. The cost would be no greater than a typical fast-feeder, but the quality would be much higher. It could easily be extended to a similar "premium-quality" lunch with a small menu. The store would be less than half the size of a typical quick-serve restaurant, so you could slip it into a free-standing spot on a main arterial. The opportunity exists for the right entrepreneur.

Another huge potential for innovation exists in the realm of home electronics and our increasingly digitized world. As of today, Apple Computer is the only vertically integrated computer company with a high-touch retail concept, and Apple has only a tiny slice of the customer demographic. As a designer, I admire the highly polished, sophisticated environments of the Apple stores, just as I admire the sleek elegance of the company's individual products. Apple's core market is designers and artists, and the stylishness of its stores definitely appeals to that group. But I wonder if the museum-like charm will appeal to enough average consumers to have a big impact on market share. So far, judging by the traffic I see in their stores and their rapid growth to $1-billion-plus in sales, I believe that they are increasing their market share through the iPod and similar new consumer devices.

With Gateway's departure from the retail arena, the "high-touch" approach to consumer electronic devices remains a totally open opportunity on the PC side of the business. Here is a multibillion-dollar market and not a single major manufacturer—not Dell, HP, or IBM—has a consistent face-to-face, high-touch retail relationship with the consumer. The major PC vendors have largely killed off each other with their own "99-cent burger war." As long as fight remains based on price, they all will lose. The opportunity for an approachable, comfortable, and familiar environment—the one Gateway briefly pioneered—still exists. My personal "Aha!" for this concept did not come so much from our research for Gateway as from my family's own experience. It took my wife—with help from an experienced audio-visual expert—four days to get TIVO hooked up to our home entertainment system. Much of that time was spent on hold on the telephone.

Surely some would-be retailer out there is bold enough to grab the "branded integrator" banner and run with it. The opportunity awaits for a high-tech company that wants to try a personal approach. Just as Williams-Sonoma is not about pots and pans but about lifestyle, a company focused on high-touch consumer electronics would not be about technical gadgetry but about better living.

Finding a "Social" Concept, Here and Elsewhere

A final opportunity lies in our social fabric. In a world in which people work harder and harder—often in physical isolation—and in which they feel threatened by potential terrorist acts or other kinds of violence, the notion of community becomes ever more important. A new concept has opened in Los Angeles called The Pumping Station. It is neither a gas station nor a body-building gym, but a place where women come to breast-feed their babies communally. You enter through a courtyard into what looks like a yoga studio. The common room is on the left, where women sit on the floor and nurse their babies together. Baby carriages are lined up in the corridor. A baby clothing shop is on the right. In the back are consultation rooms where parents can get personalized advice for their nursing problems, learn how to use a breast pump, and so on. The communal connection has something special to it. Even as a male I felt it immediately. I ended up here, by the way, because a friend's wife had just had a baby and he had to pick up a replacement part for their breast pump. The Pumping Station sells and rents the machines. They sell clothing, baby gear, bottles, and other accessories. What a smart idea. The concept is not about breast-feeding so much as it is about the needs of new mothers to connect with others, to learn from the experiences of others. To form bonds with people at a time in your life when you are in the midst of great change and therefore more open to forming new friendships and communities. This is an example of someone finding a niche opportunity built on the principle that people are looking for a connection to others in similar circumstances. Such community-based concepts are a wide-open field.

While needing to be grounded in each community, today's marketplace encompasses a much broader world than in the past. Anyone who really wants to be a trendsetter in the retail business, who wants to be involved in the next huge areas of growth, needs to look beyond the neighborhood and the usual marketplaces to the new marketplaces defined by burgeoning cultures and the growing intertwined global community. The most interesting retail opportunities will occur where cultural interchange whets the appetite for new and different goods and services. Three major trends become readily apparent.

- **Hispano-America.** First is the previously mentioned rise of Hispanic culture in the United States. A lot of people fail to understand how large the impact will be, or they think that it is localized to the American Southwest and West Coast, where most of the 20 million Mexican Americans have settled. However, the impact of Hispanic culture is being felt all over the U.S. Cuban Americans are concentrated in the Southeast. The million and a half people who fled political violence in El Salvador, Nicaragua, and Haiti have settled mostly on the East Coast. South American immigrants, plus Puerto Ricans and people from the Dominican Republic, have settled in the Northeast. Hispanic Americans have already overtaken African Americans as the largest minority, and the total Hispanic population is expected to increase to more than 50 million by the year 2025. All the different populations, like other ethnic populations, continue to migrate to other parts of the country in search of work. Where they settle, they inevitably affect the lifestyle, the politics, the schools, the economy—that is to say, the retail environment. The Hispanic population is apt to have a profound, positive impact on the retailer that identifies and meets their needs as consumers.

- **China.** With one-sixth of the world's population and an economy growing at greater than a 10 percent rate, China represents the greatest potential economic opportunity for businesses of any kind in the next decade. China is also likely to have the fastest-growing middle class and, after some years, the largest total middle class, of any country. As government restrictions have loosened in the last decade, private retail trade has blossomed. Department stores and shopping centers proliferate, and the first seeds of Western commerce—McDonald's, Pizza Hut, KFC, and other fast-feeders— have long since sprouted. Although China's desire to grow its own industries will make it difficult for many Western companies to penetrate the market, opportunity abounds for virtually every retail category, as increasingly sophisticated Chinese consumers seek out the best-known brands in the world.

- **Russia.** Another country with an educated, emerging middle and upper class, Russia may hold the most *actual* promise of any market outside the United States. The country has historic ties with Europe, and its current government seeks more business investment from the West. I recently traveled to Moscow under the auspices of a Moscow-based company, Business Transparency and Integrity International (BTII), run by an attorney in New York named Neil Getnick. A former prosecuting attorney, Neil has won major cases involving white-collar fraud and was hired by New York City to oversee the construction cleanup of the World Trade Center after the terrorist attack. BTII's mission is to create and promote a more trustworthy atmosphere for ethical business practices in Russia. Because Russia's business environment has been problematic at best since the collapse of Communism, Russia's leading business association, the Russian Union of Industrialists and Entrepreneurs, wants to put in place a system in which foreigners have confidence that financial investments are safe—and that both outside investors and their local business partners are on the up-and-up. BTII will vet the financial arrangements for new retail and other business concerns.

We have already met with several major U.S. retail chains with the goal of putting together the right kind of deals that would make sense for expanding their particular businesses. The trip to Moscow was something of a very preliminary site visit, to evaluate both the physical and the economic lay of the land. What strikes the retailer's eye is an urban lifestyle quite similar to most other European capitals. Many European brands already have stores in Moscow, but there is only a sampling of American retailers. Department stores have many European product brands but few American ones. One of the U.S. brands opening in Russia will be Jennifer Lopez's new lingerie retail concept, evidence that some new entrepreneurs can "see the whole field" and are willing to go long. Moscow's café lifestyle would be amenable to all kinds of urban retail concepts that flourish on American streets. The city is surrounded by a beltway similar to those around most large American cities. Every intersection is rife with possibility. Russians love their dogs—any kind of retail pet-oriented concept would find a receptive market. ... The list goes on and on.

A sudden swerve in the political environment obviously could affect business in Russia or China, and the outbreak of major violence in one of the volatile regions of the world could obviously constrain trade. But the hard business fact is that 95 percent of the world's population resides outside the U.S., and most of the growth opportunities for an established retail business are bound to be beyond America's borders. For the retailer who takes the time to learn the language and culture, the prospects are alluring.

Beginning retailers will be able to take advantage of the Hispanic trend in the U.S. and the Baby Boomer trend mentioned earlier. It is much less likely that a new retailer, with one or two stores in Milwaukee or Chapel Hill, North Carolina, will be able to seriously entertain a jump to Moscow or Beijing. (Such a move would violate the hub-and-spoke strategy by taking the retailer into an area that cannot be supported operationally!) The only advice is that you will know when you are ready to consider this kind of major move. Meanwhile, keep your eyes open for partners who might be interested in, and are capable of, taking your concept to another market. Blue C Sushi, for instance, has joined with another company to take its concept out of the American Northwest and into another region of the country.

Surviving Through Invention

In whatever way Wal-Mart, Costco, Amazon, and other price/value leaders proceed, they will continue to pressure the "general retailer," a category that is on the endangered list and likely to become extinct. As should be clear by now, to succeed in the future the smaller retailer needs to have a niche that is defensible against national brands and attractive to landlords. One niche is the specialty retailer, involving high-fashion branding and expertise. The other niche is the targeted lifestyle retailer, which is personally relevant to consumers, reinforcing their lifestyle and connecting with them politically, socially, and environmentally. (The connection is so important that some consumers go so far as to base their business loyalty on the political contributions of companies and senior executives.) Every retailer, especially one poised for growth, needs to be a specialty retailer or lifestyle retailer. The essence of both positions is high touch and human engagement. High touch is not about size, but about detail and quality. Constant innovation in product and constant reinvention of the concept are equally important to prevent a downward drift in market positioning, an almost inevitable byproduct of expansion and of competitors replicating any sign of a successful concept. However good, a static concept will ultimately fade to generic and fail.

Although all the generic concepts have been done—and re-done—the market remains receptive to interesting and distinctive concepts. A number of them have been covered here, which reminds me. Recall the ice-cream store that went belly up in Chapter 1, "It's About Your Values?" A well regarded local Mexican restaurant has succeeded in the same location. Blue C Sushi? In its first year of operation, the restaurant was named one of "Seattle's Best" by the local newspaper and was cited by *The New York Times* as one of four "must-see" places for visitors to go in Seattle. Potbelly Sandwich Works, Omaha Steaks and Oakley continue their rollout plans, following a disciplined financial and locationing strategy that will protect their downside and project their upside. Each of these is an original. The need for originality is why you have repeatedly read the words "core values," "on trend," "authentic," "unique," and "high quality" in this book. The need to execute on these principles consistently is the reason for the word "discipline" in various forms. Tying all of these ideas together is the single word, "innovation." Long-term growth is simply not going to happen without innovation as a core component. Brand acceptance will belong to the storekeeper who can parlay the right demographic and cultural trends into new, concrete ideas. Brand acceptance belongs to the storekeeper who has the vision to see the whole world and expand the market out of the usual areas—whether into inner cities or out to rural areas or other countries—and remain locally relevant through innovative designs and products. The founder and leaders—all employees—must be willing and feel empowered to innovate and to push the envelope when it comes to creativity. This constant innovation is one reason why the hip-hop brands are so popular. They are constantly evolving. They are unafraid of change; in fact, reflecting their market, they are eager to change. The leadership of every retail organization must push the envelope with constant innovation and instill the idea of innovation deep into the organization. To succeed, a retailer must expand the concept in all directions, must constantly *push-push-push* to stay ahead of the competition, to never rest in the effort to improve product, service, design, and the differentiated *brand positioning*.

CHAPTER 17

Defining Your Mission in the New Age of Retail

RETAIL FOR ME is more than a job. It is a mission. In a sales world reputed to be going digital, I am a brick-and-mortar guy. Other businesses may be stimulating, but nothing quite compares with the real-world buzz of retail. Everything about it has a creative or sensory component. Creating a new concept has both an intellectual and visceral appeal. Retail design excites people's senses and influences their behavior. An architect by training, I am particularly drawn to this part of the work. The anticipation of a new store is embodied physically in the whine of the circular saw and the pounding of hammers. All the details—from choosing the furnishings and finessing the small touches to solving day-to-day operational problems—provide a level of satisfaction you will not find in other kind of business. All companies deal with numbers, but fine-tuning a retail concept's economic model is particularly rewarding. Tracking the numbers carefully to understand the evolution of the concept results not only in new product directions, but also in things happening on the street in three dimensions. Profits manifest themselves not just as numbers on a spreadsheet but as a new generation of physical establishments.

Most of all, retail has the one thing that no other company has—not a product development company, not a Web company, not a wholesaler. That is the constant flow of people, of interaction in the flesh. Retail provides a total shopping experience, and the need to make that experience special is what makes retail different. Pleasing a customer face to face is fulfilling in a way that no other business is.

We are entering the New Age of Retail, in which all but the price/value leaders must succeed by creating a unique experience. So many opportunities for innovation exist. We have touched upon just a few in these pages—obvious opportunities, waiting to be filled. So many untapped markets remain, in this and other countries. The whole industry offers exciting prospects for anyone willing to take a chance.

Too many retailers, however, are mired in the old way of doing things. They do not seem to have the sense of urgency imparted by a sense of mission. They seem stuck in the "job" part of the business, the workaday difficulties that come from running every business. They seem unaware of the opportunities; or, if they are aware, they do not have the imagination or will to rise out of the generic no-man's-land that defines too many companies and too much of the retail industry and develop the fresh approach.

As a result, retail has a lot of mediocrity. We have dumbed down our expectations. As an industry, we lack the killer instinct, the passion to succeed, to be the highest quality, to invest a little more, to innovate—and to get a better return. Personally, I am frustrated by people accepting mediocrity as the default and not even knowing they have done so. I cannot accept the mindset. Even when retailers sense that change is in the air and that they need to adapt to it, when they want to understand the growth opportunity and to improve their brand positioning, they too often falter before the task. Sometimes the cost of upgrading a concept or upgrading the systems that would improve decision making is too great for their generally conservative natures. Granted, sometimes the cost is substantial. If a major chain spent $100,000 to redesign and remodel each of its stores, the cost would run into the hundreds of millions, if not thousands of millions, of dollars. Even if the changes will more than pay for themselves, the decision is a daunting one to undertake.

Most often, however, it is not the finances that stymie retailers, but their own organizational structure and the inadequacies of their own senior management. Sometimes the present management team lacks the capability to rethink and re-imagine a retail concept—the most difficult work of a hard business—or the team is simply overwhelmed by the constant pressure of daily crises. As a result, however much a company wants to be a market leader, it never gets ahead of the market. Organizational drag too often ensures that retailers act in safe, conventional, and self-defeating ways. Focused on what has gotten them where they are, or what has worked for somebody else, retailers become afraid to change the formula. They do not see that the "formula" is what limits their future (and gets them blocked from cities such as San Francisco—who wants another look-alike store?). Competitors can and will copy a formula—in a headlong rush. Many of the "new" concepts I see pitched are old concepts with a new name. It is safer to go along with what humans are used to. The idea of *not* trying to change human behavior is different than offering exactly what your competitor already has. Build on existing behavior, but offer an interesting variation to establish a niche, or provide an up-tick in quality of product, service, or experience. Too many "new" concepts are just an effort to pick up part of a market that someone else may already dominate.

One purpose of this book is to educate the existing retail community on the possibilities, to show how fresh thinking and a fresh approach can change the rules for any retail concept. The only way to lead is to be committed to new ways of thinking about your concept and new ways of executing your plan. The only way to avoid falling into the middle of the pack is to continue pushing ahead. If they can't catch you, they can't copy you. Retailers must be willing to take a risk, as long as the risk is well considered and the financial impact closely examined. Retailers must address their management shortcomings openly, honestly, and aggressively. The way to the future is not through formula but through core values and mission, which should provide the vision and stability that retailers seek in the "formula," along with a commitment to innovation, which prevents the concept from sliding into a commodity.

Evolving to Meet Hard Times

Make no mistake, the market is tough. A dozen or more name-brand retailers have gone out of business in the last few years and more are teetering on the edge. Rents for premium locations have skyrocketed, close to doubling in the last ten years. Higher rents are one reason that generic mom-and-pop operations face more difficult times. A truth that is unpleasant for everyone but landlords is that occupancy costs will continue to increase and the smaller merchant will be squeezed the most. Larger retailers have the economies of scale to absorb these costs, and landlords will invariably continue to seek the national chains with the best credit. The nationals enable landlords to obtain better financing and to expect higher sales volumes. Very few landlords will turn away a national chain in the same category for a local concept, saying: "Mrs. Smith, you're a great dress designer, we believe in you." After landlords have filled enough of their spaces with national brands, then they will be better able to gamble on smaller local concepts.

This harsh reality means that small retailers need to look at retail differently than they might have ten or 20 years ago, when a single shop in a nice location was a reasonable alternative. The fight for Grade A locations will become ever more intense. To play in Grade A space, the small retailer needs to take one of several approaches. Having a compelling differentiated offering is one way along with complementing other tenants and uses in a way that makes you attractive to landlords. Thinking in terms of a growth concept is one way—becoming a brand presence on the local level at least. Otherwise, the choices are financial: coming in with bigger deposits or paying higher rents, enough to overcome a landlord's doubts about your attractiveness.

One good bit of news for small retailers is that some mall operators are beginning to invest in startup retail concepts as a way of differentiating their malls, making them less generic. The investment can be advantageous to both parties. The retailer gets financial resources and a good mall location, and the mall operator has an investment in a business that it can largely control through location, capital investment, and rent. Offsetting this positive development is the purchase of retail chains by mall or shopping center developers and the consolidation of major mall ownership by a handful of major companies. If a developer owns a certain concept, will it let a competing retailer into its properties? If a retailer rejects an unfavorable lease in one mall, will the retailer be locked out of other malls owned by the same company? The potential conflicts could be serious, and government intrusion into the industry is not unforeseeable.

Maintaining Values, Updating Concept

Occupancy costs are not the only reason that margins for most concepts will continue to shrink. The "99-cent burger wars" continue among the price/value retailers in all categories. Amazon, though just beginning to show a profit, announced more price cuts as a way of stimulating business. Wal-Mart has moved aggressively online, raising an interesting scenario: Wal-Mart and Amazon may become the Clash of the Titans, or Amazon may become just another "small-town" retailer steamrolled by the Wal-Mart machine. Even before opening its online store, Wal-Mart sold more DVDs than any other company in the world, including Amazon. Is there enough room on the Web for two major discount brands? Stay tuned.

For Wal-Mart's physical stores, the question is one of growth, quality, and goodwill. Sam Walton's little country store, created to enable poor people to buy nice goods at decent prices, faces withering criticism for unrestrained growth, low wages and inadequate health care, and a host of allegations related to hiring, discrimination, and the environment. As the nation's largest employer, Wal-Mart is bound to be a lightning rod for issues related to employment, global trade, unfair competition, and growth. But the most ferocious resistance all over the country stems from its supercenters. Nearly twice the size of the already large previous stores, the supercenters take up four to five acres of space and require another twenty to twenty-five acres of parking. They are sometimes part of larger big-box developments that require as many as 60 acres, taking cinder-block-and-asphalt unsightliness to an epic scale, the epitome of the lament, "pave paradise, put up a parking lot."

Even as they stay true to their core values, concepts must evolve with the times, with consumer needs, and with consumer desires and expectations. One thing consumers expect is different behavior from an industry leader than from a scrappy startup. It is one thing in 1962 for Wal-Mart to bring inexpensive shopping to a rural town. It is another thing 40 years later to bring visual blight to the open land next to a town or suburb. It is one thing to pay low salaries when you start in an impoverished region where other salaries are even lower. It is another thing 40 years later to be the largest company in the world and offer pay and benefits below the industry norm. Sadder still, Wal-Mart loses 46 percent of its 1.4 million employees every year. Someone in the company must realize that better pay and benefits would cost less than the staggering expense of *replacing and training more than 640,000 people every year*. Retention of experienced employees throughout the store would also improve the customer experience far more than the greeters out front, however friendly. Costco, the country's sixth largest retailer, pays its hourly employees above the industry wage. Perhaps it is only a coincidence that Costco has the greatest sales per square foot of any large format retailer and turnover of only 17 percent versus 46 percent for Wal-Mart. Costco sees long-term employee retention as one of its competitive assets.

Rather than scramble to address complaints on an ad hoc basis, Wal-Mart would be better served to go through the ideate/create/ execute process described in this book, re-examining the proper way to apply its core "heartland values" in the new age of retail. Remember that you can extend your concept only into the welcoming arms of your customers. How many communities have to fight the supercenters before Wal-Mart recognizes that customers welcome the value but not the huge, plain box in which it comes wrapped? Sam Walton went big in order to provide the first two benefits of retail: goods to customers and jobs to employees. For 50 years, that has been enough. But in giving working people good products at low prices, did Mr. Sam intend to antagonize America? When the first Wal-Marts were built, they were big and bright and spiffy—welcome additions to small towns with little economic activity. Wal-Mart's corporate size and its economic efficiencies have served its core value of improving the standard of living for its customers, but these are not the only ways of improvement, and low prices are not the only measure of the quality of community life. It is time for the company to fulfill the third role that retail plays: creating a sense of community. Wal-Mart should be a place where people *want* to gather, like Main Street on the old town square, as well as place they need to come for bargains. With this one change, Wal-Mart would solidify its position as a committed local citizen instead of being perceived and resented as an uncaring absentee landlord.

Creative design, more on the notion of a village than a warehouse, can enable Wal-Mart to become in look and appeal the 21st Century "town center" for shopping that the company already is in sales. Value engineering, the Kit-of-Parts approach, the company's buying power, and its magnificent inventory system can enable Wal-Mart to roll out the designs at a cost level in keeping with its mission. For a company that can bring to bear the scale of resources that Wal-Mart can, there is no question that community-pleasing design, scale, and execution are possible. Nor is there any question that this is the next step to improve each community's standard of living. It is a question only of imagination and will.

Redefining the Customer Experience

As Wal-Mart must change the visual and overall sensory experience of customers with its stores, every operator in the New Age of Retail must find new ways to engage the customer. The secret has to do with time—the real and perceived time experience by customers. Not too long ago, my wife wanted to redecorate our guest bath in anticipation of her mother's visit. We picked out a new mirror, a soap dispenser, a knick-knack shelf, among other items, and these selections led to us buying new linens. The store visit was high touch, and it was fun to choose the different accessories. This part of the retail experience was leisurely, as it should be. When I got home I discovered that the mirror was damaged. The problem meant another trip to the store, paperwork to fill out, and then a review of the bills in the following weeks to ensure a proper credit. This part of the experience could have been quicker.

As computer technology becomes increasingly woven into the fabric of retailing, smart operators will find ways to use new "in-store brains" to slow and improve the *shopping* experience while expediting the *processing* of payments, credits, and the like. Back-office technology will enable real-time replenishment of stock to reduce inventory costs and to ensure that customers have the products they want, customized as they need, when they want them. Front-office technology, such as virtual reality, will enable customers to "try on" more things, whether clothes or the arrangement of furniture or a home entertainment system in a room. Retailers will be able to "ping" customers away from the store on messaging devices to alert them to sales—the digital equivalent of Kmart's old in-store advertisements of a "blue-light special." Wi-fi technology has already been a huge success for Starbucks and McDonald's and other retailers, enabling customers to connect wirelessly to their home or office computer systems while extending a break from the office. Growth opportunities exist for retailers that enable their customers to use cell phones and other digital devices to order food or drink as they approach the store and not have to wait in line. Consumers can already order takeout food online and have it waiting for them when they reach a restaurant. Soon, consumers will be able to order all of their commodities online—groceries being the most obvious category—and pick them up at a drive-through window. Established supermarkets are experimenting with home delivery; only technology will enable this "old-time" service to be cost effective.

In-store processing of purchases will become ever faster, a matter of great importance for volume retailers. Most people with a full shopping cart want to get out of the store and home as soon as possible. For hundreds of years, customers have had to bring their wares to a counter to be rung up for payment. More and more stores are going to self-scanning checkout, but most people use self-scanners only when they have to, to avoid long lines in front of human cashiers. Because the idea of self-scanners is to reduce labor costs as well as to improve service, retailers should consider offering a small discount to customers using the devices. The approach, which would be no more costly than coupons or a club card, would attract older customers on fixed incomes who otherwise might be disinclined to try new technology. Retailers might also consider redirecting some of the labor savings from self-scanners into improved customer service.

Efforts to ease customers into using self-scanners illustrate the difficulty that comes with attempts to change consumer behavior. Successful new concepts will build on existing behavior or expand on it in some way, and any concept rooted in the idea of changing existing behavior has a strong likelihood of failure. The change could involve location, hoping customers will drive out of their way to your shop; or time, hoping customers will try a category in a new day-part; or culture, hoping customers will try something totally outside their existing norm. Asking customers to drive in the opposite direction of their normal traffic flow is not a winning strategy. Developing an egg-based dinner concept, as opposed to a breakfast concept, would be tough. So would trying to convince people to eat quiche for dinner on a regular basis. American coffee shops can expand their concepts to include tea and scones, but it is highly unlikely that a U.S. retailer could create a stand-alone, tea-and-scones concept here. Americans simply do not drink much tea, in comparison to the United Kingdom and Canada, where tea is a tradition. In being original, you have to be sure that you are not the only one to whom your concept appeals.

One behavior that the small retailer wants to be sure to retain is the close interaction with customers. For a smaller, more intimate retail experience, the proprietor does not necessarily want to use technology to whisk the customer out the door. The communication at the counter is part of the intended experience, the way to say good-bye in a meaningful, brand-reinforcing way. The challenge becomes how retailers expedite the mechanics of purchase without short-circuiting the social interchange. The scanning and tallying of the purchase will become invisible. One day soon, typical retail customers will simply walk out of the store, and a scanner will identify all their purchase items, tally the cost, and automatically debit the person's store account or a specially identified credit or debit card on their person. However, the insta-scan scenario also means that retailers have to become more creative and more attentive (but not intrusive) during the sales process. In other businesses, salespeople freed of paperwork quickly shift to more value-added services and analysis. The same will happen with retail employees who are no longer trapped behind the counter. Functioning as consultants instead of cashiers, sales staff in the future will need to be better trained and to be more polished to provide more personal service. More human touch will need to occur during the sales process, rather than at the end of it, to seal the deal and encourage a return. The stop at the counter will not be needed to make a personal connection unless the stop includes additional services, such as gift wrapping. Every retailer will need to grapple with how technology fits into the vision and values of what the brand can deliver. The dynamic is to understand how to connect technology directly to sales in a way that speeds transactions, or indirectly by strengthening the communal aspect of your establishment. Technology should not be considered strictly in terms of efficiency but in terms of how it will shape the customer experience.

Using History to Establish the Future

Technology will be a small but important part of retail's future. The greater part will come from a redefinition of mission, or from a return to retail's original mission. Retail, in the form of merchants selling to individuals, is as old as human settlements. The bazaars of many cities—recreated in the U.S. as farmers' markets and "Saturday markets"—are little different today from those of the Middle Ages; and those of the Middle Ages were little different from those beneath the walls of the earliest Stone Age towns. You would be hard-pressed, in fact, to state with any certainty whether the retail stalls sprang up around the city walls, or the city rose around retail activity at humanity's earliest trading route intersections or river landings. No doubt a department store in some form was doing a bustling business in Babylon or Beijing thousands of years before the Bon Marché, the first modern one, began operation in Paris in the mid-1860s. Retail plays a large part in the economic activity of every nation. Consumer spending has been 70 percent of the U.S. Gross Domestic Product every year since 2000, and was never lower than 66 percent in the 1990s. Most of that spending is at retail.

Further, trade has always been an inextricable part of the human adventure. Cinnamon, at one time the rarest of spices, made its way from Malaysia to the courts of Persia more than 3,500 years ago, eventually reaching Greece and Rome. Two millennia later, the great Age of Exploration was not a scientific exercise, but a search for faster, cheaper, safer trade routes. When Columbus sailed West instead of East, he did not seek the New World, but a direct route to the Old World, unencumbered by the taxes and duties imposed by other nations and the *baksheesh* ("tips") required by pirates, gangs, and other "entrepreneurs" along the way. The relationship between commerce and national power brings up another point. When clans, tribes, or cultures meet, one of two things happen: They exchange goods or bullets. Mutually beneficial trade has always been a pleasing alternative to war.

Commerce is as old as civilization, perhaps the main impetus for civilization, and its benefits are both simple and profound. At its heart, retail is about three things: to provide a product or service to people; to provide jobs; and to build a community or create a new community from two disparate ones. This is where the future of retail lies.

Whether someone is buying eggs in a dusty village on the edge of nowhere or a silk dress in the most expensive store in a major city, retail is the fundamental way people obtain goods. Retail is also one of the ways many people are introduced to the work world. Whether it is emptying boxes and restocking greeting cards for Mr. Levy on the weekends, surviving the rush hour at McDonald's, or taking an entry-level job on the floor of a clothing shop, retail has always been a way for new workers to develop a work ethic, increase interpersonal skills, and learn the value of money. A few years ago, a young man got a job with a local retailer. He was personable and responsible once he got there, but he was not always punctual. He could not understand what the big deal was about being a few minutes late, or missing part of his shift. When he was promoted, his world changed. Having to find replacements or cover for the missing employees, he could not believe that employees showed up late—and sometimes not at all. For the first time in his life he got some perspective on personal responsibility, on how the actions of an individual affected those around him. It is an age-old lesson that each of us has to learn. A training ground for most other professions, retail is also a wonderful career in itself, whether your interests are in selling, operations, finance, design, or the creation and development of an entirely new concept.

Retail is also one of the primary ways people interact socially, which is why retail must do more than move merchandise. The first Roman forum, a shop-lined marketplace, evolved into a major city center with areas for games, political and religious gatherings, and eventually civic functions. Other market towns served as the Wal-Mart of their era, drawing people from miles around to obtain the goods they needed and increasing the social cohesion of the region. Coffee houses were the gathering places for the American revolutionists and, in different coffee shops, their Loyalist opponents. The idea of retail creating a sense of place, of becoming a gathering spot, a way to bring people together, is neither modern nor a marketing shtick. It is the essence of the retail experience. At a time of many artificial concepts, the creation of a sense of place is an important way to differentiate your brand from others because it is integral to the human experience.

Improving Community Life

It is no stretch to say that every retailer's vision should be to improve community life. Offering a deli sandwich on a street corner or enabling a family to buy a DVD or a gallon of milk without driving 20 miles helps make life a little more pleasurable for the people of the neighborhood. When you sell things that people need, at a fair price, you change the world for the better, just a little bit. Other human touches build on these positives. Your act can be as simple as an array of flowers by the front door that brightens the day of customers. It can be as complex as support for community concerts or education programs. Ben & Jerry's Homemade, Inc., the socially conscious purveyor of frozen desserts, operates a dozen PartnerShops around the country that hire disadvantaged teens. The chain waives its $30,000 franchise fee for the nonprofit organizations that run the stores. PartnerShops retain their profits to support their other programs. Profits tend to be somewhat less than the usual franchise because of added training costs, but the value of gainful employment to the teens and their cities is immeasurable.

Small retailers can give back to the community in big and small ways—offering time, in-kind goods, or money to civic projects, supporting community events, or sponsoring a kids' baseball or soccer team. Especially for the small entrepreneur, the best way to separate yourself from regional or national competitors is to bind with local causes in some form, shape, or manner. It's good for the community. It's good for business. It's good for the heart.

Improving community comes with improved designs that replace the generic, ho-hum looks of so many retail concepts. We know that the population will continue to grow, to infill, to expand. We as retailers have a tremendous opportunity to reshape the urban and suburban landscape through just a small application of creativity. Urban areas already have many interesting architectural features. The issue is to take advantage of them. Inner cities, the most blighted areas, have the most economic and aesthetic potential, if only we look. Suburban areas should be a fresh canvas for interesting retail design, but they almost never are. It is not clear who decided that suburbs should be featureless, or that sophisticated suburban residents would prefer their neighborhood businesses to be lacking in visual and architectural character.

A major intersection in Woodinville, a suburb of Bellevue, Washington, makes the point. An architect can come up with a typical mini-center design without much thought or variation on what has come before. The conventional design has buildings on three sides and a large, visually unpleasant parking lot in the middle. It would be convenient for cars but not pedestrians. It would look no different than a thousand other small strip centers. And it would sail through the planning process. A slightly altered design put a functional street through the center, encouraged people to walk, and created gathering places, such as the amphitheater. Voila, a strip center becomes a village. *See Figure 17-1.* However, the people-friendly design would have more trouble getting through the planning process than a people-averse design. As we saw in San Francisco, the reason is that zoning rules that restrict tacky development are written in a way that also restrict artful development. The result is the safe, cheap, cookie-cutter look we all know so well and unfortunately have grown to accept. In a perfect world, planners would welcome innovative design. In the real world, developers need to work with—and sometimes challenge—planning commissions, politicians, and local citizens. These obstacles can be considerable. It is hard to blame developers for usually taking the path of least resistance.

Change begins with the retailers and their designers pushing for something better and opting to lease space in well-designed, pedestrian-friendly centers. The extra time and investment is worth it, evidenced by the success of mixed-use urban developments that promote pedestrian-friendly open spaces, compatible retail concepts, and supportive residential use, which might be condominiums, town homes, or single-family housing. Mixed-use developments are highly adaptable to local environments. Some have retail and light commercial use on the first and sometimes second floor and residential use on the upper floors of a single complex, or in a remodeled building originally built for another use. Others have residential units adjacent to commercial and retail complexes. Parks or greenbelts are common. Such designs reduce parking needs and vehicle travel, contribute to the local economic base, develop a close-knit community, and encourage development in existing areas over vacant property on the edge of urban areas. Mixed-use development has turned a grungy and largely vacant industrial district into the vibrant Pearl District in Portland, Oregon. Minneapolis has created mixed-use developments near two light-rail stations, in an

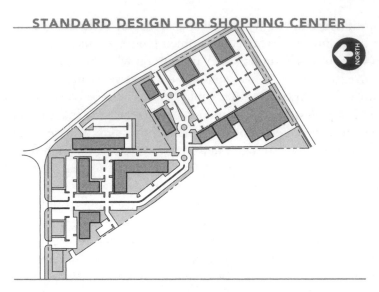

STANDARD DESIGN FOR SHOPPING CENTER

SITE PLAN TO ENHANCE PEDESTRIAN EXPERIENCE

COMMONS

AMPHITHEATER

Tiscareno Associates

FIGURE 17-1

A typical site plan (top) for a small shopping center in Woodinville, Washington, creates disconnected buildings separated by parking lots. The design encourages quick visits by automobile. A more thoughtful design for the same center (bottom) includes 150 residences as well as retail shops. Pedestrian access throughout the entire property, an amphitheater, a commons (bottom right), and other gathering spots create a unique sense of place that will increase sales because the village-like atmosphere encourages people to walk, mingle, and linger.

entire city block near the railroad depot, in an historic district, and along the Mississippi River. The river development features 53 rental units, of which 12 are affordable housing; three town homes for sale to private individuals; and about 8,000 square feet of commercial space including a restaurant, a coffee shop, and one small retail shop—a project that is human in scale. Other favorites of mine include Mizner Park, an early example of mixed use in Boca Raton, Florida; Santana Row in San Jose, California, a development across from a major mall; and The District, in Henderson, Nevada, a higher-density area from which residents can walk out to a shopping street. Such examples are still uncommon, and most require some sort of municipal support in the form of tax breaks or development dollars. However, all of these ventures add to the livability of the city while creating unique locations for retail activity. City planners—please wake up!

Beginning and Ending With Core Values

Creating a compelling brand begins with a founder's vision. "So bitchin' it hurts" is how Oakley phrases it. The core personal values translate into company values. (For Oakley, the vision began with Jim Jannard's desire to create functional, wearable art combining cutting-edge technology and design. The vision has led to a range of outdoor-related products that have garnered more than 800 patents.) Seldom do those values involve money, or at least not the quick buck. Of the many successful companies in the world, almost none mention profit as part of their mission statement. They understand that profit flows naturally from fulfilling the mission. A reasonable return is implicit in all business, including retail activity, and this book underscores the importance of honing a profitable economic model. But if profit is your *raison d'être* instead of being the reward that comes from providing a value to customers, then you are in the wrong career. If all you want is a big paycheck, other jobs are far less aggravating than running a retail business. You have to love what you sell—dresses, bikes, plants, medicine, cars, boats, watches, chocolate sundaes, holiday ornaments, and so on. The product doesn't matter, only that you love the concept. If you don't love retail, stay out of it. Good retail is high touch, high energy, high involvement. Without your commitment, you, your employees, and your customers will all end up feeling empty.

Retailers who treat this business as a job instead of a mission can discourage others who see a richer meaning in its activities. But then you meet some of the creative people who have graced these pages, people who have the imagination and courage to do something new and the willingness to bring in the right talent to accomplish it. Such people reinforce my belief that retail is exciting, fun—fresh! The choice for the retail industry is the death spiral of commoditization and price wars or the life spiral of creativity, quality, and differentiation. To push the envelope, you have to actually pilot the ship and *engage*, to embark on bold but eminently achievable steps that will bring in the New Age of Retail. Retail has always been detail, but the New Age is about innovation and execution, with attention to detail in both.

Values in mind, the would-be retailer must make no little plans, must go long, must own Main & Main, and must push the envelope when it comes to innovation. The retailer must ideate the concept in as large a way as possible, both in terms of defining the concept and defining the size and location of the market. Early on the retailer must create the strategic plans and bring in the strategic leaders who can create and execute on the concept. Entrepreneurial zeal cannot overcome a sloppy approach to building a business; the retailer must have a solid economic model and a disciplined growth strategy. Part of the strategy includes a locationing process built on the most up-to-date scientific analysis, beginning with the national market and working down through major metropolitan areas, the trade zones within those areas, and finally to the one physical location that best maps to the concept.

The retailer for the New Age is the one who can create a gathering place, an emotional touchstone for an increasingly impersonal world. The New Retailer can create or redefine a concept, give it high-touch element, an intimate experience that takes retail back to its origins and also propels it into the future. The New Retailer can engage customers with physical design and visual appeal, increase the entertainment level, use technology to humanize service as well as to expedite transactions, and take shopping to a higher level of personal satisfaction. The New Retailer can constantly turn inward to refresh the core values while turning outward to find new ways to express those values. The New Retailer can create an enduring brand by seeing through the eyes of the customer and building the brand presentation—and everything that supports that presentation—in response to what the customer sees. All of these steps are necessary for the retailer to create and sustain a brand. In today's world, brand is paradoxically one of the most fleeting values and one of the most permanent values in the marketplace. Well-informed consumers have no qualms in rapidly switching from one brand to another, whenever products become similar in quality. At the same time, the company that shows its willingness to constantly innovate and to properly treat its customers can maintain market leadership and brand position. A direct, personal connection with the customer— a meaningful engagement—is the kind of differentiation that few retail competitors will be able to match.

Retail has never been an easier business to enter or a tougher business in which to succeed. Only people with core values and a strong sense of mission need apply. But for retailers with a passion for the business, the desire to take on a challenge, and a sincere willingness to improve their communities, only one choice is possible, and that's Goethe's: "Boldness has genius, power, and magic in it. Begin it now."

Index

Symbols

3M, 10
80/20 rule for merchandising, 114

A

Abercrombie & Fitch, 104
accessibility, site selection, 236
acquisition
    expansion, 195-196
    necessary systems (organizational
    development), 144-146
ADA (American Disability Act), 283
adidas
    core values, 7, 26
    Dassler, Adi, 7
    targeted lifestyle retailers, 31
ADT (Average Daily Traffic), 236
AEC (Alliance Entertainment
    Corporation), 157
aerial photo-mapping software, 231
Allard, James (Blue C Sushi),
    development of core values, 13
Alliance Entertainment Corporation.
    See AEC
Altoids, 40
Amazon, 29
American Disability Act. *See* ADA
analyses, financial, 176
angel investors, 160
angel networks, 161
annual reports, 177-178
Anthropologie, 303
Apple, design and layout of products
    (merchandising), 102
area owned management, 194
Armani, 4
As Is provision (leasing real estate), 276
ascendancy (hub and spoke model),
    210-211
authenticity (ideation), 29
    high-touch experiences, 34-36
    retail positions, 31-32
Average Daily Traffic. *See* ADT
average sales volume per store, 178

B

Baby Boomer generation, trend
    evaluation, 37-39
*Balance Sheet Basics: Financial
Management for Non-Financial
Managers* (Spurga), 176
Baldwin, Jerry, 214
Banana Republic, 31
Barnes & Noble, 30
Barneys, 99
Behar, Howard, 141
Best Buy, 32
Big Box concepts, 32
Bizminer, 177
Bizstats, 177
Blue C Sushi
    core values, 13-14
    design and development, 64-67
    construction management, 89-93
    ideation validation with research, 45
    investors, 160
    locationing, 60
    mission statement, 16
    restaurant software, 145
The Body Shop, 31
brand, 4
    core values
        Blue C Sushi, 13-14
        ideation, 6
        qualitative human aspects, 12-13
        Starbucks, 14
    defining principles
        mantras, 18-24
        mission statements, 14-18
    design and development, 49
        brand touchstones, 72-76
        budgets, 86-88
        construction management, 89-93
        cost versus brand establishment,
          93-95
        locationing, 51-60
        material choice in terms of
          customer appeal, 88-89
        model and prototype reviews,
          84-86

one-off store design versus multiple rollouts, 64-67
 reinventing brand, 69-72
 target markets, 81-82
 unique value, 76
extension, 41-45
image and presentation, 4-5
imprinting, 9
organizational development, 142-144
unique positioning, 5
Bread & Circus store, 226
breve bar, 72
brokers, real estate
 commission structures, 266-267
 market plans, 264
BTII (Business Transparency and Integrity International), 309
Buckner, Robert W., *Site Selection: New Advancements in Methods and Technology,* 244
budgets, store design and development, 86-88
Built to Last: Successful Habits of Visionary Companies (Collins), 11
Bumps for Boomers program, 38
Business Transparency and Integrity International. *See* BTII
buying real estate versus leasing, 262-263

C

CAM (common area maintenance), 273
Cargill, 26
Cartier, 31
Chico's FAS, Inc., 178
China, cultural interchange, 309
Circuit City, 32
city building codes, 57
Claritas (data-gathering company), 178, 223
closed storefronts, 98-99
co-locating with similar brands, 239-241
The Coffee Connection, acquisition by Starbucks, 196
COGS (cost of goods sold), 170-171
Coldwater Creek, 179
Collins, Jim
 Built to Last: Successful Habits of Visionary Companies, 11
 Good to Great, 155

commission structures, real estate brokers, 266-267
commoditization, 172
common area maintenance. *See* CAM
community life improvement (New Age of Retail), 324-327
company-owned stores, expansion, 193-194
competitive landscape, expansion, 211-216
consignment investors, 166
consolidating functions for growth, 141
construction management, store design and development, 89-93
conventional locationing versus timeless locationing, 53-59
core values
 brand, 6
 New Age of Retail, 317-319, 327
 retail development
  adidas, 7
  Blue C Sushi, 13-14
  mantras, 18-24
  mission statements, 14-18
  qualitative human aspects, 12-13
  Starbucks, 10-14
corporate image, 4-5
cost of goods sold. *See* COGS
Costco
 design and layout of products (merchandising), 102
 engagement of the senses, 100
 merchandising, 115
 price/value retailers, 32
covenant to remediate (leases), 279
Crate & Barrel stores, 104
cultural interchange, innovation opportunities, 307
 China, 309
 Hispano-America, 308
 Russia, 309-310
customers
 demographics, 305-307
 experiences, 319-321
 store design appeal, 88-89
 service, 121-128
  employee hustle, 127
  high touch, 128
  Les Schwab Tire Centers, 124
  management attitude toward employees, 125-127

process, 125
product knowledge, 123
respect for personal space, 122
Westfield Shoppingtown family,
123

D

Dassler, Adi (adidas founder), 7
data-gathering companies, demographic
analysis for growth, 223
defining principles, retail development, 10
Blue C Sushi, 13-14
mantras, 18-24
mission statements, 14-18
qualitative human aspects, 12-13
Starbucks, 14
Dell Computers, 142
Dell, Michael, 142
demographics
growth, 219-226
data-gathering companies, 223
landlord reports, 222
suitability model, 223
thematic mapping, 222
innovation, 302
Starbucks expansion, 205
trend evaluation, 37
Dent, Harry, *The Roaring 2000s:
Building the Wealth and Lifestyle
You Desire in the Greatest Boom in
History,* 38
design, 49
brand touchstones, 72-76
budgets, 86-88
construction management, 89-93
cost versus brand establishment, 93-95
locationing, 51-60
conventional versus timeless, 53-59
sense of place, 60
material choice in terms of customer
appeal, 88-89
model and prototype reviews, 84-86
one-off store design versus multiple
rollouts, 64-67
reinventing brand, 69-72
target markets, 81-82
unique value, 76
Dick's Deluxe burger, 296
differentiation (ideation)
authenticity, 29

high-touch experiences, 34-36
retail positions, 31-32
trend evaluation
Baby Boomer generation, 37-39
brand extension, 41-45
demographics, 37
megatrends overview, 38-39
niche concepts, 41
validation of concept with research,
45
doppio, 72
due diligence (investors), 162-163
Dun & Bradstreet, 177

E

early binding decisions, 165
early termination clauses (leases), 269
earnings before interest, taxes,
depreciation, and amortization
(EBIDTA), 176
eBay, non-touch environment, 29
EBIDTA (earnings before interest, taxes,
depreciation, and amortization), 176
Eckerd Drugs, 195
economic model, 169
expansion, 198
expenses
cost of goods, 181
cost of sales, 181
occupancy costs, 182
pro forma financial statements,
183-184
projections, 182
gross margin, 170
commoditization, 172
differentiation, 172-174
examination of COGS, 171
net income, 170
annual reports, 177-178
average sales volume per store, 178
differentiation, 172-174
financial analyses, 176
fuel for growth, 174
out-of-area market research,
179-181
pro forma financial statements,
175-176
retail financial groupings, 172
Edelstein, David, 64
educational courses, expansion, 186

Elephant Pharmacy
   educational courses, 186
   expansion of existing trends, 42
eMachines (Gateway), 24
emotions, induction of (merchandising),
   99-105
   design and layout of products,
     102-103
   financial resources, 105
   lighting, 101
   mood, 103-104
   theater of retail experiences, 101
employees, organizational development,
   149
   hiring heart over resumé, 151-158
   matching motivation with values, 156
   strategic plans, 142-144
   telling the company's story, 158-160
Epsteen, Michael, locationing rules,
   233-234
ESRI BIS (data-gathering company), 223
excess vacancy provision (leasing real
   estate), 277
exclusive specialty retailers, 31
exclusive use provision (leasing real
   estate), 278
execution for expansion (strategic plans),
   131
   acquisition of necessary systems,
     144-146
   applying internal strengths to create
     external results, 147-148
   financial results of planned expansion,
     135
   growth targets, 137-141
   initiatives and objectives, 133
   opportunity, 132
   organizational development, 142-144
   store development plan, 133
executive summary (site surveys), 281
expansion (growth)
   acquisition, 195-196
   additional sales through Internet, 186
   area-owned management, 194
   ascendancy (hub and spoke model),
     210-211
   availability of strategic partners, 216
   brand soldiers, 217-218
   cautions, 187-188
   company-owned stores, 193-194
   competitive landscape, 211-216

demographics analysis, 219
economic model, 198
educational courses, 186
evaluation of potential customer base,
   216-217
franchising, 191-192
hidden wellsprings, 186
innovation, 291-311
   cultural interchange, 307-310
   customer demographic, 305-307
   demographics, 302, 305-307
   license, 300-301
   maintaining premium position,
     302-305
   McDonald's, 297-299
   shift to softness, 295-297
   timing, 301-302
joint ventures, 196-197
licensing, 192-193
locationing
   hot-spot mapping, 252-256
   local and regional destinations,
     256-258
   market tiers, 247-252
   real estate expansion, 258
mail order business, 187
multiple rollouts, 188-191
net income, 174
Omaha Steaks, 204
optimization, 208
"own your home" first methodology,
   207
real estate management, 144
Sam Goody, 204
service model, 199
Starbucks
   availability of strategic partners,
     216
   brand soldiers, 217-218
   demographics, 205
   evaluation of competitive
     landscape, 211-216
   evaluation of potential customer
     base, 216-217
   hub and spoke model, 210-211
   market tiers, 206-207
   MSAs (Metropolitan Statistical
     Areas), 205
strategic plans
   acquisition of necessary systems,
     144-146

applying internal strengths to create external results, 147-148

financial results of planned expansion, 135

growth targets, 137-141

initiatives and objectives, 133

opportunity, 132

organizational development, 142-144

store development plan, 133

summary of process, 219

target markets

market planning, 221

metropolitan trade areas, 221-226

proxies, 228-231

sales estimates, 221-244

site selection, 221, 231-244

traffic flow, 226-228

Wal-Mart, 203-204

wholesale business, 187-198

expenses

cost of goods, 181

cost of sales, 181

occupancy costs, 182

pro forma financial statements, 183-184

projections, 182

extension, brand extension, 41-45

F

Fannie Mae, 26

FedEx, merger with Kinko's, 43-44

Fenker, Richard M., *The Site Book: A Field Guide to Commercial Real Estate Evaluation*, 244

financial analyses, 176, 241-244

Financial and Business Statements (2d Edition) (Friedlob and Plewa), 175

financial groupings (retail), 172

financial models, net income, 175-176

financial resources, merchandising, 105

financial systems, 144

first store

design and development

brand touchstones, 72-76

budgets, 86-88

construction management, 89-93

cost versus brand establishment, 93-95

material choices, 88-89

model and prototype reviews, 84-86

one-off store design versus multiple rollouts, 64-67

reinventing brand, 69-72

target markets, 81-82

unique value, 76

locationing, 51-53

conventional versus timeless, 53-59

sense of place, 60

Flamholtz, Eric, pyramid of organizational development, 138

Flax, Leonard, 102

food service, 306

Foot Candy, 106

formal lease agreements, 271

Foundation Design (Blue C Sushi store design), 64-67

four-wall contribution. *See* net income

franchising, 191-192, 211

Free People, 303

Friedlob, George Thomas, *Financial and Business Statements (2d Edition)*, 175

fuel for growth, 174

Furla, 31

G

G&A costs (general and administrative costs), 170

Gateway Computers, 21-22

gazumping, 162

general and administrative costs. *See* G&A costs

Geographic Information Systems. *See* GIS

Gerstner, Lou, 157

GIS (Geographic Information Systems), 222

Gloria Jean's, 211

"going long" with retail concept, 137

investors, 160

consignment, 166

due diligence, 162-163

mismatches with founders, 163-166

sweat equity investors, 166

organizational development, 149-151

hiring heart over resumé, 151-158

telling the company's story, 158-160

Good to Great (Collins), 155
Goodyear, 4
government regulations, 58
Grade A locations, hot-spot mapping, 232
Grade B locations, hot-spot mapping, 232
grande markets, 206
groceries, 172
gross leases, 275
gross margin, 170
   commoditization, 172
   differentiation, 172-174
   examination of COGS, 171
Growing Pains (Flamholtz), 138
growth. *See* expansion

H

hazardous material provision (leasing real estate), 279
hearth design, Gateway Computer stores, 22
heating, ventilation, and air conditioning. *See* HVAC
Heritage store (adidas), 7
high touch
   customer service, 128
   ideation, 34-36
   retail offerings, 29-32
high-volume businesses, 172
hiring employees
   hiring heart over resumé, 151-158
   matching motivation with values, 156
   strategic plans, 142-144
   telling the company's story, 158-160
Hislop, Mike, 84
Hispano-America, cultural interchange, 308
The Home Depot, 32
home electronics, 306
Hoover's Online, 162, 177
hot-spot mapping, 230-232, 252-256
house style (design), 70
Howard Johnson, 41
HP (Hewlett Packard), 26
hub and spoke model (ascendancy), 210-211
HVAC (heating, ventilation, and air conditioning), 282

I

iconography, 295-296
ideation, 6
   authenticity, 29
      high-touch experiences, 34-36
      retail positions, 31-32
   Gateway Computers mantra, 21
   high touch
      experiences, 34-36
      retail offerings, 29-32
   opportunities, 27-29
   trend evaluation
      Baby Boomer generation, 37-39
      brand extension, 41-45
      demographics, 37
      megatrends overview, 38-39
      niche concepts, 41
   validation of concept with research, 45
Il Fornaio Café and Bakery, 19-20
Il Mulino, 103
Illuminations, 98
image, brand image and presentation, 4-5
imprinting, 9
in kind investors. *See* sweat equity investors
In-N-Out Burger, 296
incenting real estate brokers, 266
increasing margins (merchandising), 114-116
individual investors, 161
ING Direct, 43
initial public offerings. *See* IPOs
initiatives (strategic), 133
inner-city retail ventures, 197
innovation, 291-311
   cultural interchange, 307
      China, 309
      Hispano-America, 308
      Russia, 309-310
   customer demographic, 305-307
   demographics, 302
   license, 300-301
   maintaining premium position, 302-305
   McDonald's, 297-299
   shift to softness, 295-297
   timing, 301-302
InsiderVC, 162

institutional investors, VCs (venture capitalists), 161
Internet, expansion of sales, 186
investors
  angel investors, 160
  Blue C Sushi, 160
  consignment, 166
  due diligence, 162-163
  individual, 161
  institutional, VCs (venture capitalists), 161
  mismatches with founders, 163-166
  sweat equity investors, 166
IPOs (initial public offerings), 190

J

Jack in the Box, 298
Johnny Rocket restaurants, 100
Johns, Jasper, "The Map" painting, 259
Johnson Development, 197
Johnson, Earvin Magic, 197
joint ventures (expansion), 196-197
Jumpstart, 15

K

Kate's Paperie stores, 102
Keeping the Books: Basic Record Keeping and Accounting for the Successful Small Business (Pinson), 176
Keil, Bryant (Potbelly), 62, 150
kick out clauses (leases), 269
Kinko's, merger with FedEx, 43-44
kiosk-style formats (Starbucks), 72
Kit of Parts approach (multiple rollouts store design), 65-66, 74-76
Krispy Kreme, 143
Kroger, 178

L

land-banking, 263
large-store format, adidas, 7
layout of products, engaging customer senses, 102-103
leasing real estate
  kick out clauses, 269
  legal forms for ownership, 268
  lenient subleasing rights, 270
  locationing, 285

negotiations, 271-275, 286
  formal lease agreements, 271
  gross leases, 275
  landlord collection, 274
  LOIs (Letters of Intent), 271
  operating expenses, 273
  rent increases, 274
provisions
  As Is, 276
  excess vacancy, 277
  exclusive use, 278
  hazardous material, 279
  radius, 278
  rent commencement, 276
  sidewalk seating, 278
  site plan, 277
  square footage, 276
  sublet issues, 280
  tax issues, 279
  transfer/assignment issues, 280-281
  Use, 276
short leases, 268
site surveys, 281-284
unsecured leases, 268
urban shops, 285-286
versus buying, 262-263
legal forms for ownership (leases), 268
lenient subleasing rights (leases), 270
Les Schwab Tire Centers, 124
Letters of Intent. *See* LOIs
Levitan, Dan, 161
licensing, 192-193
limited liability corporations, 268
limited partnerships, 268
local destinations, 256-258
Location, Location, Location (Salvaneschi), 244
locationing, 51. *See also* site selection
  city building code considerations, 57
  co-locating with similar brands, 239-241
  conventional versus timeless, 53-59
  Epsteen, Michael, 233-234
  hot-spot mapping, 252-256
  leasing real estate, 285
  local and regional destinations, 256-258
  Main & Main strategy, 69
  market tiers, 247-252
  real estate expansion, 258

sense of place, 60
target markets, site selection, 231-235
logos, 98
LOIs (Letters of Intent), 271
Lombard, Ken, Johnson Development, 197
Lost Arrow Corporation, 26

M

mail order businesses, 187
Mailboxes Etc., merger with UPS, 44
Main & Main strategy (locationing), 69
management
construction (store design), 89-93
organizational development, 149-151
hiring heart over resumé, 151-158
matching motivation with values, 156
telling the company's story, 158-160
systems, 144
mantras, translation of core values into action, 18-24
Gateway Computers, 21-22
Il Fornaio Café and Bakery, 19-20
Omaha Steaks, 20
"The Map" painting (Johns), 259
margin increases (merchandising), 114-116
market plans
establishing target markets, 221
real estate brokers, 264
market tiers
locationing, 247-252
Starbucks expansion, 206-207
The Market, 50
Mary Kay, 26
Massey, Wright, 71
material choice, store design and development, 88-89
Maveron, 161
McDonald's
acquisitions, 195
expansion of existing trends, 41
failed innovations, 294-295
iconography, 295-296
innovative ideas, 293-294
McKinsey, 26
megatrends overview, 38-39

merchandising, 97
closed storefronts, 98
comforts, 106-108
conveying store message, 109-110
customer service, 121-128
employee hustle, 127
Les Schwab Tire Centers, 124
management attitude toward employees, 125-127
process, 125
product knowledge, 123
respect for personal space, 122
Westfield Shoppingtown family, 123
logos, 98
margin increases, 114-116
meta-merchandising, 99-104
design and layout of products, 102-103
financial resources, 105
lighting, 101
mood, 103-104
theater of retail experiences, 101
observation of similar retailers, 116-118
placement of products, 110, 114, 119
seating, 106
storefronts, 98
view corridors, 108
wall graphics, 106
wayfinding, 108-109
window spaces, 98-99
Merck, 10
Merrill Garden Intrawest, 40
meta-merchandising, 99
design and layout of products, 102-103
financial resources, 105
lighting, 101
mood, 103-104
theater of retail experiences, 101
Metropolitan Statistical Areas. See MSAs
metropolitan trade areas
proxies, 228-231
site selection, 231-235
co-locating with similar brands, 239-241
on-site inspections, 236-239
target markets, 221-226
traffic flow, 226-228

mission statements
New Age of Retail, 314-315
community life improvement,
324-327
core values, 327
evolving to meet the times,
316-317
historical nature of trade, 322-323
maintaining values, 317-319
redefining customer experience,
319-321
translation of core values into action,
14-18
Blue C Sushi, 16
Starbucks, 14-15
Miura, Shinichi, 150
models, store design, 84-86
mood, engaging customer senses, 103-104
MSAs (Metropolitan Statistical Areas),
205
hot-spot mapping, 252-256
local and regional destinations,
256-258
market tiers, 247-252
multiple rollouts
expansion, 188-191
versus one-off store design, 64-67

N

Natural Wonders, 303
Nature Company, 303
negotiations (leasing real estate), 286
formal lease agreements, 271
gross leases, 275
landlord collection, 274
LOIs (Letters of Intent), 271
operating expenses, 273
rent increases, 274
net income, 170
annual reports, 177-178
average sales volume per store, 178
differentiation, 172-174
financial analyses, 176
fuel for growth, 174
out-of-area market research, 179-181
pro forma financial statements,
175-176
Nevin, Joe, Bumps for Boomers program,
38

New Age of Retail, sense of mission,
314-315
community life improvement, 324-327
core values, 327
evolving to meet the times, 316-317
historical nature of trade, 322-323
maintaining values, 317-319
redefining customer experience,
319-321
Nike
merchandising, 116
wholesale/retail expansion, 198

O

Oakley
computerized inventory system, 144
expansion to retail operation, 190
wholesale/retail expansion, 198
objectives (strategic), 133
Occasio bank concept (Washington
Mutual), 304
occupancy costs, 182
Old Navy, 305
Omaha Steaks
growth, 204
mantra, 20
wayfinding (merchandising), 109
on-site inspections (site selection),
236-239, 255
one-off store design versus multiple
rollouts, 64-67
operating expenses, lease negotiations,
273
operational systems, 144
optimization, 208
organizational development, 149
hiring heart over resumé, 151-158
matching motivation with values, 156
strategic plans, 142-144
telling the company's story, 158-160
organizational model, Starbucks, 140-141
out-of-area market research, 179-181
Outback, 194
"own your home" first methodology
(expansion), 207

P

P&L (profit-and-loss) statements, 169
partnerships, 268
Peet's Coffee and Tea, 214
Peet, Alfred, 214
Pei Wei restaurant chain, 103
Pep Boys, 204
percentage rent, lease negotiations, 274
personnel, organizational development, 149
   hiring heart over resumé, 151-158
   matching motivation with values, 156
   strategic plans, 142-144
   telling the company's story, 158-160
photo-mapping software, 231
Piecora, Danny, 185
Pike Place Market (Washington), first Starbucks, 50
Pinson, Linda, *Keeping the Books: Basic Record Keeping and Accounting for the Successful Small Business,* 176
placement of products, merchandising, 110, 114, 119
Plewa, Franklin James, *Financial and Business Statements (2d Edition),* 175
point-of-sale registers. *See* POS registers
POS (point-of-sale) registers, 103, 113
postal codes, thematic mapping, 222
Potbelly Sandwich Works
   customer service, 127
   high-touch experiences, 35-36
   locationing, 62
   merchandising, 107
Prad, 31
presentation, brand image, 4-5
Pressler, Paul, 157
price leaders, 302
price/value retailers, 32
pro forma financial statements, 175-176, 183-184
products
   brand image, 4-5
   knowledge (customer service), 123
   layout, 102-103
   placement for merchandising, 110, 114, 119
profit-and-loss statements. *See* P&L statements
projections (expenses), 182
prototypes (store design), 84-86
provisions (leasing real estate), 276
   As Is, 276
   excess vacancy, 277
   exclusive use, 278
   hazardous material, 279
   radius, 278
   rent commencement, 276
   sidewalk seating, 278
   site plan, 277
   square footage, 276
   sublet issues, 280
   tax issues, 279
   transfer/assignment issues, 280-281
   Use, 276
proxies, 228-231
The Pumping Station, 307
pyramid of organizational development (Flamholtz), 138

Q

qualitative human aspects, core values, 12-13
quality control, franchising, 191
quality leaders, 302
Quiznos, 194

R

"Race Is On" competitors, 212
radius provision (leasing real estate), 278
real estate. *See also* locationing; site selection
   brokers
      commission structures, 266-267
      market plans, 264
   expansion, 144, 258
   leasing, 261
      kick out clauses, 269
      legal forms for ownership, 268
      lenient subleasing rights, 270
      locationing, 285
      negotiations, 271-275, 286
      provisions, 276-281
      short leases, 268
      site surveys, 281-284
      unsecured leases, 268
      urban shops, 285-286
      versus buying, 262-263
   locationing, 51-53
      conventional versus timeless, 53-59
      sense of place, 60

Real Estate Investment Trusts. *See* REITs
regional destinations, 256-258
REITs (Real Estate Investment Trusts), 262
remediation (leases), 279
Remlinger's Farm, 187
rent commencement provision (leasing real estate), 276
rent increases (lease negotiations), 274
research, validating ideation, 45
resources, site selection, 244
retail
    brand
        core values, 6, 10-14, 24
        defining principles, 14-24
        image and presentation, 4
        imprinting, 9
        store experience, 5
        unique positioning, 5
    exclusive specialty retailers, 31
    price/value retailers, 32
    targeted lifestyle retailers, 31
retail financial groupings, 172
return on investment. *See* ROI
revenue, pro forma financial statements, 176
The Roaring 2000s: Building the Wealth and Lifestyle You Desire in the Greatest Boom in History (Dent), 38
ROI (return on investment), 175
rollable elements, store design, 66
Rosen, Steve (Blue C Sushi), development of core values, 13
Rouse Company/General Growth Properties, 189
Russia, cultural interchange, 309-310

S

S-corporations, 268
SADI (Superior Achievement in Design and Imaging) Award, 24
sales estimates, establishing target markets, 221, 241-244
Salvaneschi, Luigi, *Location, Location, Location*, 244
Sam Goody
    engagement of the senses, 100
    growth, 204
scheduling site surveys, 281-284
Schultz, Howard, 14

SCORE, 177
seasonality, generation of cash flow, 182
"See Ya" competitors, 212
senior concepts in retail, 39
senior management, organizational development, 149
    hiring heart over resumé, 151-158
    matching motivation with values, 156
    strategic plans, 142-144
    telling the company's story, 158-160
sense of mission, 314-315
    community life improvement, 324-327
    core values, 327
    evolving to meet the times, 316-317
    historical nature of trade, 322-323
    maintaining values, 317-319
    redefining customer experience, 319-321
senses, engagement of (merchandising), 99-105
    design and layout of products, 102-103
    financial resources, 105
    lighting, 101
    mood, 103-104
    theater of retail experiences, 101
service model, 199
service providers, sweat equity investments, 166
short leases, 268
short markets, 206
sidewalk seating provision (leasing real estate), 278
Simon Property Group, 189
The Site Book: A Field Guide to Commercial Real Estate Evaluation (Fenker), 244
site plan provision (leasing real estate), 277
site selection. *See also* locationing; real estate
    establishing target markets, 221
        hot-spot mapping, 252-256
        local and regional destinations, 256-258
        market tiers, 247-252
    growth, 231-235
        co-locating with similar brands, 239-241
        on-site inspections, 236-239
        resources, 244

Site Selection: New Advancements in Methods and Technology (Buckner), 244

site surveys (leasing real estate), 281-284

SKUs (stock keeping units), 114

Sleeth, Bill (Vizwerks), 80

Small Business Administration, 177

smash-and-grab thieves, 99

Smith, Orin, 72

sole proprietorships, 268

Sony, 26

specialty retailers, 172, 311

Spurga, Ronald C., *Balance Sheet Basics: Financial Management for Non-Financial Managers,* 176

square footage provision (leasing real estate), 276

Staples, 43

Starbucks

  acquisition of The Coffee Connection, 196

  brand image and presentation, 4

  breve bar, 72

  core values, 10-14

  Costco wholesale account for coffee beans, 186

  development of mission statement, 14-15

  doppio, 72

  growth and expansion, 205

    availability of strategic partners, 216

    brand soldiers, 217-218

    competitive landscape, 211-216

    demographics, 205

    evaluation of competitive landscape, 211-216

    evaluation of potential customer base, 216-217

    execution, 136-140

    existing trends, 41

    hub and spoke model, 210-211

    market tiers, 206-207

    MSAs (Metropolitan Statistical Areas), 205

  kiosk-style formats, 72

  Lincoln Center connection, 56

  Main & Main locationing strategy, 69

  organizational model, 140-141

  Pike Place Market, 50

  targeted lifestyle retailers, 31

  Vancouver, B.C., 55

  wholesale/retail expansion, 198

Starbucks Foundation, 15

Sticky Fingers Ribhouse, 187

Stinson, Shauna (Vizwerks), 80

stock keeping units. *See* SKUs

storefronts, 98

strategic partners, 216

strategic plans

  acquisition of necessary systems, 144-146

  applying internal strengths to create external results, 147-148

  financial results of planned expansion, 135

  growth targets, 137, 141

  initiatives and objectives, 133

  opportunity, 132

  organizational development, 142-144

  store development plans, 133

subleasing rights (leases), 270, 280

Subway Sandwich franchise (Bend, Oregon), 127

suitability model, demographic analysis for growth, 223

Superior Achievement in Design and Imaging Award. *See* SADI Award

sweat equity investors, 166

T

tall markets, 206

Target

  design and layout of products (merchandising), 102

  price/value retailers, 32

target markets

  market planning, 221

  metropolitan trade areas, 221-226

  proxies, 228-231

  sales estimates, 221, 241-244

  site selection, 221, 231-235

    co-locating with similar brands, 239-241

    hot-spot mapping, 252-256

    local and regional destinations, 256-258

    market tiers, 247-252

    on-site inspections, 236-239

    resources, 244

store design, 81-82
  traffic flow, 226-228
targeted lifestyle retailers, 31, 172, 311
Taubman Company, 189
tax issues (leasing real estate), 279
taxes, insurance, and common area
  maintenance. See TICAM
tenant brokers, 266
Tenant Improvement Allowance. See TIA
theater of retail experiences, 100-101
thematic mapping, 222
TIA (Tenant Improvement Allowance),
  284
TICAM (taxes, insurance, and common
  area maintenance), 273
Tiffany's
  closed storefronts, 99
  exclusive specialty retailers, 31
timeless locationing versus conventional
  locationing, 53-59
Tommy Bahamas, 64, 304
Top Pot Doughnuts, 186, 198
touchstones (brand touchstones), 72-76
traditional retailing, 172
traffic flow, 226-228
transfer/assignment issues (leasing real
  estate), 280-281
trends, ideation
  Baby Boomer generation, 37-39
  brand extension, 41-45
  demographics, 37
  megatrends overview, 38-39
  Merrill Garden Intrawest, 40
  niche concepts, 41

U

U.S. census reports, 223
unique positioning, brand image and
  presentation, 5
unique value, design and development, 76
unsecured leases, 268
UPS, merger with Mailboxes Etc., 44
Urban Outfitters, 303
urban shops, 285-286
Use provision(leasing real estate), 276
utility players, 157

V

value leaders, 302
value meals, margin increases
  (merchandising), 115
VCs (venture capitalists), 161
venture capitalists. See VCs
Victoria's Secret
  merchandising, 104
  targeted lifestyle retailers, 31
view corridors (merchandising), 108
visibility, site selection, 237
Vizwerks, 80

W-Z

Waitt, Ted, Gateway Computers mantra,
  21-22
Wal-Mart
  core values, 26
  growth, 203-204
  high-touch experiences, 34
  price/value retailers, 32
Walgreens
  average sales volume per store, 178
  Capitol Hill location (Seattle), 59
wall graphics, 106
Walt Disney Corporation, 10
Walton, Sam
  growth of Wal-Mart, 203-204
  high-touch experiences, 34
Washington Mutual, Occasio bank
  concept, 304
wayfinding, 108-109
Web vendors, 29-30
Weisman, Eric, 157
Westfield Group, 189
Westfield Shoppingtown family, 123
Whole Foods Market
  average sales volume per store, 178
  innovation, 303
wholesale business expansion, 187, 198
Williams, Chuck (Williams-Sonoma), 34
Williams-Sonoma
  exclusive specialty retailers, 31
  high-touch experiences, 34
window spaces (merchandising), 98-99

Will It Fly?
How to Know if Your New Business Idea Has Wings ... Before You Take the Leap
BY THOMAS K. MCKNIGHT

Will it fly? That's the #1 question facing everyone with a new business idea. Now, there's a systematic way to answer that question ahead of time-before you invest one dime. *Will It Fly?* introduces the Innovator's Scorecard, the first intuitive, practical tool for assessing and refining new business ideas. Created by one of the world's leading entrepreneurial consultants, this is the fastest and most confidential way to identify the strengths and weaknesses of your proposed business. Thomas McKnight's Innovator's Scorecard addresses 44 key facets of business success, from market demand to competition, pricing to management competence, finance to exit strategies. For every element, you learn what to evaluate, how important it is, how to uncover the necessary information, and how to improve their score. By answering these questions, you can fine-tune your ideas to reduce risks; protect your family and friends from losing money; quickly evaluate dozens of new ideas; and dramatically improve odds of success.

ISBN 0130462217, ©2004, 368 pp., $24.95

Clued In
How to Keep Customers Coming Back Again and Again
BY LEWIS CARBONE

Every customer has an experience with your product or brand. It can be good: it can be bad. In most businesses, however, the experience that the customer has with your product or brand is not managed in any systematic and sound way to build long-term profitability. The result is that companies lose the opportunity to leverage the value that exists in each of their customers. This is the first book that will show companies how to "engineer" the experiences of their customers, so that those customers will have a fruitful experience with your products and will want to come back

ISBN 0131015508, ©2004, 304 pp., $25.95